Credits

Author
Miko Coffey

Reviewers
Chris Cox
Ryan Reed

Commissioning Editor
Usha Iyer

Acquisition Editor
Sam Wood

Content Development Editor
Athira Laji

Technical Editor
Edwin Moses

Copy Editors
Stuti Srivastava
Sameen Siddiqui

Project Coordinator
Harshal Ved

Proofreaders
Ting Baker
Simran Bhogal

Indexer
Monica Ajmera Mehta

Production Coordinator
Arvindkumar Gupta

Cover Work
Arvindkumar Gupta

About the Author

Miko Coffey has been building websites since 1995. Having first been introduced to the Internet through cyber-art projects such as SITO's HyGrid (`www.sito.org/synergy/hygrid`), she soon developed a zeal for creating things on that new-fangled thing called the World Wide Web.

After graduating from the University of Texas at Austin, Miko moved to London, where she continued designing and building websites as part of her career in marketing. During these early years, she spent a lot of time trying to convince her employers that this whole "web" thing was really going to take off and that they should definitely let her create websites for them. Over time, she started to specialize in online marketing, moving beyond design and into more tactical and strategic work in areas such as email marketing, search engine optimization, content strategy, and user experience. As she worked her way up to senior management positions by day, by night, she continued to keep a hand in web design, building websites and blogs for personal projects or for friends and family.

By 2007, having spent 2 years as the head of Digital Media for NESTA, the UK's largest innovation organization, Miko decided it was time to use her skills and experience to work for a broader client base by doing freelance work. She also wanted to get back to her design roots. Through her previous experience of managing web teams, she'd been exposed to quite a few content management systems over the years, most of which were too complex and expensive for her smaller business clients. Having been frustrated by the cost and learning curve associated with these larger systems and the lack of finesse offered by smaller ones, she started looking for something that would be easy enough for her least-technical clients to use, flexible enough for her to apply her custom designs, and powerful but affordable. It was at this point that she discovered Squarespace, and she hasn't looked back since.

Building Business Websites with Squarespace 7

Master the tools and techniques of using Squarespace to create professional websites

Miko Coffey

BIRMINGHAM - MUMBAI

Building Business Websites with Squarespace 7

First published: April 2015

Production reference: 1300315

Published by Packt Publishing Ltd.
Livery Place
35 Livery Street
Birmingham B3 2PB, UK.

ISBN 978-1-78355-996-1

www.packtpub.com

Cover image by Jarek (milak6@wp.pl)

Miko has spent the last 7 years using Squarespace to create websites for her clients at Using My Head (`www.usingmyhead.com`), where her focus is on "helping people do things better online." She strives to keep her digital marketing skills as sharp as her design skills, because the combination of the two is what allows her to add the most value to client projects. She has worked with a range of sizes and types of organizations, from The Royal Society for the Arts to Channel 4 to small start-ups and nonprofits. Her passion is to enable people to communicate better online by demystifying the often confusing online landscape and giving people the skills and tools they need to make their work easier, their bumps smoother, and their lives better.

Half Japanese and half American, Miko currently lives in Brixton, South London, with her super-creative husband / DJ / VJ / generally awesome man, Mark, and their two cats, Kuma and Toshi.

Acknowledgments

This book is dedicated to my mother, Nobuko, and my grandmother, Fukiko. I can only aspire to be half as positive, inspiring, and joyful as you both are. To my mother especially: thank you for encouraging me to be the best that I can be and for showing me how to laugh at myself.

I'd also like to thank my husband, resident comedian, cat singer, and rock-solid support system, Mark, for sticking by me through all of life's storms and sunshine. You mean more to me than I can say in these little words on paper.

Last but not least, a big shout out to my "Underwire" gals, Jane and Kirsty, for lifting me up in all the right places.

About the Reviewers

Chris Cox is a UX engineer who is currently working at Google in New York City, where he prototypes and writes code using a variety of languages. Originally from California, he spent over 8 years developing software for the construction industry. In 2007, he decided to venture out on his own by starting a consulting company providing web and mobile development services.

Shortly afterwards, he became one of the early employees of Squarespace, which brought him to New York. While there, he developed Squarespace's original blogging mobile apps and the Note app for iOS, and then subsequently, he became the lead engineer of version 5 of their website-blogging platform.

Ryan Reed serves as the pastor to students and families at the Hillside Church of Marin in Corte Madera, CA. A native Californian, he attended Alderson Broaddus University in West Virginia. He received a full-tuition scholarship to attend Princeton Theological Seminary in Princeton, NJ. He earned two degrees: master of divinity and master of arts in adolescent development and faith formation. He was awarded the Bryant J Kirkland Excellence in Practical Theology Award at Princeton for his contribution and dedication to the field of practical theology. Currently, he sits on the board of coalition for healthy youth in Marin County and maintains a significant online presence in these fields. You can read his writings and learn more about his passion at `http://www.ryanreed.me/`.

He is married to the love of his life, Stacy, and they celebrated the birth of their first child, Hannah Grace, in January 2014. When not serving in his professional capacities, he enjoys living life with his family, reading, and mountain biking the beautiful trails of Marin County.

www.PacktPub.com

Support files, eBooks, discount offers, and more

For support files and downloads related to your book, please visit www.PacktPub.com.

Did you know that Packt offers eBook versions of every book published, with PDF and ePub files available? You can upgrade to the eBook version at www.PacktPub.com and as a print book customer, you are entitled to a discount on the eBook copy. Get in touch with us at service@packtpub.com for more details.

At www.PacktPub.com, you can also read a collection of free technical articles, sign up for a range of free newsletters and receive exclusive discounts and offers on Packt books and eBooks.

https://www2.packtpub.com/books/subscription/packtlib

Do you need instant solutions to your IT questions? PacktLib is Packt's online digital book library. Here, you can search, access, and read Packt's entire library of books.

Why subscribe?

- Fully searchable across every book published by Packt
- Copy and paste, print, and bookmark content
- On demand and accessible via a web browser

Free access for Packt account holders

If you have an account with Packt at www.PacktPub.com, you can use this to access PacktLib today and view 9 entirely free books. Simply use your login credentials for immediate access.

Table of Contents

Preface

Squarespace is a powerful website builder and content management system that allows you to create polished websites that look fantastic on both desktop computers and mobile devices, without needing the help of a web designer or developer. Everything is created and managed through a standard web browser, which means that you don't need to purchase, download, or install any specialist software. You don't even need web hosting, because your Squarespace subscription includes hosting as well as access to all of the Squarespace tools and functions in one place, for one price. You can also get a custom domain name (or use an existing one) and manage your blog, online shop, media gallery, and website statistics through Squarespace, making it your one-stop shop for everything you need for your website.

Why choose Squarespace

Squarespace is not the only website builder/CMS on the market; you may have heard of or considered using similar web-based tools such as Wix, Weebly, or Jimdo. You may have also compared Squarespace to more traditionally installed CMSes, such as WordPress, Drupal, or Joomla. In terms of power, flexibility, functionality, and ease, Squarespace sits somewhere in between these sets of competing products. For example, it's not as simple as something like Weebly, nor as complex and technical as something like Drupal. I believe that Squarespace offers the perfect balance: something that's very easy to set up, pretty easy to use, highly flexible, and incredibly powerful. You can create something that looks great without having to work too hard, and you have the option of digging deeper and applying advanced customizations if you want to.

Like other web-based tools, you don't have to worry about technical stuff such as servers or performing maintenance upgrades: they seamlessly take care of that for you behind the scenes. Yet, unlike some other web-based tools, Squarespace has been around for over 10 years, has an industry-leading 99.98 percent uptime, and uses multiple servers on the award-winning Peer 1 network to ensure your site's reliability. You also get access to 24/7 support, and for all but the cheapest Squarespace subscription plans, unlimited storage and bandwidth, without "throttling" (delays). This means you won't have to worry about caps on uploading or a slow/inaccessible site if you expect high volumes of traffic. Add to this the many third-party integrations that are available—such as email accounts, social media feeds, credit card processing, email newsletters, and more—and it's easy to see why Squarespace is a solid choice for business websites.

About this book

This book is a practical guide to planning, designing, building, launching, and managing a website for your business with Squarespace 7. You will learn how to use all of the Squarespace tools to control the layout, appearance, structure, and functions of your website, starting from the inception stage, all the way to monitoring and managing your site after the launch. More than just a how-to manual to create a website, this book also includes helpful design resources for finding and choosing images, fonts, and logos as well as online marketing advice about things such as increasing your site's visibility in search engines, driving traffic to your website through social media and ensuring your site visitors can perform their objectives quickly and easily.

Whether you've had some previous experience or you've never built a website before, this book leads you through a tried and tested, step-by-step process that is designed to help you create your Squarespace website in the most efficient manner possible. By following the chapters in order, you'll be more likely to launch your website on time with the least amount of hassle.

With the release of Squarespace 7, the company has dramatically boosted the support and online help available, and the user support community is rapidly growing. However, this latest version of Squarespace is a bit more complex than previous versions, and the increased flexibility and power of Squarespace 7 has made things less intuitive in some areas. Even by following Squarespace's training videos or help guides, it's not always clear what is the best method or order to do things, and sometimes, the terminology or techniques can be confusing for "non-techies". This book will guide you through every step of the way, in the right order, clearly explaining the how, why, and the effect of every action you'll perform.

What this book covers

Chapter 1, Setting Up for Success – Your Website Toolkit, introduces the process we'll follow to build your website and gives you advice on planning and gathering the raw materials you'll need for the rest of the book.

Chapter 2, Getting Started with Squarespace, sets up your Squarespace account, configures some basic settings, and takes a tour through the Squarespace system.

Chapter 3, Working with Squarespace Templates, provides an overview of the Squarespace templates and helps you choose the best one for your needs.

Chapter 4, Creating Your Site Framework: Pages, Items, Collections, and Navigation, takes you through the different types of Squarespace pages and containers, enabling you to create an empty shell ready for filling with content.

Chapter 5, Adding, Editing, and Arranging Content in Your Web Pages, talks about Squarespace Blocks and how to use them, and you'll add basic content to the pages you created in the last chapter.

Chapter 6, Using Blocks to Add Functionality, Rich Media, and Special Features, covers the more advanced types of blocks, allowing you to add functions, features, and multimedia to your website.

Chapter 7, Selling Online or Taking Donations with Squarespace Commerce, talks about how to set up and use Squarespace Commerce to create an online shop or manage donations on your website.

Chapter 8, Tailoring Your Site's Look and Feel, shows you how to adjust the aesthetics of your website, such as fonts, colors, and logo, to match your brand and target audience.

Chapter 9, Going Live with Your Website and Driving Traffic to It, performs all the final preflight checks before launching your website and helps you learn how you can use Squarespace features to promote your website through social media.

Chapter 10, Managing Your Squarespace Website, covers how to monitor your website activity with Squarespace Metrics, managing comments, inviting contributors to help you manage your site, and using Squarespace mobile apps to monitor and publish while on the move.

Chapter 11, Moving beyond Standard Squarespace Tools, teaches you how to add code to your site to expand its functions or control its appearance in ways you can't with the standard built-in tools. You'll also learn where to find code, guides, and help from Squarespace, the community of users, or from a professional designer/developer.

Appendix A, Getting Help with Squarespace, provides the list of resources that can be accessed through the Squarespace Help Center.

Appendix B, Squarespace Templates in a Nutshell, contains charts displaying the key features of all of the Squarespace templates.

Appendix C, List of Online Resources Used in This Book, gives a chapter-wise list of online resources used in the book.

Who this book is for

This book is for anyone who wants to learn how to use the latest version of Squarespace to create a website from scratch and take it through to go-live. You don't need any prior experience with Squarespace or building websites in general. As everything is done using Squarespace's simple, browser-based interface, you don't need to know how to code HTML or CSS—although any prior experience with these may come in handy if you want to perform advanced customizations. If you have used Squarespace 5 or other website builders/CMSes, this book will help you understand the key differences and teach you how to do things the new Squarespace 7 way, which may be very different from what you are accustomed to.

This book has been written with business users in mind, so the content and steps are designed specifically for websites that will be used to promote, market, or sell products and services. It's suitable for start-ups and sole traders who need to build their own website as well as for marketing, design, IT, or communications staff within organizations that want to use Squarespace to create or move their website, so they can manage it internally without needing to rely on a web designer / editor / producer.

Although professional web designers/developers who want to learn about Squarespace could use this book, it's not pitched at that level. You do not need to have any technical skills beyond basic computing skills such as knowing how to use a web browser, social networking site, or word processor.

Conventions

In this book, you will find a number of text styles that distinguish between different kinds of information. Here are some examples of these styles and an explanation of their meaning.

Code words in text, database table names, folder names, filenames, file extensions, pathnames, dummy URLs, user input, and Twitter handles are shown as follows: " For example, if you enter `Jane Doe` as your name, your site's Squarespace address will be `http://jane-doe.squarespace.com`."

A block of code is set as follows:

```
<p> This sentence will appear on a new line, with an empty
    line space above it.</p>
```

New terms and **important words** are shown in bold. Words that you see on the screen, for example, in menus or dialog boxes, appear in the text like this: "Click on **SEO** to load this section into the side panel."

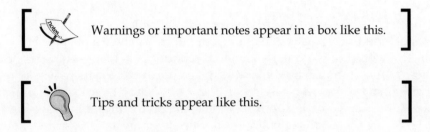

Warnings or important notes appear in a box like this.

Tips and tricks appear like this.

Reader feedback

Feedback from our readers is always welcome. Let us know what you think about this book—what you liked or disliked. Reader feedback is important for us as it helps us develop titles that you will really get the most out of.

To send us general feedback, simply e-mail feedback@packtpub.com, and mention the book's title in the subject of your message.

If there is a topic that you have expertise in and you are interested in either writing or contributing to a book, see our author guide at www.packtpub.com/authors.

Customer support

Now that you are the proud owner of a Packt book, we have a number of things to help you to get the most from your purchase.

Downloading the support files

You can download the support files for all Packt books you have purchased from your account at http://www.packtpub.com. If you purchased this book elsewhere, you can visit http://www.packtpub.com/support and register to have the files emailed directly to you.

Downloading the color images of this book

We also provide you with a PDF file that has color images of the screenshots/diagrams used in this book. The color images will help you better understand the changes in the output. You can download this file from `https://www.packtpub.com/sites/default/files/downloads/ImageProcessingwithOpenCV_Graphics.pdf`.

Errata

Although we have taken every care to ensure the accuracy of our content, mistakes do happen. If you find a mistake in one of our books—maybe a mistake in the text or the code—we would be grateful if you could report this to us. By doing so, you can save other readers from frustration and help us improve subsequent versions of this book. If you find any errata, please report them by visiting `http://www.packtpub.com/submit-errata`, selecting your book, clicking on the **Errata Submission Form** link, and entering the details of your errata. Once your errata are verified, your submission will be accepted and the errata will be uploaded to our website or added to any list of existing errata under the Errata section of that title.

To view the previously submitted errata, go to `https://www.packtpub.com/books/content/support` and enter the name of the book in the search field. The required information will appear under the **Errata** section.

Piracy

Piracy of copyrighted material on the Internet is an ongoing problem across all media. At Packt, we take the protection of our copyright and licenses very seriously. If you come across any illegal copies of our works in any form on the Internet, please provide us with the location address or website name immediately so that we can pursue a remedy.

Please contact us at `copyright@packtpub.com` with a link to the suspected pirated material.

We appreciate your help in protecting our authors and our ability to bring you valuable content.

Questions

If you have a problem with any aspect of this book, you can contact us at `questions@packtpub.com`, and we will do our best to address the problem.

1
Setting Up for Success – Your Website Toolkit

Making a website using the Squarespace platform is one of the easiest and most cost-effective ways to create a professional, polished website in a short amount of time. However, starting any website project without doing the groundwork can lead to confusion, missed deadlines, and just plain bad websites. This chapter covers everything you need to do before you even sign up for Squarespace to ensure that your website project is successful. We will cover the following topics in this chapter:

- The right way to make a website
- The different components of a website
- How to create an effective Website Toolkit, which includes the following:
    - Writing your website plan
    - Creating idea boards
    - Creating your sitemap
    - Gathering your raw materials

Understanding the process of making a website

Constructing a website is a lot like constructing a building, and many of the steps and processes are similar conceptually. To construct a building, we first need to consider what type of building it will be: a hospital, shop, house, office, or any other building. Who will use it? What functions will be performed there? This will tell us what shape, size, and structure the building needs to take. We then need to gather our raw materials before the construction can start. Once we have put together the shell and framework, we can start installing the core elements, such as plumbing and fixtures, which make the building operational. Finally, we apply the paint and furnishings and are ready for the opening day.

These are the same steps we will use in this book to construct your website. First, we will set the main objectives for your site, its purpose, your audience, and the types of functions that visitors will perform there. Next, we will gather the materials needed to create your site, such as text, images, and graphic elements. We will then select a site template, fill the template with your content, and customize the site's appearance, thus making it ready for launch.

This chapter focuses on the first two parts of the process: defining your site and gathering references and materials. These two parts make up your **Website Toolkit**, and you will refer back to the Toolkit time and time again throughout the project. You might find it tempting to skip ahead to the hands-on parts of the book. This is understandable, but be warned; every building needs a solid foundation, and every successful website needs a solid Website Toolkit. Starting here and spending time getting your foundation right will really pay off later.

A good Website Toolkit will make the rest of the project easier and quicker, keep you focused, and help smooth the road when things get bumpy (and they will get bumpy). Don't rush through this part of the process.

You might also be tempted to jump around and perform the steps in a different order. Just remember: you wouldn't paint the walls before installing the electricity in a building. Likewise, it doesn't make sense to focus on font sizes and fine-tuning colors before you have a site framework with some content in it. Now, if you have ever worked with a design agency on a website project, this may sound different to the order of their process. This book is laid out in this way because you are probably not a web designer by trade, and you don't need to impress your client with pretty visuals to win the contract.

If you are a designer, feel free to use this book in the manner that makes the most sense to your business model. However, for all the non-designers out there, following the order laid out in this book will make it far more likely that you launch your site on time, in full working order. It's easy to get bogged down in design details, so we'll leave this until the end, ensuring that all the major elements are sorted first.

Understanding website concepts

Before we dive into building your Website Toolkit, let's start by breaking down a website into components so that you can better understand how to make one. Each component is distinct, but some are closely related to one another, and it's easy to mix them up. The sum total of all the components put together makes up the process of designing and building a website, which is the final goal of this book.

Structure

Structure refers to the way in which the different elements of a web page or website are put together. In the web industry, we often use tools such as **sitemaps** and **wireframes** to define a site's structure. A sitemap is simply an outline that shows the hierarchy of web pages in terms of navigation. You can think of a sitemap like a table of contents in a book, or an organizational chart.

A wireframe is a schematic drawing of a web page, showing where the main elements of the page sit. Wireframes show only the relative size and position of content and functions; they do not include visual elements such as color or images nor do they contain real blocks of text. You can think of a wireframe like a pencil sketch.

Functions

A **function** is an action-oriented part of a website, for example, a shopping cart, inquiry form, or downloads. Functions always relate to actions that we want our website users to perform, and it's important to know from the beginning what these are and what priority each function has. Functions are enabled and restricted by the technology we use. So, in our case, the set of functions available to us is defined by what is possible using the Squarespace system.

Content

This one is pretty self-explanatory. The **content** of a website refers to the text and other media (such as PDFs or videos) that sit within each web page. Sometimes, the content will be provided by someone other than you, such as a marketing or communications staff member, or from a third party, such as a photographer, stock photo agency, or copywriter. Often, the content will need to be reformatted or reworked in order to make it suitable for use on a website.

Aesthetics

Many people would refer to **aesthetics** as *design*. However, other components such as structure (the size and placement of things) and content (photographs or length of text) also play a role in design. Therefore, it's easier to keep things distinct if we avoid this term, which can be broadly interpreted, and instead narrow our focus down to the way things look and feel. This means we are talking about colors, fonts, and graphic elements such as lines and patterns, not content or structure. The *feel* part of look and feel is quite important but harder to define. This is the tricky bit: it refers to how the website appeals to your emotions. Authoritative, refreshing, playful, vibrant, or zen are just a few examples of emotive words that can describe a site's *feel* or overall impression. These words will be critical in helping you choose colors, fonts, and other visual elements to fit with your desired impression. They will also play a role in content choices such as types of photography, tone of voice, and writing style.

Writing a website plan

Now that we understand the different components of a website, we can start to lay out the project plan or roadmap for this project. Your website plan keeps you focused, ensures that your messages are right, and sets the overall direction of your project. Your website plan is one of the most important parts of your Website Toolkit, so take your time on it, get it right, and keep it close to hand so that you can refer back to it easily.

 You can download a sample website plan template from this book's support bundle page on the http://www.packtpub.com/support website.

The website plan is laid out for you in the following sections, along with some sample answers and helpful questions to ask yourself so that you can ensure that you are on the right track when writing yours. Some of this information may already be available in your business, such as within your branding guidelines or annual reports. Don't just leave it there; put it into your website plan. For smaller businesses or those without such documents, there's no time like the present to sharpen up the way you communicate about your business, so let's get started. Many of the items included here can be used for other communication projects too.

About your business

The first section of your website plan summarizes your business and how it should be presented online.

Business overview (the "elevator pitch")

Describe your business in 2-3 sentences. Focus on what you do, what makes you different, and what your strongest selling points are. What are the key reasons your customers choose you instead of the competition?

Here's an example: Floribunda is a boutique florist that specializes in supplying unusual varieties of flowers to the wedding and catering trade. We create truly unique and distinctive arrangements by including colors and types of flowers that aren't available through any other florist in the tri-county area. Unlike other local florists, we have direct links with the best growers and only ever select the freshest, highest quality blooms.

Slogan (a.k.a. tagline or strapline)

Now, condense it down even further: does your business have a slogan or strapline that clearly defines what you offer in terms of uniqueness, benefits, or features? If not, you may find it useful to write one, as it will come in handy for your website. Ensure that it is no more than 10 words long, and open up thesaurus.com if you need word inspiration. Think about some of your favorite brands and the kinds of short, punchy phrases they use to communicate about their business.

The following are some examples:

- **Lastminute.com** – Book cheap, last-minute travel deals
- **Qantas Airlines** – All-inclusive airfares on Australia Pacific's best airline
- **Oxfam International** – The power of people against poverty

Brand image

List your company's brand values. If you don't have some already, think about how you would like your business to be perceived and list 4-5 descriptive words or phrases that you want people to feel about your business when they encounter your website.

Some examples are fresh, confident, down to earth, powerful, simple, rational, fun, energetic, cheeky, inexpensive, relaxed, quirky, luxurious, trustworthy, edgy, youthful, and refined.

About your audience

This section describes who will be coming to your website and why.

Your customers (the site's target audience)

Describe your typical customers. Pay special attention to their demographics (income, interests, gender, and age) and comfort with technology. If your website is a business-to-business site, exactly what sort of companies are you hoping to attract, and which level and type of staff members will access your site? If you have more than one type of customer, split them into primary and secondary audiences.

It may help you to think about your customer as a single individual, including his/her life experiences, job, favorite TV shows, brands, or books. How often does s/he go online, and what websites does s/he visit? In the web industry, we call this a **user persona**, and we always think about what this person would want or do, whenever we are developing the site.

 Be specific when defining your target audience. "Women" is not a target audience. "Upper middle-class French women over 50 with smartphones" is much better.

Primary purpose

What is the main reason that your target customers would come to your website? What action do you want them to perform? If there is more than one desired outcome, please prioritize them.

Some examples include buying a product, joining your online community, downloading a brochure, sending an enquiry, or calling your company.

About your website

The *About your website* part of your website plan helps you focus on what you want your website to do and includes some considerations you may need to take into account for this project.

Goals

What are the main goals you have for your website? What business objectives are you hoping to meet through this project? If this website will be replacing your old site, what do you want to be different/better about this one?

Some examples include generating sales, increasing leads, improving brand awareness, and reducing emails to your customer support team.

Functions

Thinking about your customers and the primary purpose described in the previous section, list the functions that your website will need to perform, in order of priority.

Some examples are: online shop, newsletter signup, RSS feed, and calendar of events.

Content

Briefly summarize the source, volume, and type of content for your site. Where will the content (text, images, downloadable files, videos) come from? Approximately how much content do you have in terms of number of pages? Is it available now? If not, when will it be ready? If it's coming from an existing source, will it need to be adjusted in any way to make it fit for your website?

 A content preparation checklist is included in this book's support bundle on the http://www.packtpub.com/support website.

Integration

Are there any pre-existing systems or tools that your website will need to integrate with or link to?

Some examples include credit card payment gateways, social media sites, and email newsletter systems.

Site management

Briefly summarize how the site will be managed. Who will be responsible for keeping the site updated? How often will it be updated? If you will have a blog, who will moderate the comments? If you will have an online shop, how will the fulfillment and inventory process be handled?

About this project

The last part of your website plan is about the logistics of this project.

Project team

Who will be involved in this project, and what role will each person play? Even if you are doing this on your own, it's useful for you to note the project roles, because you will need to allow time for them in your schedule.

Some role examples are: final decision maker, content provider, proofreader, tester, designer, copywriter, cost approver, and project manager.

Project timelines

When do you want your website to go live? Are there any key dates to bear in mind (for example, big meetings or holidays)? Setting a realistic timeline is important, and the amount of time your project will take depends on many variables. When setting your target date, review what you have written in your plan so far, as follows:

- **Content**: How ready is it? Always allow time to reformat and adjust it.
- **Functions**: How many and how complex are they? For example, if you need to set up an online shop, think about how many products you will need to configure.
- **Team**: Will everyone you need be available at the drop of a hat?

Remember to factor in your own availability or any other restrictions. Based on all of this, you should be able to come up with an estimated date. Now, add 30 percent extra time to this estimate, as contingency. Put this date in your calendar… in pencil.

Always set a preferred go-live date. Even if you don't have a specific date in mind, it can be useful to set an arbitrary date as your target to give you something to aim for, and to keep the project momentum.

Project budget

What is your budget for this project? You will need to budget for your Squarespace subscription, domain name (Squarespace includes one for free if you pay your subscription annually), and you might also want to set aside some money for things such as stock photo licenses and logo design. Remember, you don't need web hosting with Squarespace, so you won't need to budget for that.

 You have just completed the first—and the most important—part of your Website Toolkit: your website plan. You may want to print out your plan and put it in a folder next to your computer. You will need to refer back to it often.

Gathering materials, ideas, and inspiration

Now that you have your website plan and you know where you are headed, the next steps are to do some research and put together the rest of your Website Toolkit. The following sections can be carried out in any order, with some parts leading naturally to others as you work.

Creating idea boards

An **idea board** is a collection of ideas or inspiration that you can use as reference when creating your site. An idea board is similar to the concept of a **mood board** in fashion or interior design, but you will use them for more than just inspiration on color and style (mood), and ideally, you should have multiple boards for your website project.

Online tools such as `https://www.pinterest.com/` or `https://evernote.com/` allow you to collect things from around the Web and store them in different boards (Pinterest) or notebooks (Evernote). Although Pinterest is the easiest to use, Evernote allows you to store screen grabs with annotations such as arrows or circles, in addition to photos and web links. Either tool will work for your website project idea boards. The following screenshot example shows a private Pinterest board that was used for planning the `http://www.square-help.com/` website:

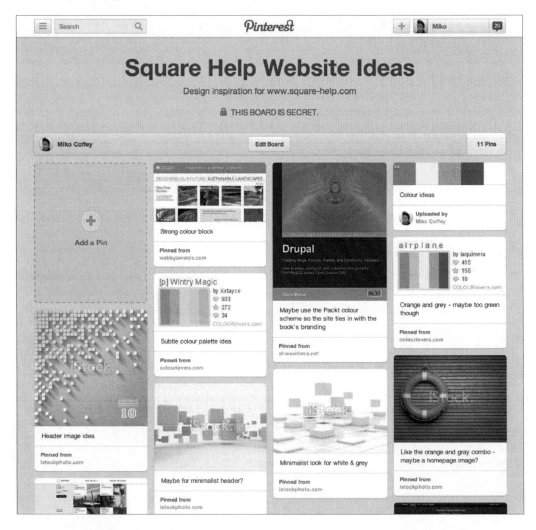

Your idea boards will be used for the work we'll do in the rest of this book, so it's a good idea to start them now and continue to add to them and edit them as you move through the early stages of your project.

Website inspiration

Just as an architect studies existing buildings and draws upon them for inspiration, I encourage you to start your research by looking at other websites to find out what you like and what you think would work well for your target audience.

 Visit http://winners.webbyawards.com and check out the winners in the Best Practice, Best User Experience, and Best Visual Design categories for inspiration of websites to help inspire you.

When looking at other websites, remember the four components of a website: structure, content, function, and aesthetics. If you find a site you like, mentally break it down into these components and try to figure out exactly why you like the site. Which of the four components are really working well on the site?

Play close attention to the following:

- **Call to action**: Is it clear what action the website owners want site visitors to perform?

- **Page elements**: Does the page have a clearly defined header, navigation area (possibly more than one), body, footer, and/or sidebar that would work well on your site?

- **Audience fit**: What elements of the site make it work well for its target audience?

- **Brand image and perception**: What emotive words do you feel when you look at the site? How does the choice of words, images, and aesthetics support this?

 Keep good, clear notes in your idea boards. Consider creating an idea board for each of the four different website components, or add a text note or screen grab that shows what component(s) you like when you add the site to your idea board so that you can easily remember them later.

Don't just look at your competitors' sites; doing so means you will likely focus too much on content alone. Try to expand your research into other categories. After all, your target customers are probably visiting a wide variety of websites.

Other resources for inspiration

Whereas looking at other websites is an activity that can help you narrow down your preferences, looking at things such as colors, fonts, and imagery can quickly become overwhelming and seemingly endless due to the sheer volume of choices available. We'll tackle these elements in earnest in *Chapter 5, Editing, and Arranging Content in Your Web Pages*, and *Chapter 8, Tailoring Your Site's Look and Feel*, where you'll be introduced to some resources and tools to help make things easier. For now, just make a note of any aesthetic elements you like as you go along, and be rest assured that we'll do more research and hone things down when we start building your site.

Creating a sitemap

Your sitemap lays out the overall structure of your website, acting as a blueprint for building. The sitemap is the foundation of your **information architecture**, which is a fancy word to describe the way in which visitors move around your site. Good information architecture is essential to enable your target audience to take the desired actions on your site. If visitors can't easily find what they need, they will leave—in an instant.

Even if you start out by writing things on paper, it's a good idea to make an electronic version of your sitemap, because you will be able to copy/paste page titles directly into Squarespace later.

Some people like to use software such as Microsoft PowerPoint, Apple Keynote, or Google Drive Drawings to layout their sitemap in a flowchart (organizational chart) style. Others prefer to use a word processor and create the sitemap as a text outline. Whichever way you choose, remember the following tips.

Don't make your customers work hard

Remember your customers' primary purpose and ensure that your site structure makes it easy for them to perform that action. Put yourself in their shoes and think about what they expect to see in your site, and where.

This is especially important if you are creating a website to replace an existing one. Don't just copy your existing site structure; take the time to revisit your site through the eyes of a customer.

Break it down

You may have many or just a few pages for your website. Either way, it's worth remembering that not every page or link is created equal. You can use a footer or sidebar on your website to house links to the less important information, such as terms and conditions, newsletter signup, or delivery information.

If you have several key areas, you might want to break them down into subpages to keep each page short and sweet.

Keep it simple

Don't use jargon or uncommon words as labels for site pages or sections. A first-time customer won't know that *The Scoop* is your news page, *KDD Lite* is the internal name for one of your services, or *Gimme Gimme Gimme* is your online shop section. You have less than 2 seconds to show your customers what they came for; don't make them have to think about what things mean.

Try to use common words such as *Home*, *Shop*, and *Contact*, because today's web users are accustomed to these labels. Unless your brand or product names are well known, consider using more general terms as labels for the pages or sections.

Even if one of your brand values is quirkiness or playfulness, you can convey this through your text, images, and visual elements—keep your navigation labels clear and concise.

Consider action words

One trend in website navigation is to use action words. This can make your site feel more inclusive and dynamic, and encourage your visitors to perform certain tasks. If you do this, be careful to ensure that the words are still clear and concise. The following table shows some examples:

Passive words	Equivalent action words
Newsletter	Sign Up
Store	Go Shopping or Buy Now
Enquiry Form	Contact Us or Get In Touch
About Us	Meet the Team
Location	Find Us
Membership	Join Now

Include notes or wireframes

As you go along, include any notes to yourself that you need to remember, such as cross-linking pages between sections or links to external sites such as Facebook.

You might find it easier to keep some notes in separate schematic drawings for certain pages. If so, go ahead and make some page wireframes (sketches) in addition to your sitemap. Tools such as `https://moqups.com/`, `http://lumzy.com/`, or Google Drive Drawings can create simple wireframes and are useful if you need to share your ideas or get approval from colleagues.

Once you have finished your sitemap and wireframes, have someone else look them over to sense-check. This could be a colleague or friend, ideally someone who fits your target audience.

 Avoid reinventing the wheel. Refer back to the websites in your idea boards when working on your own sitemap.

Gathering raw materials

One of the most time-consuming parts of creating your Website Toolkit is likely to be gathering your raw materials. You might have some of the materials you need already, or you might need to get them from someone else. Starting the process now rather than later in the project means you/they will have enough time to pull everything together in the right format without causing delays to your overall timeline.

Create a folder called `Materials` in your Website Toolkit folder. Take a moment now to run through each of the following sections, and place copies of your materials inside. If your materials are not ready yet, now is the time to get the ball rolling on sourcing and finalizing them. You don't necessarily have to have everything 100 percent complete before moving on to the next chapter, but you should definitely start gathering materials now, and continue to fine-tune things as you progress into the early stages of building your website. Refer to the content preparation checklist (included in this book's support bundle) to help with your content gathering.

Branding

If your company has a logo, approved brand colors, and fonts, you'll have a head start on your site's look and feel. If you don't have these things, don't worry; you can create them or source them inexpensively.

Logo

If you don't have a logo yet, you have a few options:

- Create a text-based logo as part of your site design. There are hundreds of fonts to choose from in Squarespace, so you can simply create your logo on the fly directly in the Squarespace system as part of the designing process later.

- Use Squarespace Logo (`http://squarespace.com/logo`) to create a simple logo design yourself. Squarespace subscribers can create a logo for free with Squarespace Logo. Alternatively, try the logo creation tool at `https://www.graphicsprings.com/` to make your own logo.

 We'll cover Squarespace Logo in more detail in *Chapter 8, Tailoring Your Site's Look and Feel*.

- Pay a graphic designer to create a custom logo for you. If you don't know a designer, try an online marketplace such as `http://www.guru.com/`, `http://99designs.com/`, or `https://www.freelancer.com/` to find one.

- Use a stock illustration as your logo. Most of the main stock websites such as `http://www.istockphoto.com/` or `www.shutterstock.com` offer illustrations for a very reasonable cost. Try searching for the word "logo" or "icon" in the **Illustrations** category. You might wish to collect a few different options on an idea board before committing to buy your final choice.

If you already have a logo or will be sourcing one, it's important to get a copy in the right format:

- **File format**: `.png` or `.jpg` format
- **Color space**: RGB or sRGB (not CMYK, which is used for print only)
- **Resolution**: 72 dpi/ppi (pixels per inch)
- **Maximum dimensions**: 1500 pixels wide

The dimensions and resolution are not as important as the other formatting options, as you can adjust the size in Squarespace's image editor later, if necessary.

Colors

If your company has brand colors, you will need to get the colors in the RGB or hex format. RGB (red, green, blue) is the method that backlit screens such as computer monitors or smartphones use to present colors. **Hex (hexadecimal)** color is a 6-digit alphanumeric way of presenting RGB colors, used in web design. Squarespace can use either RGB or hex colors.

The following is an example:

- **Color**: dark gray
- **Hex**: #333333
- **RGB**: rgb (51,51,51)

 Store your color references in a `.txt` file so that you can easily copy/paste them into Squarespace later.

If you don't have brand colors or you need to source additional colors, we'll do so in *Chapter 8, Tailoring Your Site's Look and Feel*.

 You can convert CMYK colors to RGB or hex format using an online tool. Search for `cmyk to rgb converter` in your favorite search engine.

Fonts

Once we start building the site, you'll be able to choose fonts from the *300+* fonts available within Squarespace, but some companies have specified fonts in their branding guidelines—and some require paid licenses for use. If your brand includes fonts such as these, you might need to source similar alternatives from the fonts that Squarespace offers, unless your brand uses Typekit fonts, which can be integrated and used on your site. We'll cover fonts in more detail in *Chapter 8, Tailoring Your Site's Look and Feel*. For now, make note of any special fonts associated with your brand, and find out about any licensing issues so that you'll have plenty of time to resolve them before the go-live date.

Text content

If you will be migrating content from another website to your new site or drawing from printed materials such as brochures, it's a good idea to carry out an audit of that content with your new sitemap as your guide. Regardless of whether you will be writing from scratch or reformatting the existing text, remember the following:

- As a general rule, search engines prefer web pages that have at least 250 words.

- Use as many words as necessary to convey your message, but keep your text focused.

- Use short paragraphs and dividing elements such as subheaders and bullets to help break up long pages. Consider breaking really long pages into multiple pages.

- Keep in mind your brand image and your site's desired *feel* when writing; ensure that your writing style, tone of voice, and choice of words reflect the image you want to convey.

Photos

If you already have photographs that you want to use on your site, do a quick review of them with your brand image and site's desired *feel* in mind.

 Unless you will be using them for very small thumbnails or icons only, all images should be at least 800 pixels on their longest side and, ideally, 1500 pixels on the longest side.

Squarespace caters for all sizes of screen, from large computer monitors to small phones, and it will resize images automatically to fit. There are also cropping and other image-adjustment tools built into Squarespace as well.

If you don't have photos yet but want to source some, have a look at http://www.istockphoto.com/, http://www.thinkstockphotos.com/, https://creativemarket.com/, or http://www.shutterstock.com/ for ideas. You should probably hold off on purchasing photos until you have selected your template in *Chapter 3, Working with Squarespace Templates*, but you can create a shortlist of photos in an idea board.

Downloads

If you will be offering any downloadable files on your site, ensure that they are formatted in an accessible way.

 Use PDF for documents, MP3 for audio, and ZIP for multifile folders.

Avoid file formats that will require users to have platform-specific or niche software to open them.

 Name your files in a logical way that will make sense to your customers. Use hyphens or underscores instead of spaces, as web browsers can have problems with spaces.

- Good: `jump-sportswear-price-list.pdf`
- Not so good: `020333871 V3 final-aug2014.doc`

Videos or audio streams

Squarespace does not offer video hosting or streaming, but you can embed videos hosted on other sites such as `http://www.youtube.com/` or `http://vimeo.com/`. You can also embed streaming audio from sites such as `http://soundcloud.com/` into a Squarespace web page.

 Create a `.txt` file and paste the links to your videos or audio streams into the file so that you will have quick access to them later.

Summary

You've now made a good start on creating your Website Toolkit, which will act as the foundation for everything we'll do in the rest of this book. It can take time to gather all of the materials and background research that goes into your toolkit, so don't worry if you don't have absolutely everything compiled at this stage. You can keep adding to it as we move into the next chapter and beyond.

You've done a lot of hard work so far, learning the concepts of making websites and doing your research, so have a well-deserved cup of tea before diving into *Chapter 2, Getting Started with Squarespace*, where we will finally get you signed up and started in the Squarespace system. We'll then introduce all of the key areas of the Squarespace interface so that you will know how to find your way around.

2
Getting Started with Squarespace

Now that you have started preparing your Website Toolkit with all the essential ingredients you'll need for your website, let's get signed up with a Squarespace account so that you can start working on your site. In this chapter, you'll learn your way around Squarespace and be introduced to the main controls that you will use to create your website. We will cover the following topics:

- Signing up and logging in to Squarespace
- Finding your way around Squarespace
- Understanding the main site editing and management tools
- Adjusting basic account and site settings

Signing up for a Squarespace account

All you need in order to sign up for Squarespace is a valid email address. Squarespace includes a free trial period, so you don't even need a credit card to get started—you can set up payment with your credit card later at the end of your trial period.

To sign up for your Squarespace account, perform the following steps:

1. Go to www.squarespace.com.
2. Click on the **Get Started** button.

   You will then be presented with a selection of templates to choose from. Don't worry too much about choosing the right template at this point, because we'll cover templates in the next chapter. Choose any template for now.

3. Click on the thumbnail image for your chosen template.

4. On the resulting screen, click on **Start With This Design**.

5. Enter the information in the **First Name** and **Last Name** fields.

 Whatever you enter here will be your Squarespace Site Name, which is also used to create your site's unique `Squarespace.com` address. For example, if you enter `Jane Doe` as your name, your site's Squarespace address will be `http://jane-doe.squarespace.com`.

Ideally, you should enter a form of your business name instead of your personal name. It's worth noting that you can use a custom domain name, such as `www.janedoe.com`, instead of your Squarespace Site Name, so don't fret too much about what you enter while signing up, especially if you plan to use a custom domain name when you launch the site. You can also change your Squarespace account name later, if you need to (we'll learn how to do this in *Chapter 9, Going Live with Your Website and Driving Traffic to It*).

Squarespace will insert a hyphen between whatever you put as **First Name** and whatever you put as **Last Name**.

First Name	Last Name	Squarespace Site Name / address
Jane	Doe	`http://jane-doe.squarespace.com`
Business	Websites	`http://business-websites.squarespace.com`
This-is	Hyphenated	`http://this-is-hyphenated.squarespace.com`

Squarespace account names must be between 3-25 characters long, and they can have numbers, letters, and hyphens.

 Even if you plan to use a custom domain name later, for now, you will access your site using your Squarespace Site Name, so ensure you write down and remember what you've chosen.

6. Enter your valid email address in the **Email** field.

 This is the email address that will be used for all communication and support with Squarespace, so ensure the address you use is one that you personally check regularly.

If you already have an account with Squarespace, you can link this new site to your existing account. Just enter the same e-mail address and the same password that you used for the other account here.

7. Enter a secure password in the **Password** field. It probably goes without saying, but you should always ensure you use a secure, unique password—ensure you remember what it is.

8. Click on **Finish & Create Site**.

The system will now check whether the Squarespace Site Name is available, and if so, it will automatically create your account and your Squarespace website. You will now see a floating **Welcome** box that invites you to answer a few questions to help set up your new website according to the purpose of your site.

To perform the initial set up for your new Squarespace website, click on **Next** and answer the questions on screen, as follows:

1. Under **Site Purpose**, select **Business**, and then click on **Next**.

2. Under **Site Title**, put the name of your business, and then click on **Next**.

3. Under **Business Information**, enter the address for your business if you want this information to be visible to the public. If not, you can skip this and click on **Done**.

This will close the dialog box and you will then be logged in to the backend administrative part of your website, called the **Squarespace Site Manager**.

Finding your way around Squarespace

In order to familiarize you with the Squarespace tools, let's take a quick tour of the main Squarespace editing areas, starting with the Squarespace Site Manager. The Site Manager is where you perform all tasks to set up and manage your website, and the Site Manager home screen is where you will land whenever you log in to your site.

The Site Manager home screen is shown here and is split into two parts:

- **Side panel**: This is present on the left-hand side of the screen. This is where the different control menus appear. The side panel in this screenshot shows you the **Home** Menu, which allows you to navigate to the main areas of Squarespace. Each area gives you access to different sets of tools. The contents of the side panel will change depending on which area you are in.

- **Preview screen**: This is present on the right-hand side of the screen. This large space is where you preview your website, edit content, make adjustments, and view the results. The Preview screen in this screenshot shows you a preview of the website homepage. The Preview screen always shows you a preview of the part of the site that you are working on.

You will notice that the preview screen on your computer shows something very similar to the homepage that you saw when you selected which template to use. That's because Squarespace preloads your template with demo content to make it easier for you to see and understand how different elements work with your template.

Understanding the Site Manager interface

The parts of the Site Manager interface can expand/contract depending on the type of activity you are performing. For example, the side panel will automatically expand to accommodate charts when you are viewing your site statistics (and therefore, the Preview screen will shrink accordingly). You can also hide the side panel entirely to fill the screen with your site preview. You can do this using the Expansion Arrow in the top-left corner of the Preview screen, shown here:

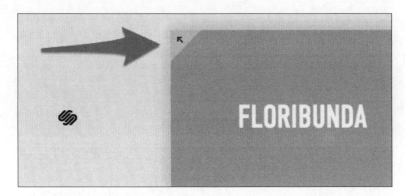

Clicking on the Expansion Arrow will:

- Expand the Preview screen to fill the browser window
- Disable all editing tools, allowing you to view and interact with your website just as your public visitors do

When in fullscreen preview, you will notice that the Expansion Arrow is still visible in the top-left corner, but the arrow points in the opposite direction. Clicking on the arrow will collapse the Preview screen, revealing the side panel and re-enabling the editing tools. You will toggle between these views a lot when working on your website, so take a moment now to try this. Fullscreen preview is very useful for testing content or design changes, so you can see things exactly as they will appear to your visitors on desktop computers.

However, you can also preview how your website will appear to visitors who use tablets or mobile devices using Squarespace's built-in Device View. You activate Device View by simply dragging the right or left edge of your browser to shrink the width of the window. As you shrink the width, the tablet view will trigger first, and if you continue to drag, the mobile view will trigger once you reach a certain narrower width. Tablet and mobile views display an outline silhouette of the device around the outside of the Preview screen:

Device View showing a mobile preview

Be aware that if you embed code into your pages using advanced customizations, they may not work while you are logged into your site, even in fullscreen preview. We'll cover advanced customizations in *Chapter 11, Moving beyond Standard Squarespace Tools*.

Understanding Annotations

Unlike some content management systems or blogging platforms, Squarespace allows you to make content changes directly on the page you are viewing. This means that you do not need to access a separate area to adjust content; you can make changes in the Site Manager by clicking on the area you wish to change in the Preview screen. Squarespace highlights editable areas using the Annotations system. Annotations appear when you hover your mouse over an editable part of your web page, and they show you the name of the element, a link to the tools you can use to make adjustments, and a border around the element that you'll be adjusting. Here's an example of an Annotation:

Take a moment now to hover over various parts of the page showing in your Preview screen to familiarize yourself with Annotations and to get a glimpse into the types of things we will adjust later. Just hover for now — don't click on anything yet, because we will need to perform a couple of steps before we dive into making adjustments. Instead, let's continue on our tour.

Using the Home Menu

The Home Menu in the side panel links to the following seven areas:

- **Pages**: This area displays your site structure and allows you to easily add, remove, and reorganize pages in your site's navigation.

- **Design**: The **Design** area is where you control the aesthetic appearance of your website.

- **Metrics**: The **Metrics** area shows you the statistics of your website traffic and how people are using your site.

- **Comments**: The **Comments** area is where you can access and approve blog comments if you have enabled the comment functionality.

- **Settings**: This is where you set up your site's technical configuration and manage user accounts. It is also where you set up payment for your Squarespace subscription.

- **Commerce**: This area is where you manage all aspects of your online shop, such as orders, inventory, and shipping.

- **Help**: This link opens the Squarespace Help Center in a new window, where you can search for help in the Knowledge Base, or contact Squarespace directly for assistance.

At the bottom of the Home Menu, you'll see a round user icon and your name. Clicking on your user icon opens a shortcut box where you can quickly jump to your user profile to edit it, log out of the Squarespace editor, add a new Squarespace site to your account, or switch between Squarespace sites (if you have more than one associated with your account).

The first six areas in the Home Menu are where you set up, add, adjust, and remove things on your website, so let's take a quick look at each one in turn. The subsequent chapters will cover each one in more detail, but for now, we'll introduce each area and its purpose to give an overview of the entire Squarespace system.

Using the Pages area

When you click on the **Pages** link in the Home Menu, you will notice that the content of the side panel changes to display a list of the pages on your website. As you have not created any real pages yet, you will see the pages that came with your demo site, along with the word **Demo** next to each of them. You will also notice a link and arrow at the top of the panel that you can use to return to the Home Menu. Here's an example of the **Pages** panel:

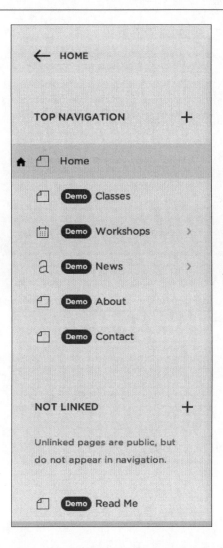

You will use the **Pages** area to control the site structure. Here, you can add or delete pages and set the type of page (for example, blog, image gallery, or standard text page). You can also control the site's menus here, including reordering pages and creating submenus (drop-down menus).

Click on the **Home** link at the top of the screen now to return to the Home Menu so we can continue the tour.

Using the Design area

When you click on the **Design** link in the Home Menu, you will see the following menu appear in the side panel:

As you can see from the Design Menu items, the Design area is where you can input a logo, switch to a different template, adjust the visual style of your website or certain pages within it, and perform other adjustments to control the appearance of your website.

Return to the Home Menu now, and then return to it again after each of the following sections to carry out the rest of our tour.

Using the Commerce area

When you first click on the **Commerce** link in the Home Menu, a dialog box will open to tell you some about the basic requirements of using Squarespace Commerce. Click on the **Get started with Commerce** button at the bottom of the box to close it and reveal the main **Commerce** menu, as shown in the following screenshot:

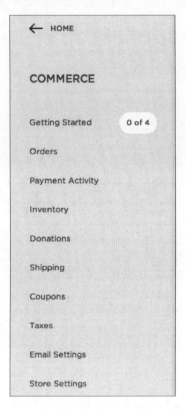

If you plan to sell goods or services, take donations, or offer paid subscriptions, the **Commerce** area is where you will set up and manage all commerce-related functions for your website.

Currently, Squarespace Commerce is only integrated with the **Stripe payment gateway**, which is only fully supported in USA, UK, Canada, Australia, and Ireland. *If you live in a different country or do not want to use Stripe, you will only be able to use a very limited set of Squarespace Commerce tools.

At the time of writing this, Stripe is also being made available in other countries in the Beta mode, so visit www.stripe.com/global to see whether your country is supported today.

You can use Commerce to do the following:

- **Manage products**: Create products; set options such as sizes, prices, or colors; organize your products into categories; and track the inventory of your products

- **Manage orders**: Track orders, handle fulfillment, and set shipping options

- **Manage your finances**: Set up your online payment gateway, taxes, and currency and offer discounts through promo codes

- **Manage customer communication**: Configure the e-mails that your customers receive, set return and privacy policies, or link your store to your e-mail newsletter system

Using the Metrics area

Clicking on the **Metrics** link will load the following menu in the side panel:

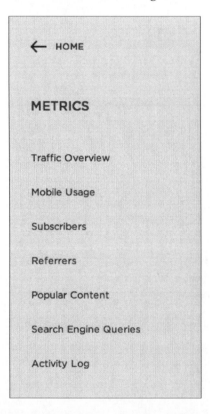

Once your website is live, you will want to check the Metrics reports often, so you can see how people are using your site and make adjustments if necessary.

You will use Metrics reports for the following:

- **Monitoring website traffic**: See how many visits your site has received in the past day, week, month, or year—and whether visitors are viewing on mobile devices or standard computers.

- **Understanding how people find your website**: Check which sites are sending traffic to your site and find out what search terms people are using to look for your site in Google and other search engines.

- **Understanding what content your customers like—and don't like**: Compare the popularity of each of your site's pages to determine whether you need to change your site's content or structure to improve it.

 You can also use Google Analytics with your Squarespace website, if you prefer. We'll cover this in *Chapter 10, Managing Your Squarespace Website*.

Comments

Click on the **Comments** link in the Home Menu to expand the side panel to show the following **Comments** panel:

At present, the Comments panel is empty, but if you have a blog on your site, you will use this area to approve comments, respond to them, remove them, or mark comments as spam.

Settings

The next area accessible from the Home Menu is the **Settings** area. When you click on **Settings**, you will see the following menu in the side panel:

You will mainly use the **Settings** area at the beginning of your project to configure your site and set things up before you start building and populating your site with content. We'll carry out many of these activities in the next part of this chapter.

You can use **Settings** to set up the following:

- **Information about your business**: You can enter business-related information, such as your company name and slogan, and indicate where your business is located.

- **Information about your Squarespace account**: This is where you set your subscription plan, payment details, and account name.

- **Control access and visibility**: You can enable a custom domain name, set up some important features for search engines, or lock public access to your website.

- **Social media sharing**: Here is where you can link to your Facebook page or allow visitors to share your content within their social networks.

- **Additional authors**: You can add user accounts here to allow colleagues to contribute content and manage the site.

You probably won't need to use most of the more technical or advanced settings unless you later find that you want to do some complicated things with your site (usually with the help of a Squarespace developer).

Logging in and out of Squarespace

Now that we've gone through an overview of the six main site management areas in Squarespace, it's a good time for one final stop on our introductory tour: logging in and out of the Squarespace editor.

If you've followed this chapter up until this point, you should still be logged in, so we'll cover logging out first. You can log out by following these steps:

1. Ensure you are in the Home Menu and click on the user icon at the bottom of the side panel.

2. In the pop-up shortcut box, click on the **Logout** button.

You will now be logged out and automatically directed to the public view of your website.

 If you are still on a trial account, you will see a message indicating this instead of seeing your website's pages. This is because trial sites are not public yet.

Logging in

There are three different ways to log in to the Squarespace editor: two of them can be done on your Squarespace website, and the last one can be done on Squarespace's own website.

In all cases, you will need to enter your e-mail address and Squarespace password, so ensure you have them handy.

> On the login screen, you will have the option to tick the **Stay Logged In** box. If you tick this box, Squarespace will automatically log you in whenever you visit your website even if you close your browser or shut down your computer.

Logging in by pressing Esc

The easiest way to log in is to use a keyboard shortcut whenever you are on any page on your Squarespace website:

1. Open your Squarespace website in your web browser (`http://your-account-name.squarespace.com`).

> If you are on a trial account, you will need to choose **Visitor Access** on the black lock screen and then enter the code shown to open the public view of your website.

2. Hit the *Esc* key on your keyboard.

> You can use this method even if you have set a custom domain name. Instead of going to `http://your-account-name.squarespace.com`, just go to `http://www.customdomain.com` and hit *Esc* to log in.

> If you plan to use videos or slideshows on your website that will be viewed in fullscreen mode, you may want to disable the ability to log in via *Esc*, because the *Esc* key is also used to enter/exit fullscreen mode in media viewers. You can disable it in **Settings**.

Accessing your site's login page

The login page for your Squarespace website can be accessed directly by going to `http://your-account-name.squarespace.com/config`.

You may want to add this URL to your bookmarks, so you can log in quickly in the future.

You can use this method even if you have set a custom domain name; just visit `http://www.customdomain.com/config` instead.

Logging in via the Squarespace site

You can also log in from the `www.squarespace.com` site: click on the **Login** button in the top-right corner.

If you manage multiple Squarespace sites under one account, you will be logged into whichever site you were last working on. Once logged in, you can switch to another site using the shortcut box that appears when you click on your user icon in the Home Menu.

This is the method to use if you have forgotten your Squarespace Site Name. Once logged in, your Squarespace Site Name will show in your browser's URL bar, so don't forget to write it down.

Adjusting basic site settings

Before you get too far down the line with your project, it's a good idea to set up some of the basic things related to your website. Have your website plan from your Website Toolkit handy, and let's get started.

All of the items we'll set up are in your **Settings** area, so log in and navigate to that area.

Adding Basic Information

Click on the link to open the **Basic Information** panel. As part of the initial setup, you should have already selected **Site Type**, so we can skip that and move on to **Site Description**. You can paste your Business Overview from your website plan here. Certain Squarespace templates show you this information on the homepage or sidebar.

Site Description as it appears on the Aviator template

Next, decide whether you are happy for your website to be shown in Squarespace's index, and check the **Promotion/Indexing** box accordingly.

Finally, click on the **Business Information** link to load this section into the side panel. You may need to click on **Save** in the dialog box to store any changes you made to **Site Description** first. Review the screen notes regarding your business contact details, and fill in the parts that are applicable to your business. When you are finished, click on the **Save** button at the top of the screen to store your changes.

Use the navigational arrow links at the top of the side panel to return to the **Settings** menu now and after all of the upcoming **Settings** adjustments.

Setting your site's language and region

Open the **Language & Region** panel to set your language and time zone, as this will affect the display of any time- or date-based content (such as blog post dates). To change the time zone, click on your location in the map. You should also set the country in the **Geography** drop-down menu, as this setting affects the default currency and certain other commerce-related items. Save your changes and return to the **Settings** menu.

Setting up the SEO options

Click on **SEO** to load this section into the side panel. The first setting in the **SEO** section is **Search Engine Description**. This is an important field, because whatever you put here will be shown on search engine results pages. This text appears below the link to your site, so make sure it entices people to click. Use a variation of your Business Overview from your website plan here.

Using My Head - London **Squarespace** design and support
usingmyhead.**squarespace**.com/ ▾
Squarespace web designer and trainer for London, UK and beyond. I make **Squarespace** websites and train clients on how to manage them.

The gray text is the Search Engine Description as it appears on Google search results

Google will only display the first 150-155 characters, so use short sentences and check your character count if you don't want the end to be cut off.

You can use an online character counter such as `http://charactercounttool.com/` to calculate the number of characters in your text.

The rest of the settings on this page can be left as is for now. You'll have a chance to come back and adjust them later if necessary, but the default settings are fine to get started.

Keeping your site private until its launch

Squarespace hides your website from the public during your free trial period, but it's unlikely you will complete your website and have all the finishing touches applied before your Squarespace trial ends. Therefore, you need to take measures to ensure your site stays private and hidden from the public regardless of whether you are in your trial period or not. You can do this by setting a **Site-Wide Password** in the **Security** section.

You may want to use your normal Squarespace account password here, so you don't have to remember another one. However, if you will be showing your site to colleagues, choose a different password and don't forget to write it down.

Setting up your subscription plan and billing

At this point, you are using a free Squarespace trial account, so you don't have to choose a subscription plan yet, but it's worth covering here as it is part of your basic site setup. Feel free to use up your free trial (currently, this is 14 days), and come back to this bit when you are ready to choose your plan and set up your billing information.

Choosing the right subscription plan

Squarespace currently offers three different subscription plans, each with different levels of features and functionalities. As Squarespace often adjusts what is offered with each plan, check `www.squarespace.com/pricing` to see what's currently available and to see the current prices for each plan.

The Squarespace subscription plans are in the order of the least used to most used features: **Personal**, **Professional**, and **Business**. Your free trial account is set to the highest level, which is Business.

All Squarespace plans include:

- Access to the full set of Squarespace editing and site-building tools, including the full range of site templates
- Fully integrated e-Commerce
- The ability to create all types of pages: standard pages, blogs, and galleries
- Plenty of storage space for images and other files
- The hosting of your site, with plenty of bandwidth for most sites
- A free custom domain name if you pay yearly

Everything we cover in this book applies to all levels of Squarespace plans, so browsing the table of contents will give you a good idea of all the features you get as the standard. The differences in the subscription plans are mainly about restricting the number and volume of things and allowing you access to do more complex things with your site.

The Personal plan

The Personal plan places limitations on the number of pages, products, and contributors you can have on your site and how much storage and bandwidth you can use.

The Personal plan includes all of the standard features listed previously, with the following limitations:

- A maximum of 20 pages on your site

 20 pages may not seem like enough, especially if you want to have a blog or news section on your site. However, Squarespace does not count individual posts in this 20 page limit; your blog as a whole counts as only 1 page.

- Sell only 1 product with multiple variants such as size or color and/or accept donations through Squarespace Commerce
- A maximum of two contributors (for example, authors or shopkeepers) with access to the site's administration area
- A maximum of 2 GB file storage space for your images and downloads
- A maximum of 500 GB bandwidth per month (the amount of traffic your site can have)

The personal plan is suitable for most small businesses that do not need to sell products online or for nonprofit organizations. The restrictions on file storage and bandwidth do not really affect most small sites, unless you offer large file downloads on your site or expect to have very heavy traffic peaks at certain times of the year.

The Professional plan

The Professional plan relaxes the restrictions of the Personal plan, and should you wish to have a highly customized site, it gives Squarespace developers full control of the code that affects the design of your site.

The Professional plan includes all of the standard features, plus:

- Unlimited pages, contributors, storage, and bandwidth
- Sell up to 20 products
- Access to the Developer platform (refer to *Chapter 11, Moving beyond Standard Squarespace Tools*, for more detail)

The Professional plan is suitable for businesses that need to have a lot of content on the site or for boutique-style shops that have a small number of products to sell online.

The Business plan

The Business plan removes all restrictions and offers integration with third-party tools for improved online shop workflow.

The Business plan includes all of the features of the Professional plan, with the following extras:

- Sell unlimited products
- Automated shipping label printing by ShipStation
- Real-time US Postal Service shipping calculations
- Integrated accounting by Xero

The Business plan is suitable for businesses with a lot of products to sell online or any business that wants to streamline their online shop processes—especially those based in USA, as most of the third-party tools are US-specific.

Setting up your billing information

In order to keep your account and website active, you will need to set up regular billing by credit card before the end of your trial period. You can pay monthly or annually.

 Squarespace rewards customers who pay annually by giving a 20% discount and a free custom domain name, so annual payment is the most cost-effective option.

Open the **Billing & Account** section and perform the following steps to set up your subscription:

1. Click on **Upgrade** to open the **Select a Plan** screen.

2. Choose your option under **Plan Level and Billing Period**.

3. Enter the credit card that you wish to be charged.

4. Click on **Update Payment Information**.

 If you need an invoice for tax or accounting purposes, you can view all invoices associated with your account by clicking on the **Invoices** link in the **Billing & Account** menu.

Summary

You've now completed all of the essential administration setup for your site, so you are ready to start constructing your site. As mentioned in *Chapter 1*, *Setting Up for Success – Your Website Toolkit*, we'll be following a similar process as constructing a building: first, we'll put together the framework, then we'll install the core elements that make the site do what it needs to do, and lastly, we'll apply the visual finishing touches that make the site unique to you.

The next chapter focuses on one of the most critical decisions you will make in this project: choosing the right site template. The site template is what determines the overall shape of your website and what functions and structural elements it can have. In our building analogy, the template is what dictates whether the building can be a single story house, a hospital, a high-rise office building, or type of building.

Before choosing your template, it's essential that you understand the website concepts we talked about in the previous chapter, and it's even more helpful if you have done your research and have some idea boards bursting with inspiration. If you need to go back and do this, now is a great time for a little refresher before you dive into *Chapter 3*, *Working with Squarespace Templates*.

3

Working with Squarespace Templates

Choosing the right Squarespace **template** for your website is one of the most important decisions you will make on this project. The template dictates the overall structure of your site's pages, sets the starting point for your site's look and feel, and in some cases, restricts the types of pages, content, and other elements that you can have on your site. To help you make the right choice, in this chapter, we will cover:

- The characteristics of a Squarespace template
- Template variables and how they can restrict you
- An overview of the different templates available in Squarespace
- Browsing and exploring templates
- Installing and applying templates
- Using template Preview Mode

Understanding Squarespace templates

Squarespace templates are basically readymade kits for website design. Each template contains certain stylistic and structural elements that you can apply to your website. It may help to compare them to kits of Lego toys: each one is unique, and each comes with certain pieces that you can use to create something that looks very much like the picture on the box. Although you may be able to use your imagination to create other things using these pieces, there are certain restrictions that apply depending on the kit you have purchased. For example, if you buy a kit to make a castle, it is unlikely that you will be able to build a very good racecar—and vice versa. Some kits have many different pieces, offering a lot of complex options. Others have fewer pieces or pieces with very specific shapes and therefore, less scope for creativity.

Squarespace templates are similar, as they can be used to create websites that look very much like the sample website shown for each template. Or, you can use your creativity to deviate from the sample site, but there will be restrictions on how far you can go depending on the template you have chosen.

Characteristics of a Squarespace template

Each template has several different characteristics that will affect your site's design and structure. These three characteristics are page structure, visual style, and special features. Some elements of these characteristics will be set in stone, while others have variable options to allow you to adjust the template. Let's go through each of the template characteristics in more detail so that you can understand how they will affect your site.

Page structure

Page structure refers to the position of the core elements on the page. If you chose to make wireframes for your site part of your Website Toolkit, you may have already sketched out a desired page structure. Or, you may have some ideas for page structure from the sites you researched in your idea boards.

Many people may be inclined to think of page structure as the same thing as page layout. However, when it comes to Squarespace, this can end up causing confusion. The page structure is set across the entire site and usually applies to every page on the site, regardless of the type of page or the content sitting within that page. Page structure is determined by the template and cannot be changed without switching templates. Your site navigation is an example of a structure element.

In Squarespace, page layout refers to the way the individual content elements are arranged on a specific page, not sitewide. The text and photos on a page are layout elements. You can think of page structure as macro level and page layout as micro level. Page structure applies to elements that are reused on many pages, while layout only applies to the content elements on one page.

The following main components of page structure are set and controlled by the Squarespace template. There are others, but these are the main ones you will notice when comparing templates.

Before we define each component, here is a diagram that may help you understand how they all fit together:

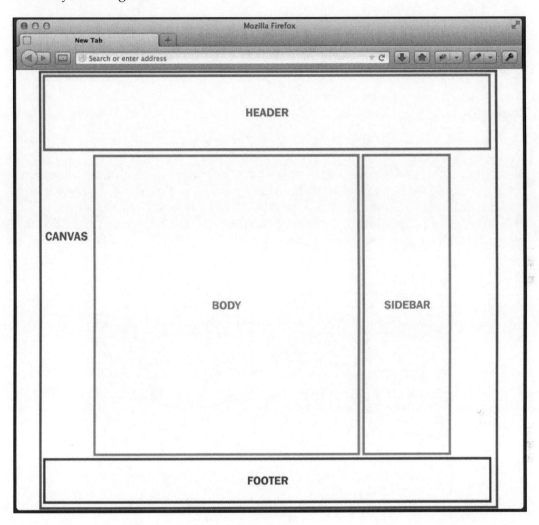

 The names used here correspond to the names used in the Squarespace Style Editor. Advanced users familiar with HTML should not confuse these terms with actual HTML tags, such as <body>.

Canvas

The **canvas** is the part of the web page that contains all of the content, visual, and navigation elements. The canvas is usually the main outer container within which everything else sits. However, the canvas is not always the full width or height of your web browser window: sometimes, template designers leave borders around the edges of the canvas to allow a background image, color, or pattern to show behind the canvas.

Header

Most templates have a **header** at the top of the page that contains the main site navigation and the logo or site title. In the web industry, we often refer to the main navigation area as a navigation bar—or **navbar** for short. Many templates separate the navbar from the rest of the header using a visual separator, such as a horizontal line or a different background color. The header may also contain a header image, also known as a **banner** image. Depending on the template, the header may also display the site's tagline or other short text.

Header shown on the Five template

In certain templates, there is no header at the top of the page; instead, the logo and navigation appear vertically along the left-hand side of the page, as shown in this example:

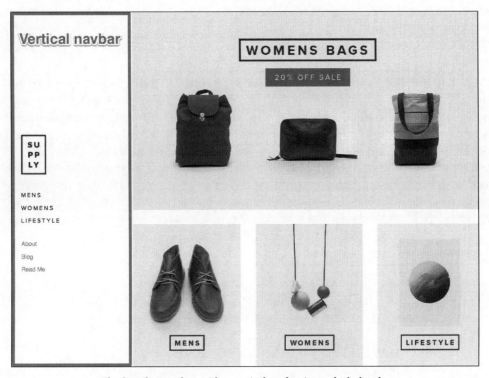

The Supply template with a vertical navbar instead of a header

Body

The **body** contains all of the main content and functions of the page, usually comprising text, images, and video. In Squarespace, each chunk of content is referred to as a content block. Content blocks can be arranged within the page body in many different ways—for example, in multiple columns or with text wrapping around images. This is how you control the page layout. We will learn a lot more about content blocks in the next chapters.

The body usually sits below the header and above the **footer**.

Footer

The **footer** sits along the bottom of the page and usually contains general information such as a copyright notice or link to social media profiles. The footer can also contain nearly any other type of content block, such as a short description of the site or a newsletter signup form.

Sidebar(s)

A template may include one or more **sidebars**, which are narrow columns that sit next to the body. Sidebars often contain short content blocks, such as testimonial quotes or a list of blog post categories, and they can sometimes be separated from the body by a dividing line or a different background color. It's easy to confuse a sidebar with a column of content within the page body, but remember that sidebars are structural, not layout, elements. This means that a sidebar appears in the same place with the same contents on multiple pages, like headers or footers. However, unlike headers or footers, which usually appear on every single page, some templates specify that the sidebars only be shown on certain page types, such as blog pages. Most blogs on the Web use sidebars, as do many news sites. The following screenshot displays a sidebar:

Example of a sidebar, shown here on the Galapagos template

Visual style

The second characteristic of a Squarespace template is the visual style. In Squarespace terms, style refers to the aesthetics of your website—that is, the colors, fonts, patterns, backgrounds, and borders applied to the different elements of your site.

All templates specify the default colors, size, and placement of the core page elements. It is then up to you to adjust these things according to your own taste to make your site unique. The level of control you have varies from template to template, but as a general rule, you will be able to adjust the following:

- The color of text and backgrounds
- The font choice and size of text
- The alignment, padding (spacing), and size (height or width) of elements
- Decoration, such as borders or dividing lines

You may also be able to turn the display of some elements on or off, such as social media icons in the footer.

In some templates, the designer has specified each individual element to a very granular level—for example, setting the color and font for headings, subheadings, and sub-subheadings separately. In other templates, the designer has set things very broadly, which means there are fewer things that you can control.

In all templates, you will notice that the default style of the template is quite subdued, with most templates having a white background and simple, dark gray text. This is so you will not be influenced by strong colors or stylized fonts when choosing your template. Instead, you can focus on choosing a template based on its structure and features, which you cannot change, instead of the visual style, which you can change.

Special features

The final characteristic of a Squarespace template is its special features: a broad category that covers many types of settings that may apply to a template. Because Squarespace allows customers to build many different types of website—from personal blogs to online shops to photo galleries—some templates have features that make these templates more suitable for one type of site over another. Some special features may only be available with one or two templates, but there are some that appear in more templates, so let's examine each of these more common special features to learn more about what they can do for you.

Different homepage

Some templates have a different page structure and visual style for the home page than the rest of the site. This often takes the form of a large, fullscreen image that occupies all of the homepage canvas and is useful for creative businesses.

Homepage in the Frontrow template

Secondary navigation area

Some templates are geared toward sites with lots of pages. These templates often include a secondary navigation area—or even a secondary and tertiary navigation. Sometimes, this appears as a navigation area within the footer for things such as terms and conditions or return policies. In other templates, the secondary navigation only appears when you set up a **folder** with subpages in your site's main navigation. A folder is a navigational container that is used to group a collection of pages together under one main navigation item. Normally, navigation to pages in folders only shows as a drop-down menu as part of the main navbar. In templates with a special secondary navigation setup, the secondary navigation appears as a second navbar or sidebar when you go to a page in the folder to allow visitors to easily navigate between pages within that folder. A good use for this is different categories of products. A secondary navigation area is shown in the following screenshot:

Secondary navigation on the Adirondack template

Index page

Some templates take the idea of the folder and secondary navigation even further, choosing to display the different pages within the folder visually on a special type of page called an **Index** page. An Index page is really just a special kind of folder: a collection of pages grouped together. There are two types of Index pages:

- **Grid**: This displays a grid of thumbnail images, and each thumbnail links to a different page within the Index.

- **Scroll**: This displays the full content of all pages within the Index in one long, scrolling page.

Here's an example of a grid Index:

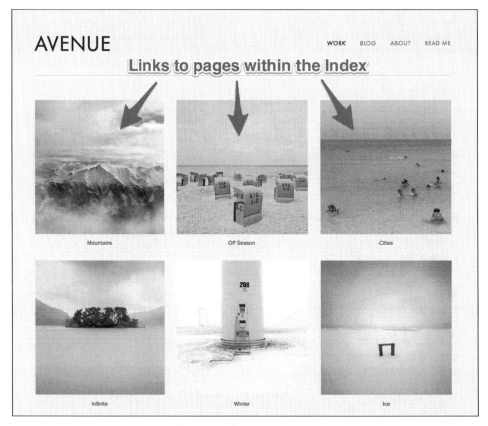

Index page in the Avenue template

The following screenshot depicts a scrolling Index:

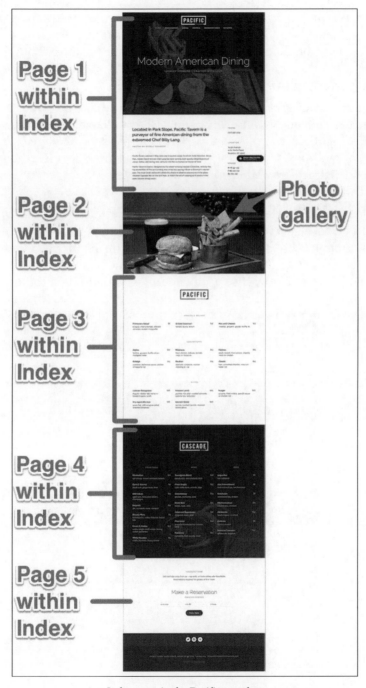

Index page in the Pacific template

In some templates, you can only have an Index collection of photo galleries; this is useful for photographers or designers with lots of projects to show. In other templates, you can only have an Index collection of normal pages; this kind of Index is useful for businesses with lots of case studies, for example. And in others, you can have an Index collection that contains either galleries or pages (or both).

Variable header images

In some templates, you can vary the header image on a page-by-page basis or turn it off entirely on certain pages within your site. Using variable header images is a good way to visually highlight an important concept on that specific page. Turning the header image off entirely is useful for pages such as contact forms, where you may want to remove distractions and keep the page clean.

Promoted Blocks in blog posts

Some templates have a special feature designed for blogs, events, or news pages with strong visual content, such as photo or video blogs. This feature is called a **Promoted Block**, and it allows you to put a large image, gallery, or video at the very top of your blog post. Some templates also apply special styling to the Promoted Block, such as showing it in full width to make it stand out even more. This is useful for drawing the eye in or making certain important posts stand out from the rest:

Promoted Block shown in the Boutique template

Fixed navigation

Some templates make the navbar **fixed**, which means that the navigation area will be visible even after you scroll. Normally, scrolling down on the page will also scroll the navigation, so it disappears off the top. With fixed navigation, the navbar sticks in place, and the rest of the page content scrolls. This is useful for sites with lots of text or images per page, such as long blog articles, or for sites that use a scrolling Index.

Choosing the right Squarespace template for your site

Now that you understand the different characteristics of a template, it's time to start thinking about which of the 30+ templates that Squarespace offers is the right one for you. In this part of the chapter, we'll outline the steps and techniques you can use to make the right decision and explore the different templates currently available.

Before we start exploring the templates, it's important to note that Squarespace keeps the design of your site separate from the content. This means that you can safely change the site template without affecting the content. Therefore, although our goal is to choose the right template from the start, you can always switch templates later, even after you have filled the site with your content, without worrying about losing your work. This makes it possible for you to freshen up your site in future, whenever you fancy a new look.

The exception to this rule is special features. If you have been using a template that has a special feature, and you switch to a template that does not have the same special feature, this *will* be affected, and you won't be able to use whatever it was that you had before. Pay extra attention to special features such as Index pages when considering templates.

Squarespace has provided several ways for you to view the different templates to help you make your choice. You can do the following:

- See a **Live Preview** of the template on a demo site. The demo site contains fake content but has been mocked up to represent a realistic business so you can get an idea of how things would look and work on a real site.

- View real-life **example sites** that use that template. For each template, Squarespace provides some links to actual websites for real businesses that have created their own sites using that template.

- Use the template **Preview** function to apply the template in the test mode on your own site. This will allow you to preview how the template works with your own content before you commit to it.

We'll cover each of these in this chapter. However, clicking around the different Squarespace templates without a plan will only end in confusion, especially as many of them look very similar at first. Therefore, it's important to do some thinking before you do any clicking.

Selecting the best template for your needs

Before you start looking at any templates, go through these steps to make the selection of your template more methodical to save time and ensure you end up with a template that is appropriate for your site.

Step 1: Consider the site's primary purpose and important functions

In your website plan, you should have written the primary purpose of your site and listed the key functions you need your site to perform. In theory, all templates offer the full set of key Squarespace functions, but certain templates will be better suited to certain functions, such as selling products or showcasing a creative portfolio. Keep your primary purpose in the front of your mind when exploring templates.

 You may want to circle this part of your website plan or write it on a sticky note and stick it to your computer. It's easy to get dazzled by fancy features when choosing templates, so this will help bring you back to your goals.

Step 2: List the special features that you want

When you were learning about the special features earlier in this chapter, you may have recognized one or more that would really work well for your site. Write them down now, along with whether they are essential or just nice to have. You may also want to refer to your idea boards to see whether there is anything in your wish list that may be available as a special feature in Squarespace.

Step 3: Identify the page structure you like best

You probably have quite a few inspiration sites in your idea boards, and once you start exploring templates, you may end up with even more ideas. Take a look at your inspiration sites now and see whether you can identify any similarities, especially when it comes to page structure. Do they all have horizontal navigation at the top? Do they have large header images? Or, maybe they use sidebars or vertical navigation. If you can see similarities, it will help you narrow things down, but don't worry if you can't find a common thread at this stage.

Step 4: Refer back to your brand and content

No matter how appealing it may appear, there's no sense choosing a template that won't work well with your content or brand. Some templates work best with small amounts of text, while others can cope well with long pages. Some are designed to showcase powerful imagery, and others focus more on powerful messages. Refer to your Website Toolkit for a reminder of what you will be putting into your site, and keep these things in mind when choosing your template.

An overview of the different Squarespace templates

Once you've gone through the four steps, and you have your notes handy for reference, you're ready to start narrowing down the choice of templates that Squarespace offers. At the time of writing, there are 32 different templates for you to choose from. To help you match the template to your needs, there's a handy chart in *Appendix B, Squarespace Templates in a Nutshell*. This chart shows you all of the main features and differences between each template in an easy-to-compare format. It's probably the most useful part of this book, so take a look now.

> As Squarespace regularly adds or removes templates and features offered with the templates, you should check out www.square-help. com/templates for the latest version of this chart, along with a more detailed list of features and specifications for each template.

Although there are technically 32 templates, some of these are variants of another template. Refer to the detailed feature list at www.square-help.com/templates to find out which templates are based on others. You'll also find notes about which templates are best for certain situations and which templates have features that are similar to others.

Browsing templates

The list of templates and key features can only take you so far when it comes to making your final selection; the next stage is to browse the templates, making notes as you go:

1. Go to www.squarespace.com/templates. You will see the same set of thumbnails that you saw when you set up your account.

To help you narrow your choices, Squarespace allows you to filter the templates by category. You will see the list of categories above the thumbnail grid, where it says **Featured**, **Business**, **Portfolios**, and so on.

2. Hover your mouse over a thumbnail to see the name of the template.
3. Pick a template to preview, and click on the **View (Template Name)** button.
4. The resulting screen gives you three different options to view the demo site and examples.

   To view the demo site in a desktop browser:

   1. Hover over the large thumbnail at the top next to the name of the template.
   2. Click on the **Live Preview** button that appears when you hover. The resulting screen will have the demo site loaded into a frame.

Next to the **Start With This Design** button at the top, you'll see the web address for the demo site. Click on the web address to open the demo site in a new browser tab. This will allow you to have multiple tabs open with several template demos or several sites that use a certain template—a great way to compare.

   To view the demo site in a mobile browser:

   3. Hover over the mobile phone image next to the large thumbnail of the template.
   4. Click on the **Mobile View** button that appears when you hover. The resulting screen will have the demo site loaded into a frame that simulates viewing the template on a smartphone.

   To view real-life example sites in a desktop browser:

   5. Scroll down to the thumbnails of customer sites using this template.
   6. Click on a thumbnail to view the example. The resulting screen will have the example site loaded into a frame.

Just as with the demo site, you can click on the web address of the example site at the top to open the example site in a new browser tab. The example site web address appears next to the **Create A Site Like This** button.

Important points to remember when browsing templates

As you browse the templates, there are a few important things that you should remember in order to make your choices most effectively:

- It's a good idea to browse both the demo site and some example sites for each template that you are considering. The demo site will only show you a single view of what the template can do, whereas the example sites will show you a broader range of what is possible with the template. Just bear in mind that most example sites have been built by professional website designers, so you may not be able to achieve everything you see on the example sites without the help of a professional.

- When choosing templates, focus on function, structure, and features. Remember that the visual style that comes with a template is only a starting point, and most of this can be changed to give dramatically different results from what you see in the demo and example sites.

- The page structure set by the template is not flexible: the structure you see is the structure you will get. As a general rule, the only things you can change about the structure are the aesthetics of each component. For example, you can change the size and color of a navbar, but you would not be able to switch from a horizontal navbar to a vertical one within the same template.

There are a couple of exceptions, but they are very rare. Check out www.square-help.com/templates for details of exactly what is possible with each template.

- All of the Squarespace templates are designed to work well on computers, tablets, and smartphones, but some templates use fancy menus or make certain structural changes to the page when viewing on a mobile device. Be sure to browse templates on tablets and smartphones, in addition to a desktop computer monitor, to see how your chosen template behaves on these devices.

 If you don't have a tablet or smartphone handy, you can simulate a smaller screen on your computer by manually dragging the right edge of your browser window to make it smaller. This is useful when viewing example sites, as they don't have the built-in Mobile View option that you can use when viewing the demo site.

- Try very hard not to confuse the four website concepts: structure, function, content, and aesthetics. It's easy to be lured into using a template because someone else's site looked amazing only to find that it was their branding or content that made it look so good.

Using the template's Read Me page

Many templates come with a **Read Me** page, which you will see as a link in the template demo site's navigation. The Read Me page usually includes details about the features that are available with the template as well as the kinds of things that can be configured in the visual style. You may find it useful to have a look at the Read Me page when you are considering templates, but you'll notice not all templates come with one.

 Most things listed in the template Read Me pages are also covered in the comparison chart available at www.square-help.com/templates. You may find it easier to use this chart, because it lists all templates and key points side by side.

Trying out a new template for your site

After you have browsed the templates and narrowed it down to a few that you like, you can install and preview the templates on your account to try them out before committing to a final template. You can install as many templates as you like. Installing a template just makes it available for you to use; it does not apply the template to your site or affect it in any way. Think of it like going shopping: you buy many jackets and have them available in your closet, but you only wear one jacket at a time.

Previewing a template is a bit like trying on the jacket before you go out: it shows you what it will look like with your outfit, but you are not committing to wearing it in public just yet. Previewing a template allows you to play around with it to find out what styles, restrictions, and features are built into the template without affecting your live site.

Installing and previewing a new template

To install and preview a new template, perform the following steps:

1. In the Site Manager Home screen, go to **Design | Template**.
2. Click on the **Install New Template** button. This will open the template browser.
3. Hover your mouse over the template thumbnail image to see the template name and click on the **View (Template Name)** button to open the template viewer.
4. Click on the **Install Template** button on the resulting screen. This should take you back into your Settings screen, where you will see a thumbnail of the template, along with any other templates that you have installed.
5. Hover your mouse over the template thumbnail and click on the **Preview** button to apply the template in Preview mode.

After performing these steps, the main preview screen will load something that looks very much like the demo site that you saw when browsing templates, and the side panel will gray out the template thumbnail and display a **Previewing** badge next to the template name, as shown in the following example:

Previewing a template does three things:

1. It loads the template in a private *test* mode, so you can see it and adjust it when you are logged in, but the public will not be aware of anything happening. Your existing live template will still be applied to the public view of your site.

2. It loads the pages and content that you have seen on the demo site into your site. You can choose to keep this demo content to use as a starting point for your own pages, or not.

3. It moves any existing pages that you have created out of your main navigation and into a temporary storage location called the **Not Linked** section. This is to ensure that the demo content and navigation work exactly like what you have seen on the demo site. You can move your pages back into the active navigation at any time.

 Because you haven't yet created any pages on your site, the third point does not apply right now, but it will apply if you change your template in future, after you have made some pages. At that time, you might be confused into thinking that your content and pages have gone missing if you don't remember this point.

You will know you are previewing a template because you will see a dark gray band at the bottom of the screen, with a message showing you the name of the template you are previewing and a **Manage Templates** link that will take you back to the **Template** panel under **Design**. The gray band is shown in the preceding screenshot but is zoomed in here:

Previewing Encore. This template is only visible to you, and navigation changes do not affect the live site. Manage Templates

Choosing your final template

Previewing templates allows you to experiment with a template to find out the specific features and restrictions it has, so you can understand whether it will do what you want for your site. It's a good idea to install and preview several templates to compare them before making your final choice.

 You can go back and install more templates to preview at any time using the **Manage Templates** link in the bottom gray band.

Ask yourself the following questions when previewing and comparing templates:

- How well does this template present the functions I need? Is it easy to find and use them?

- Does this page structure work well for my target audience and site content?

- Do the template's special features do what I want?

To answer these questions, you will need to switch back and forth between the following areas within the Squarespace system, examining the different controls and features in each template. Refer to *Chapter 2, Getting Started with Squarespace*, if you need a reminder of how to access each area.

Fullscreen preview

Clicking on the Expansion Arrow will enable the fullscreen preview. This is where you will see the visual style, page structure, and special features of your template in action, exactly how they would appear on your site. If you have made any adjustments while in the Style Editor or Pages area, you will see the effects of your adjustments here.

> Don't forget to preview your template in mobile and tablet Device View as well.

The Style Editor

You access the Style Editor from the **Design** menu under **Home**. The Style Editor is where you will get a general idea of the controls you will have over the visual style elements. While this mostly relates to colors, sizes, and fonts, you should also look out for some controls of special features here, such as fixed navigation.

Feel free to have a play around with some of the controls, but don't get carried away. Now is not the time to do detailed visual design work on your site; we'll cover that later. For now, just familiarize yourself with the controls and notice how they differ from template to template.

> The *Squarespace Templates in a Nutshell* chart in *Appendix B, Squarespace Templates in a Nutshell* shows you the overall scale of controls available within the Style Editor: XL means there are a lot of controls that you can adjust, whereas S means you have very few controls.

The Pages panel

From the Home Menu, go to **Pages** to see any special page types, such as Index pages, as well as secondary footer navigation.

Some special features and variable elements of certain templates are not controlled via the Style Editor or Pages area. These will be covered in *Chapter 4, Creating Your Site Framework: Pages, Items, Collections, and Navigation*, so don't worry if you can't immediately see the control or variable you were looking for.

Applying your chosen template to your site

Once you have narrowed things down to your final choice of template, you need to activate the template to make it live. This will apply the template that you are previewing to your site, turning off the old template that you set up at the beginning.

Making a template live

To make a template live, perform the following steps:

1. Click on the **Manage Templates** link in the gray band at the bottom of the screen. You will be taken to the **Templates** area in the Site Manager, where you will see all of the templates you have installed.

2. You will notice that the thumbnail of the template you are previewing has an overlay on it, with a large button in the middle that says **Set as Live Template**. Click on this button to activate the template.

3. You will see a confirmation message indicating that this will make the template live for all of your website visitors. Click on **Confirm**. An alert will appear to let you know this change has been applied successfully.

 As we set up a sitewide password in the last chapter, your website is currently hidden from the public. Therefore, right now, no one will see this change except you. In future, if you want to change your template, remember to make all your design changes before making the new template live.

Summary

You've now set a template for your site, which defines the direction your site's pages can take structurally and visually. The next step is to create some pages for your site, so we have somewhere to put all your exciting content and functions. In the next chapter, we will cover all of the different types of Squarespace pages and create sample pages to help you learn how each type looks and works in your template.

Remember, you can change your template at any time, so don't be afraid to come back to this chapter later if you find that the template you have chosen just isn't working the way you thought it would. Sometimes, it takes a bit of trial and error working with your actual pages and content for you to discover exactly how a certain template will affect your site.

4
Creating Your Site Framework: Pages, Items, Collections, and Navigation

When you set your site template in the previous chapter, the Squarespace system automatically created demo pages that looked like the ones you saw on the demo site. You can choose to keep these pages to use as a starting point, or you can create new pages to use as a clean slate to build your site, or a bit of both. Whatever you decide, you'll need to learn about the different Squarespace page types and how to use them in order to create the right pages to house your content and functions.

In this chapter, we will create samples of all of the main page types to learn about their distinct characteristics, and we'll organize them in different ways to learn how to adjust your site's navigation. We will start by learning about some core Squarespace page concepts, and then we'll use a series of practical exercises to demonstrate how to set up different pages and items on your site.

We will cover the following topics:

- Understanding the different types of Squarespace pages and page collections
- Creating and deleting pages
- Using demo pages as your starting point
- Understanding the various Page Settings
- Adding items to Collection Pages
- Organizing pages and setting up navigation
- Using special navigation elements

Understanding Squarespace pages

Squarespace comes with a range of different page types to suit different purposes. Some of these are very straightforward and easy to understand, while others are a bit more complex and can seem a little confusing at first. There are four main categories of pages, and they are:

- **Standard page**: This is a single, normal web page that contains no subpages
- **Collection Page**: This is a page that links to and/or contains multiple items within it, such as a Gallery or Blog
- **Cover Page**: This is a simplified, bold page with a large background image and minimal content
- **Page cluster**: This is a set of pages that are grouped together for navigational purposes.

The latter term, page cluster, does not appear in any of the Squarespace documentation, as this is a term I have adopted to help make this concept easier to understand. These are the terms we will use throughout the rest of the book, so let's dig a little deeper into each category.

 If you are using the Personal subscription plan, you can only have up to 20 pages on your site. This refers to standard pages, Cover Pages, and Collection Pages, but not individual items within a Collection Page. Individual pages within a cluster do count toward the 20-page limit.

Standard page

A standard page can contain a range of content or functional elements, such as body text, headline, image, video, or form field. The things that you put into standard pages are managed within the Squarespace Site Manager's main viewing and editing screen using content blocks, which we'll learn all about in the next chapter. You can arrange content blocks on a standard page in many different ways, simply by dragging and dropping the blocks into position and resizing them if you like. Standard pages are the most flexible type of page.

Collection Pages

A Collection Page always has **items** within it. An item is an individual, self-contained piece of content, such as a Gallery image, or a Blog post. There are different types of Collection Pages to hold different types of items. Here are the types of Squarespace Collection Pages and their associated items:

Collection Page names	Individual item within collections
Blog	Post
Gallery	Image or video
Events Page	Event
Album	Track
Products Page	Product

You can actually use a Blog or Gallery for a range of content purposes apart from just news articles or photos. Take a look at www.square-help.com/inspiration for some creative ideas on how you can adapt these collections to fit other content needs.

Each item has specific properties that you can apply, such as a description, price, or location. However, not all items have the same properties. The properties are determined by the type of item, and they are preset by the system.

Many templates come with preset visual styles and structures for the different collections and their associated items. The display can vary widely from template to template, and you usually have very little control over how the items are displayed within the collection, apart from changing the order.

Collection Pages do not usually have any content of their own; they normally only display the items (or excerpts of the items) within the page.

Certain templates allow you to display some Page Settings as content on Collection Pages. We'll cover Page Settings later in this chapter.

Cover Page

A Cover Page is a stripped-down page designed to create strong visual impact, normally used as a landing page or doorway into your main site. This is known in the web industry as a **splash page** or **splash screen**. You can also use a Cover Page as a temporary holding page until your main site has been built and launched. Cover Pages have their own special properties and design controls, and the content is added in a slightly different way than normal pages.

Page cluster

Instead of individual items, a page cluster is made up of individual pages. There are two types of page clusters available within Squarespace:

- **Folder**: This is a navigational device used to create submenus, usually, drop-down menus or secondary navbars
- **Index**: This is a special collection of pages that presents links to the pages in a visual way instead of using menus

You add, delete, and rearrange pages in a Folder or Index using the **Pages** menu.

Although Folders and Indexes are conceptually similar, they do have some very important differences:

- Folders are available with any template, but only certain templates offer Indexes.

- A Folder can contain standard pages or any type of Collection Page, but Indexes are restricted to standard pages or Galleries only.

- Designwise, pages in a Folder are no different from pages outside the Folder, so you have the same controls you would for any normal pages of this type. The only difference is that some templates display a secondary navbar somewhere on Folder pages. Indexes, however, usually have special display elements that are set by the template, and you will generally have little or no control over the display, apart from changing the order of pages.

- A Folder is not a page in its own right; it is simply a navigational device. In this sense, an Index is a bit more like a Collection Page, because it is a page—it just contains subpages instead of subitems.

 If a Folder is not really a page, why is it included here? Squarespace lumps Folders, Indexes, and all other page types together when you use the Site Manager tool. You will find them all in the **Create New Page** menu regardless of whether you want to add a Folder or add a page.

Special properties of Collection and Index Pages

Collection Pages and Index Pages are designed to hold and display multiple items, and they can hold many dozens of items… in some cases, hundreds. With so many items, it can be useful to have a way to classify items and group similar ones together. That's when **categories** and **tags** can come in handy.

Categories are used to group similar items together in a broad sense. You can think of categories like the signs you see hanging above the aisles in supermarkets. One aisle might be labeled *Meat*, and another may say *Dairy*.

Tags are more specific labels that are used to classify items or show at a glance what something is about. In the supermarket analogy, tags would be specific terms, such as sausage, bacon, cheese, milk, cream, and so on.

There's no rule about when to use a category versus a tag: for example, you could have cheese as a category and then have tags such as cheddar, sliced, strong, and so on. An item can have multiple categories and/or multiple tags as well.

You may want to consider focusing on categories first, because:

- Some templates use categories as navigational devices that are built into the template.
- All types of Collection Pages and Index Pages can have categories, but not all of them can have tags.

Not all templates make use of categories or tags, but you will usually find them displayed in blog pages at least, regardless of the template. You can also add lists of categories or tags to your pages using special content blocks, which we will cover in *Chapter 6, Using Blocks to Add Functionality, Rich Media, and Special Features*.

Adding pages to your site

The best way to understand the way pages work is to add some. When you start a new site with Squarespace, there are two ways to add pages to your site: you can start from the demo pages that come with your template, or you can add fresh blank pages. We'll learn how to do both in this section. We'll also cover the different page types and settings that apply to the pages that you create.

If you have an existing site on Squarespace 5, WordPress, Blogger, or Tumblr, you can import those pages into Squarespace 7. Refer to http://help.squarespace.com if you need to import from another site.

Everything to do with adding, removing, setting up, or reorganizing pages is done by navigating to **Pages** in the Site Manager, so ensure you are in that area before proceeding with the rest of this chapter.

Using the Pages panel

Before we start adding pages, let's take a moment to learn about the different parts of the Pages panel and what the different icons mean. When you entered the Pages panel, you may have noticed that a list of demo pages from the demo site has been loaded into the side panel under a label called **Main Navigation** or **Top Navigation** (the wording depends on the template, but they are the same). The exact items shown will vary depending on your template. Next to the name of each item, you will see an icon that depicts the type of page. You will also notice the word **DEMO** next to each page name, as shown in the following screenshot:

This is because you have not yet created any real pages; your site only contains demo pages at this point. You may also notice that some pages appear indented and display a *tree* structure. This tells you that these pages are part of a page cluster. Here is an example of **Main Navigation** comprised of real pages that shows you the full list of different page icons and their meanings:

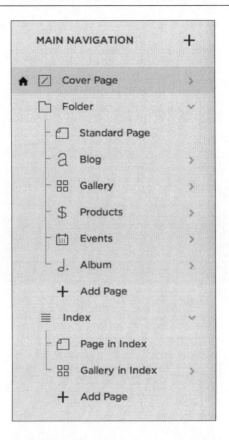

You will also notice that one of the pages has a house icon next to it to indicate that this is the site's homepage. Whatever page you have set as the homepage will be linked from the site logo or title.

At the top of the **Main Navigation** section, you will see a large **+** sign, which is the Add Page button that you use to add new pages. If you have a Folder or Index on your site, you will also see the **+ Add Page** button shown under the tree structure to allow you to add pages directly to the Folder or Index. We'll use these buttons later in this chapter.

Below your **Main Navigation** section, you may see a section called **Secondary Navigation** or **Footer Navigation** if your template offers this functionality. Refer to the chart in *Appendix B, Squarespace Templates in a Nutshell*, to see which templates have a secondary or footer navigation area.

At the bottom of the Pages menu, you will see a section called **Not Linked**. All templates have a **Not Linked** section. This is a useful place to store pages that you don't want in your site's navigation. We'll learn more about the **Not Linked** section in a few moments. Here's a screenshot showing you the **Secondary Navigation** and **Not Linked** section:

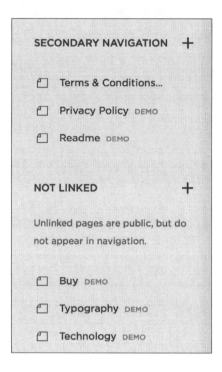

Notice that each of these sections also has a + button at the top to allow you to add pages to these areas directly.

Understanding your template's unique way of displaying page elements

As each template displays the various page types in a unique way, before you create any of your own pages, it's a good idea to study the demo pages to see the differences and learn the specifics of how your template shows certain elements. This is particularly true for Collection Pages and Indexes or any special feature pages that your template offers. Although you may have a general idea of how your template works based on your research from the previous chapter, it's a good idea to take a moment now to examine your demo pages closely, both in terms of the public display that you see in fullscreen Preview and in terms of the navigation hierarchy that you see in the Pages panel. This can save a lot of potential confusion later.

You should *always* do this *before* you have saved any of the demo pages, because some demo pages change once they are saved, and you cannot go back without uninstalling and then reinstalling the template.

Here are some of the important things to look out for when studying your demo pages:

- If you will be using a Blog, Products, Events, Gallery, or Index Page on your site, click around multiple items to see how they are shown.

- Scroll all the way down to the bottom of the page: you may notice secondary navigation or an Index grid below the main content.

- Pay attention to how images are used and displayed. In some page types in certain templates, you can hover or click on images to see more information or a larger view.

- Look closely at the Navigation menu in the Pages panel, and check how that relates to the way pages are shown to the public in Preview. This is especially important for Indexes and Folders.

- Keep an eye out for categories (and tags), especially in Blog pages but also in Indexes and Galleries, where they can sometimes appear as navigational devices in certain templates.

Using demo pages to create new pages

After studying the demo pages, you may find that one of them is pretty close to one of the pages you want for your own site. You can copy this demo page to use as a starting point for your new page, and it will usually recreate the content and layout shown in the example in your newly copied page. However, sometimes copying the demo page only recreates some of the content, or it only recreates the structure and settings without copying any content. This usually happens with Collection Pages or Indexes, so you won't be able to use an exact copy of these pages as your starting point, but you will be able to use them to get a general idea of how the template works with these page types. For this reason, let's start by copying a standard page.

Follow these steps to copy a demo page:

1. In the Pages panel, find a standard page in your **Main Navigation** section by looking for the following icon:

2. Hover your mouse over the page name and you will notice a cog icon appear on the right-hand side of the page name, as shown here:

3. Click on the cog, and you will see a popup overlay that indicates you are modifying the example content and will need to create a page copy first.

4. Click on the **Create** button. This will remove the **DEMO** tag from the icon in your **Main Navigation** section and will open the **Page Settings** panel on the right-hand side of the screen. The **Page Settings** panel floats over a translucent overlay and shows you the **Configure Page** controls, as shown here:

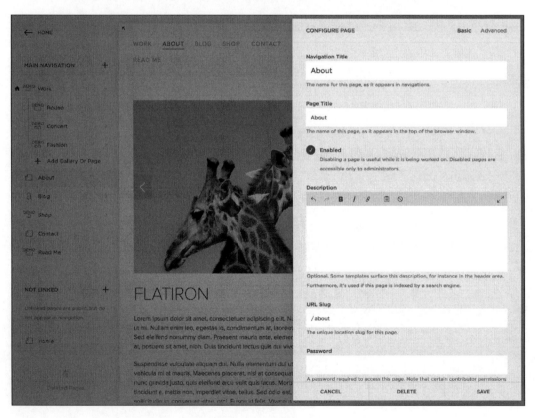

Congratulations! You just created your first web page. We will use this page as a learning tool for the next part of this chapter before moving on to creating other pages. We'll edit the content of this page in the next chapter, when you'll learn about content blocks and how to use them. For now, we'll just focus on setting up the page to learn about the various Page Settings and what they do.

Standard page settings

Now that you have a real page on your site, and as we've already opened the Page Settings panel on this page, it's a good time to learn about the different settings that apply to Squarespace pages. Some settings will apply to every page you create, other settings will only be used in certain templates, and some settings only apply to specific page types. Let's go through the different Page Settings now, starting with the settings that apply to all pages regardless of the type of page or template you are using.

Navigation Title

The **Navigation Title** is displayed in your navigation menu. In most cases, the Navigation Title and Page Title will be the same, but you may prefer to use a shorter word or phrase for your Navigation Title, especially if you have many menu items and/or long Page Titles.

 Ensure your Navigation Titles are intelligible and free of jargon. Refer to the advice about sitemaps in *Chapter 1, Setting Up for Success – Your Website Toolkit*, if you need a refresher.

Page Title

The Page Title is used in two places:

- In your browser window: at the top or in the tab
- On Google (or another search engine) search results pages, as the link that people can click to visit your site

In some templates, the Page Title can also be displayed on the web page itself as part of or below the header area.

Try to keep your Page Titles brief: a maximum of 8 words or 65 characters is a good guideline that will ensure your full title is displayed on the Google search results page.

Always ensure your Page Title is unique on your site. You do not want to have multiple pages called *Products*, as it is confusing for users and bad for search engines.

The Enabled checkbox

You can use the **Enabled checkbox** to disable or enable the page. If the page is disabled, it will not be accessible to the public. It's a good idea to keep pages disabled while you are working on them or when storing currently unwanted pages for potential future use.

In the Pages menu, disabled pages appear grayed out.

Page Layout

Some templates allow you to set sidebars on a page-by-page basis. In this instance, you may see a **Page Layout** option in your Page Settings, where you can turn the sidebar(s) on or off and choose to display it on the left- or right-hand side.

Some template designers have put the sidebar settings elsewhere in the Style Editor. We'll find out how to set up these kinds of sidebars in the next chapter.

Page Description

The **Page Description** is usually a short sentence that describes what the page is about. The Page Description will be shown on Google search results pages underneath the Page Title link.

Google displays approximately the first 156 characters of your Page Description, so make your first few words count: use this space to get your message across succinctly and entice readers to click.

In some templates, the Page Description is also shown on the web page itself, either as part of the header or elsewhere. In certain templates, the Page Description acts very much like normal page content, taking up a large portion of the web page display. In these instances, you can have multiple paragraphs and apply basic formatting, such as bold or italics, to your Page Description. Remember that even in this circumstance, the first 156 characters will be shown on Google, so choose your wording wisely.

Refer to the chart in *Appendix B, Squarespace Templates in a Nutshell*, or www.square-help.com/templates for further information about if and how your chosen template displays Page Descriptions.

URL Slug

The **URL Slug** is the unique identifier for your page and is the part of the web address that comes after your domain name. In most cases, you should use your Navigation Title or Page Title as the URL for consistency.

If your title has multiple words, always use a hyphen, not an underscore or space, between each word. This is important for search engines and makes your URLs more readable to humans as well.

Password

If you need to make certain pages on your website private, you can set a **Password** on a page-by-page basis here. This is useful for client-specific pages or pages that you want to share with others within your organization before releasing them to the public.

If you've been following the chapters in order, your entire website is currently password-protected at the site level (we did this in *Chapter 2, Getting Started with Squarespace*). Therefore, you do not need to set a password per page right now. The entire site will be hidden from public view until we make it live in *Chapter 9, Going Live with Your Website and Driving Traffic to It*.

Setting a password on a page does not remove that page from your navigation, so be careful when using this setting. You'll learn how to keep pages out of your main navigation later in this chapter.

The Thumbnail Image

The Thumbnail Image is only used in certain templates. It is most commonly used in one of three ways:

- As a header or banner image, appearing at the top of the page itself
- As a background image, filling the screen behind the canvas
- As the thumbnail image on an Index Page as the link to the page

You can use one of your own images or buy a stock image from the **Getty Images** library. We will cover uploading and buying images in *Chapter 5, Adding, Editing, and Arranging Content in Your Web Pages*.

Page Controls

These are buttons that allow you to:

- **Duplicate**: Make a copy of your page, including all content and Page Settings. This button only appears on standard pages.
- **Set Homepage**: Make the current page your homepage, which will be linked from your logo or Site Title and will be the page that visitors first land on.

 Remember, some templates have special homepages, so setting a page as the homepage may change its appearance. Refer to the chart in *Appendix B, Squarespace Templates in a Nutshell*, to see which templates have special homepages.

Page Settings action buttons

At the bottom of the Page Settings panel, you will find a set of buttons that will perform certain actions to the page:

- **Save** will save any changes you have made to the Page Settings
- **Cancel** will discard any changes and revert to the last saved Page Settings
- **Delete** will move the page into the **Recycle Bin**, where it will stay for 7 days before being removed by the system

If you have made any adjustments to your Page Settings during this walkthrough, you can click on **Save** to store them now. If not, click on **Cancel** to close the Page Settings screen.

Creating new pages

Our next task will be to create a new, blank page that you can use on your site. Let's create a Collection Page so that we can learn how these pages differ from standard pages. Refer to your Website Toolkit, and select any Collection Page from your sitemap. For this exercise, you may want to choose something other than a Products Page, as these are a bit more complex than the others.

Follow these steps to add a new page:

1. In the Pages panel, click on the **+** button at the bottom of your **Main Navigation** or **Top Navigation** section. This will open the **Create New Page** overlay, as shown here:

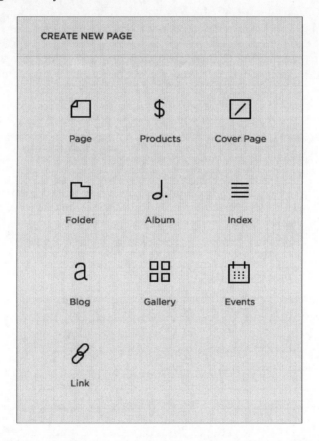

2. Select whichever Collection Page is most appropriate for your site: Products, Gallery, Events, Album, or Blog.

3. This will insert the page into the navigation in the Pages panel and open a textbox that will allow you to replace the default text with your chosen Navigation Title in the white box, as shown here:

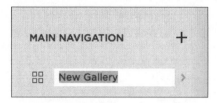

4. Type the title you want, and hit the *Enter* key to save.

You just created a completely empty, blank page. The side panel will load the collection controls, and the preview screen will fill with your empty new page.

Before we add any items to your collection, let's take a moment to learn about the special settings that apply to different types of Collection Pages. Open the settings panel by clicking on the cog icon.

You'll notice that the settings title at the top of the panel displays a slightly different wording, so instead of **Configure Page**, it now reads **Configure Blog** or **Configure Gallery**, and so on.

 Once you open the Settings panel, you will also notice that the system has automatically applied whatever you put as the Navigation Title to the Page Title box.

Collection Page settings

Most Collection Pages have extra settings in addition to the standard ones. The settings differ according to the type of Collection Page. Most of the settings can be found under the main screen, which is the **Basic** settings area. However, some settings are controlled in the **Advanced** settings area, accessed through a link at the top right of the settings window:

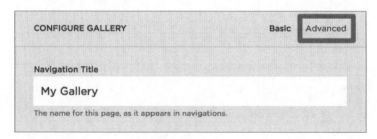

The **Advanced** area is primarily used to manage categories and tags, but you will also notice a space labeled **Page Header Code Injection**. This is used by designers/developers to apply custom code to the page, so you don't need to worry about that part right now (if at all).

Some Collection Pages have other settings that are controlled elsewhere in the Page Settings window, apart from the **Basic** or **Advanced** areas. Let's take a look at all the different Collection Page Settings.

Blog Page Settings

The following Basic settings apply to Blog pages:

- **Posts Per Page** sets how many blog posts will be shown on the Collection Page before the user must navigate forward or back within the blog to see other posts

- **Post By Email Address** generates a unique email address that you can send messages to in order to automatically post that message to your blog

- **Quickpost Bookmarklet** is a tool that you can drag into your browser bookmarks bar as a shortcut to allow you to quickly write blog posts

You can also manage your blog's categories and tags in the **Advanced** area.

You'll notice that a Blog page has an additional link next to **Advanced**, which takes you to the **Syndication** area. Your Blog page automatically comes with **Really Simple Syndication (RSS)**, so you don't need to do anything to use the default RSS feed. You'll only need to use the **Syndication** settings if you prefer to use Feedburner or an alternative feed management tool or if you will be using your blog to host podcasts and you want these podcasts to be syndicated to iTunes.

Further information on using RSS on your Squarespace site is available here:

`http://help.squarespace.com/guides/finding-your-rss-feed-url`

Further information on setting up your site for podcasting is available here:

`http://help.squarespace.com/guides/podcasting-with-squarespace`

Gallery Page Settings

Like a Blog Page, a Gallery Page can also have categories and tags associated with it. You can also use the **Post By Email Address** function with galleries.

Events Page Settings

In addition to categories and tags, an Events Page has a special setting called **Default Event View**. This determines whether the Events Page displays a Calendar or a List of events.

 You can also display an event calendar within a standard page, which we will cover in the next chapter. Therefore, you could set your Events page to display as a list but still have a calendar on your site elsewhere.

Index Page Settings

The only special settings that apply to Indexes are categories and tags.

Products Page Settings

A Products Page can have categories or tags.

Album Page Settings

Album Pages have special settings that are controlled from within the main page viewing and editing screen instead of the Settings area. These are **Album Art, Album Title, Artist Name,** and **Album Description**. In addition to these, you will also find the usual page settings under **Album Settings**, including categories and tags.

Adding items to Collection Pages

The next exercise for this chapter is to add some sample items to your Collection Page. We will create at least one sample item for the collection that you just created, so you may want to have your Website Toolkit content handy—or you can just use fake content for now, as we'll add all of your real content in the next chapter.

You can add items to Collection Pages in three different ways:

- In the side panel, click on the **+** button next to the title of the page
- In the side panel, click where indicated in the empty space below the title of the page
- In the Preview screen, hover over the main content area of the page to activate the Annotations, and then click on the **Add...** button.

The following screenshot shows you these three methods on a Gallery Page:

For Gallery or Album Pages, there is also a shortcut: you can add items quickly by simply dragging and dropping image or audio files onto the side panel area below the page title. This shortcut is especially handy if you want to add lots of files at once.

Once you have items in your collection, the side panel will be filled with the list of items, so you must use **+** or the Annotation button to add items for all Collection Pages apart from Gallery or Album Pages. On Gallery or Album Pages, you can still add items by clicking or dragging into the side panel using the square with a dotted border at the end of the list of existing items, as shown here:

When you add an item using any method apart from the drag and drop shortcut, you will open the **Edit Item** window, where you can apply the item settings for the item you are adding. Here's an example of the **Edit Event** window that appears when adding a new event item:

You can refer to the *Configuring the item settings* section in the next part of this chapter for details of the settings that apply to your item type.

For now, just input one of the key settings, such as the title or image, and click on **Save** to store a **Draft** of your item (which will not be visible to the public until you are ready), or click on **Save & Publish** to save the item and immediately make it live.

You will see the item you just created in the Preview screen, and the title of this item will appear in the side panel below the title of the Collection Page.

If you saved a Draft, your item will display a **DRAFT** badge next to its name in the side panel to remind you that it has not yet been published, as shown in the following screenshot:

Configuring the item settings

Just as Page Settings control the properties of pages, an item's settings control what is shown for that item on your Collection Page. In most cases, it's pretty easy to understand what to put in the different boxes that you see when you are setting up items. However, it's a good idea to have a closer look at the items that pertain to your site, because there are a few settings that are easy to miss or that may benefit from further explanation.

You can access the item settings in one of the following ways:

- Products or Events:
    - In the side panel, hover over the item name and click on **Edit**

　○　Or, load the item in the Preview screen, and then hover over the content area to activate the Annotations and click on **Edit**, as shown here:

- Blog: In the side panel, hover over the blog post title and click on the **Settings** button
- **Gallery**: In the side panel, hover over the Image Thumbnail and click on the cog icon
- **Album**: In the side panel, scroll down to see the **Tracks** and click on the track number

The item settings are often split into different screens, much like Page Settings. You can navigate between the different screens using the links in the top-right corner of the **Edit Item** screen.

Some settings apply to most of the different item types, so let's go through these first:

- **Categories and/or tags**: These can be set for most items in the bottom-left corner of the main **Edit Item** screen. You can either type directly to create new ones or select from the list of categories or tags that have been used previously.
- **Social** (accessed using the top-right link): This allows you to specify whether this item should be automatically posted onto your Facebook, Twitter, or Tumblr feed. We will cover this in *Chapter 9, Going Live with Your Website and Driving Traffic to It*.

As you start using items and their settings, you will get the feeling that most Collection Pages are variations of the Blog type of collection, and most items are just stripped down or amended versions of posts. For example, you will see a lot of settings on Gallery or Album items that really don't make that much sense and are not used at all—for example, the ability to have comments on an Album track or to assign an author to a Gallery image. I have not yet come across a template that displays this information, but perhaps one day, Squarespace will release a template that does. Alternately, having these fields available within the system means that people with very specific requirements to show these things could hire a Squarespace developer to make them display on their site.

For the rest of us, we don't really need to worry about configuring these settings except for certain types of items, so they are only listed here under the relevant item's settings even though you might see them on other item types as well.

Blog post settings

Here's an example of the **Edit Post** window, where you can set the Blog post settings:

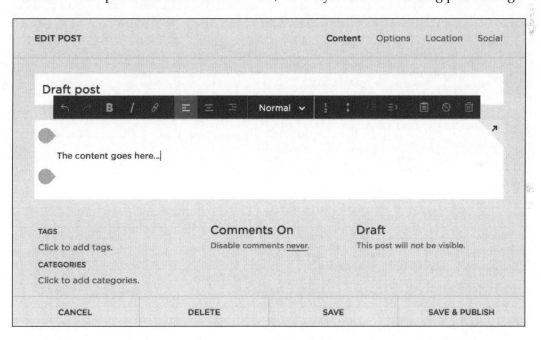

The key Blog post settings are:

- **Post title**: This acts as the link that opens the post in a new page as well as the words that appear in Google search results pages and at the top of your browser window.

- **Post body**: This is a large box that shows **Write here...** when you first open it. Here is where you insert the main post content. You will notice that a formatting bar appears when you start typing in the box to allow you to style your text. You can also use many of the same types of content blocks that you can use on standard pages. We will explain the formatting bar and the use of content blocks in the next chapter.

- **Comments On**: This appears at the bottom to let you know that people can leave comments on the post. You can turn comments off selectively on a post-by-post basis here, or you can turn comments off entirely by navigating to **Settings | General**. We will cover Comments in more detail in *Chapter 10, Managing Your Squarespace Website*.

- **Published**: The Published date will be set to the date and time when you click on **Save and Publish**. If you would like to amend this date/time, you can do so by clicking on the date and making adjustments using the pop-up calendar. Blog posts are displayed in reverse chronological order based on the Published date.

- **Post Options**: The following can be accessed by clicking on **Options** in the top-right section:

    - **Post URL**: This is automatically generated but can be manually changed here, should you wish.

    - **Author**: This is based on the user who entered the post but can be overridden here, if required.

    - **Excerpt**: Here, you can set a short summary to be shown in the blog Collection Page instead of the full post body. This can be useful if you want to show visitors snippets of many posts instead of expecting readers to scroll down long body texts of a few posts. If anything is entered in the Excerpt field, most templates will show this text in the Collection Page with a **Read More** link below it, as shown here:

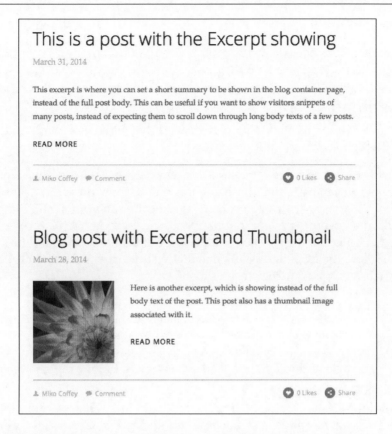

- **Thumbnail Image**: This image may also be used alongside the Excerpt instead of the full post body in your blog's home (collection) page. However, not all templates display the Thumbnail Image even if you have set one. Refer to the chart in *Appendix B, Squarespace Templates in a Nutshell,* for information on which templates display them. The preceding screenshot shows you a Thumbnail Image next to an Excerpt.

    ◦ **Source URL**: This may be useful in rare occasions if your post is referencing content on another website.

    ◦ **External Link**: You'll only need to use this if you want the title of your post to link to the Source URL instead of the actual post. This is not recommended.

    ◦ **Featured Post**: This option is currently only used by the Bedford template: it can be set to display the post in a slideshow at the top of the blog.

- **Location**: This is accessed using the top-right link. This allows you to assign an address or physical location to your post. This could be useful if you use your blog to write reviews of restaurants or to log your travels, for example. Be aware that only very few templates display location for blog posts.

Event settings

Events are most closely related to blog posts, and they have most of the same settings, with the following additions:

- **Start Date / End Date**: You should always set these dates/times for your event. You can have time-based events on the same day and/or multiday events. Events will show in chronological order on your site in **List** view (with the upcoming event that happens nearest today at the top) or by date in **Calendar** view. The settings you put for **Start Date** and **End Date** also set up the **gCal** and **iCal** icons that visitors can click on to add an event to their own personal electronic calendar.

> Only events that will happen in the future show on the List view, although some templates include a link to past events.
>
> Calendar view defaults to today's date, allowing visitors to navigate through the calendar months to see future or past events.

- **Location**: This is accessed using the top-right link. This is important for events, as all templates use **Location** to display the address and a link to a Google map for Events items.

Gallery image settings

Here is an example of the **Edit Image** window, where you can set the image settings:

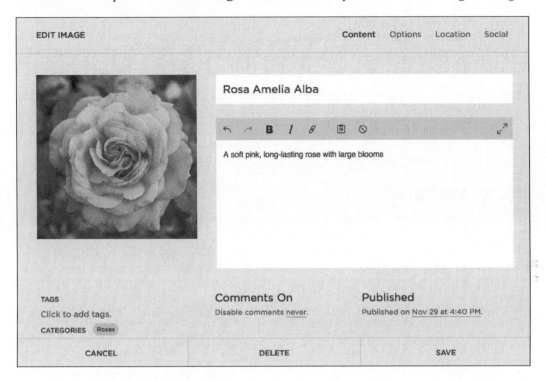

The key settings for images are:

- **Image title**: This appears in some templates either above or below the image or as an overlay when you hover your mouse over the image.

- **Description**: The large box below the image title is where you can enter a short description of the image. You will notice that there is a simplified formatting bar above this box to allow basic formatting and to add links to the description text. Some templates display the image description next to or below the title.

 Some Galleries display images in formats that may not match the dimensions of your images. In these cases, your image may be cropped to fit the space allocated by the template. We'll address how to control which part of the image is cropped in the next chapter.

Gallery video settings

Video settings are similar to image settings, with the following additions:

- **Video URL**: You will need to paste the URL from YouTube, Vimeo, or another video site into the box, and the Squarespace system will automatically locate the video and pull in the title and description from the video hosting site. You can manually override these by typing into the respective boxes.

- **Custom Thumbnail**: By default, the first frame of the video will show within the Gallery as a placeholder image until the user clicks on the play button. You can upload your own image and tick the **Use Thumbnail** box if you want to use a different image.

Product settings

We will cover Products in more detail in *Chapter 7, Selling Online or Taking Donations with Squarespace Commerce*, as many Product settings can't be configured until you set up your Squarespace Commerce account. For now, you could add a Product **image**, **title**, and/or **brief description** if you want to preview a Product.

Album track settings

The key settings for Album tracks are:

- **Track title**: You should set this for each track in your Album
- **Artist Name**: This is most useful if your Album contains multiple artists, as you can use this to set the artist for each track

Organizing items in Gallery, Products, or Album Pages

You can change the order of items in a Gallery, Products, or Album Page by clicking and dragging items to the order you want. You can select multiple items in a Gallery or Products Page by holding down the *Shift* key while clicking on items.

If you have more than one Gallery or Products Page, you can also move items from one Gallery or Products Page to another.

Here's how to move items to another Gallery or Products Page:

1. Click on the item(s) you want to move. A mini toolbar will appear at the bottom of the side panel, as shown in this screenshot:

2. In the mini toolbar, click on **Move Items**. An overlay will appear, showing you the available pages where you can move the item(s).

3. Click on the name of the page where you want to move the item(s).

4. Click on **Move Items**.

Moving Blog posts

If you have more than one Blog, you can move posts from one Blog to another using the same method as for Gallery or Products pages, with the following exception:

*   To move multiple posts, hold down the *Shift* key and then click on the items to select them.

*   To move a single post, hold down the *Ctrl* key when clicking on the item.

Deleting items

There are several ways to delete items, depending on the type of item.

Follow these steps to delete any type of item:

1. Open the item settings screen.
2. Click on the **Delete** button at the bottom. An overlay will appear, asking you to confirm that you wish to remove the item.
3. Click on **Confirm**.

Other ways to delete items are:

- In the side panel, hover over the item name, and click on the trash can icon or the **Delete** button that appears next to it
- To delete one or more items from a Gallery or Products Page, follow the same steps to move items from one page to another, except click on **Delete** instead of **Move Items**.

Creating a Cover Page

Cover Pages are different from all other page types, as they have their own content, settings, and style controls that apply to that specific Cover Page and nothing else. Cover Pages are not affected by the template you choose or by the style changes you make to that template. Instead, you control the appearance of the Cover Page independently from the rest of the website. You control the appearance of two separate Cover Pages independently as well.

Cover Pages are also special because they do not use content blocks like standard pages, nor do they contain items like Collection Pages do. The content and functions of a Cover Page are determined by the **Layout** of the Cover Page you choose. All Layouts contain the following elements:

- **Branding & Text**: This includes a logo, headline, body text, and social icons.
- **Imagery**: These are usually displayed as fullscreen backgrounds, though certain Layouts show them filling only a part of the screen. If you select multiple images, these will rotate in a slideshow (fading between slides). If you prefer not to use images, you can set a background color instead.
- **Action**: You can add buttons, navigation links, or forms to your Cover Page. If you add a form, it will open in a translucent overlay on top of the Cover Page.

Certain types of Layouts contain other elements, as follows:

- **Audio**: This type of Cover Page contains one or more audio tracks that can be played from the Cover Page
- **Video**: This allows you to embed a video that will be played in a lightbox (translucent overlay) using a large play button on the Cover Page
- **Location**: This type of Cover Page displays a large map as the main content

Not every website will have a Cover Page, as they are not appropriate for all types of businesses. However, if you'd like to add one to your website, you can create a Cover Page by following these steps:

1. In the Pages panel, click on the **+** button to open the **Create New Page** window, and select **Cover Page**.
2. Enter the name for your page and hit the *Enter* key. This will open the Cover Page panel and load the default Cover Page Layout in the Preview screen, as shown here:

3. Select the Layout you want to use by clicking on the **Change Layout** button and then selecting the one you like from the resulting set of thumbnails. You can use the drop-down menu above the thumbnails to filter the list.

4. Once you select a Layout, the Preview screen will refresh to show this new Layout. When you find the one you like, click on **Save** and then use the arrow at the top to return to the main Cover Page panel to set up your content and functions.

Setting up your Cover Page

Choosing your Cover Page Layout makes a copy of the demo content for that page, just like when you created a new standard page based on the demo earlier in this chapter. Just like a standard page or Collection Page, there are various settings that you can apply to your Cover Page. However, unlike other pages, everything to do with the Cover Page is managed in one place: the Cover Page panel. The content, aesthetics, and functions are all managed from here. You may find this a bit confusing later once you've learned about content blocks and have started applying them to other pages. Just remember that Cover Pages are different, and if you need to adjust the content on this type of page, you'll need to follow a different process than for normal pages.

Because the Cover Page settings include everything (content, aesthetics, and functions), it doesn't make sense to go through all of the settings now. You'll be better off coming back to adjust the more advanced settings, such as adding logos or forms, or adjusting visual style, after you've learned how to perform these types of adjustments in later chapters.

For now, I suggest you only perform the following adjustments, leaving the other settings until later:

- Add the text you want to display in the **Branding & Text** panel.

- Add at least one image in the **Imagery** panel.

To access the Cover Page panel at a later time, go to the Pages menu and click on the Cover Page title or the small arrow to the far right of the title, as shown here:

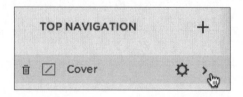

Organizing your site's navigation

Organizing pages in Squarespace is really easy. Before we start playing with your site navigation, it's a good idea to create a few more pages so you can see the effects of reorganizing things better.

Go ahead and add at least three more pages to your site either by saving demo pages or creating blank pages. It's best if you create/save standard or Collection Pages for this exercise. Refer to your sitemap in your Website Toolkit, and choose a few real pages to create now.

You can quickly create a copy of any standard page by going to Page Settings and clicking on the Duplicate Page button. The new copy will appear in the Not Linked section of the Navigation area.

Next, let's add a Folder—and if your template uses them, an Index—to your navigation.

To create a Folder, follow these steps:

1. In the Pages menu, click on the + button at the top of your **Main Navigation** or **Top Navigation** section. This will open the **Create New Page** overlay.

2. Select **Folder**.

> If you can't see Folder in the list of page types, it means you have clicked on a **+ Add Page** button that is associated with an existing Folder or Index. Cancel this, and ensure you click on the + button next to the label **Top Navigation** or **Main Navigation** instead.

3. In the resulting overlay, replace the default text with your chosen Navigation Title in the white box. You will notice that the URL below the white box automatically updates as you type. You can change this if you wish.

4. Click on **Save**.

You just created an empty Folder, ready for us to add some pages to it, as shown in the following screenshot:

Folder Settings

As mentioned, a Folder is not really a page at all; it is merely a navigational device. For this reason, there are no Page Settings other than Navigation Title and URL Slug. These are accessed by clicking on the cog icon that appears when you hover over the name of the Folder in the Pages menu.

The URL for a Folder behaves differently from the URL for all other page types. Normally, when someone visits the URL for a page or clicks on the page link in the navbar, the browser takes you to the page. However, as there is no page associated with a Folder, the URL acts as a *shortcut* or *alias*, taking you to the first page in the Folder instead.

Creating an Index

If your chosen template uses Indexes, follow the same steps to create a Folder, except choose **Index** in *step 2*.

Index Settings

Indexes have the same settings as standard pages, except they can also have categories and tags.

Rearranging pages

Changing the order of pages in your site's navigation is very simple. Here's how to do that:

1. Click on the name of the page that you want to move.
2. Drag it to the place where you want to move it.
3. Release the mouse and the page will be placed into its new position in the navigation.

Adding pages to a Folder or Index

To move pages into a Folder or an Index, perform the same steps as rearranging pages: just drag your chosen pages into the space below the Folder or Index, ensuring the page is indented before releasing. You will see the page in the Folder or Index *tree* structure:

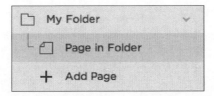

 Remember, not all page types can be added to Indexes: only standard pages or Gallery Pages can be added (the type of page allowed is determined by your template). It's also important to note that you cannot add a Folder to another Folder.

Opening and closing Folders or Indexes

If your site has lots of pages within Folders or Indexes, it can be annoying to have to scroll up and down a lot in the Pages menu. Therefore, you may find it helpful to temporarily close the Folder or Index. This will hide all the pages within that cluster. You use the small up/down arrow that appears to the far right of the Folder/Index name to open/close it. The following screenshot shows you a closed Folder and an open Index—notice the arrows on the right-hand side:

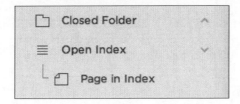

Adding pages to a secondary navigation area

As mentioned earlier in this chapter, some templates have a secondary navigation bar or footer navigation that you can control in the Pages menu. You can add, remove, or rearrange pages in this navigation exactly like your main navigation.

 Some templates automatically create a secondary navigation bar for Folder or Index Pages. You will not see this type of secondary navigation in the Navigation area in the Pages panel.

Removing pages from your site

There are three ways to remove pages from the public view of your site, ranging from temporarily turning them off to permanently deleting them.

Disabling pages

If you need to temporarily hide or remove a page from the public, the easiest way is to disable the page. This will keep the page's location in your site navigation, but will hide it so that only logged-in administrators can see it. This is useful for times when you are updating a page but have to stop before you have finished the updates. You can disable a page by unchecking **Enable** checkbox in Page Settings, described earlier in this chapter.

Storing pages for later

If you have a page that you don't want to show on your site right now but may want to use in future, you can store it in the **Not Linked** section. This removes the page from your site's navigation. If you also disable it, this is the safest way to keep a page out of the public eye, but accessible to you, on a long-term basis. Pages can stay in the **Not Linked** section for an indefinite amount of time.

If you want to keep pages in the **Not Linked** section completely hidden from the public, you must disable them. Enabled pages in the **Not Linked** section can still be accessed using the URL; they just don't form part of your navigation.

For this reason, you can also use the **Not Linked** section for pages that you want to keep public but are not important enough to be a part of your **Main Navigation** section, such as Terms and Conditions. You can simply link to these pages from your footer or any other text content.

To store a page in the **Not Linked** section, click on the page and drag it below the **Not Linked** section header, and then release it.

Disabled pages stored in the **Not Linked** section do not count in any page number limits that may apply to your Squarespace subscription.

Deleting pages

Deleting pages is a two-step process: the first step is to move the page to the Recycle Bin, and the second step of permanent removal happens automatically 7 days later. This ensures that if you accidentally remove pages, you have time to restore them if you need to. However, the safest way to remove pages is to first move them to the **Not Linked** section and leave them there for a while—perhaps a few months or longer. Then, you can periodically clear out your **Not Linked** section and move anything you know you will definitely not need into the Recycle Bin. This is the best way to ensure you do not lose any work that may come in handy later.

> If you really want to be organized, you can make Folders in the **Not Linked** section to store your unused pages. Name the Folders according to month, department, person's name, or whatever helps you keep track of pages and aids in regular housekeeping.

Moving pages to the Recycle Bin

If you are absolutely certain you want to permanently delete a page, you can move the page to the Recycle Bin in one of two ways:

- In Page Settings, click on the **Delete** button
- In the Pages menu, hover your mouse over the name of the page, and click on the trash can icon that appears on the left-hand side of the page name, as shown here:

Restoring a page from the Recycle Bin

If you have accidentally removed a page, you can follow these steps to restore it:

1. Click on the Recycle Bin icon at the bottom of the Pages panel.
2. Locate the page you want to restore.
3. Hover over the page name and click on the **Restore** button.

The restored page will be moved out of the Recycle Bin and into the **Not Linked** section of the Navigation area.

Adding external site links to your site navigation

So far, everything we have done with your site's navigation has linked to pages on your own website. However, there may be times when you want to include a link to a separate website in your navigation. This may be a link to your company's Facebook or Twitter profile, or it could be a link to an external third-party site, such as a reseller or sister organization.

Adding social media profile links

Most Squarespace templates have a special area for linking to social media profiles. This may be as part of your main navigation, your secondary navigation, or situated in the top or bottom corner of the page. In most cases, these links are presented as social icons, such as those shown here:

To connect social media accounts to your site, follow these steps:

1. From the Home menu, go to **Settings | Social**.
2. Click on **Connected Accounts** in the **Social** menu.
3. Click on **Connect Account**.
4. Choose the type of account you wish to connect.
5. Enter your account details or authorize the connection in the pop-up window.

You will see the account on the **Connected Accounts** screen, and if your template offers social icons, you can see the icon for that account in the Preview screen.

You can find more detail about **Connected Accounts**, including screenshots, in *Chapter 9, Going Live with Your Website and Driving Traffic to It.*

Squarespace includes **Email** as one of the social media accounts / icons even though it's not really a social media thing. This will allow visitors to send an email to a specified address by clicking on the icon. Be careful about using this, as spammers often look for this type of code. It's better to use a contact form instead of publishing an email address on the Web in this manner. We'll cover forms in *Chapter 6, Using Blocks to Add Functionality, Rich Media, and Special Features.*

Adding links to third-party sites

Use external links in navigation with caution: including a link that takes visitors away from your site within the main navigation is risky. Users do not usually expect to be taken to a different site, so you need to use clear labeling to indicate that is what the link does. Furthermore, moving traffic away from your own site may not be the best business move. Think carefully about whether you could put the link somewhere else, such as a footer or sidebar, or within a page in your own site that includes context to indicate why the person should visit that site instead of staying on yours.

Here's how to add an external link to your navigation:

1. In the Pages menu, click on **+ Add Page**.
2. Choose **Link** as the type.
3. Enter the title you want to show in the navigation, and enter the website's URL below it.
4. Click on **Save**.

 You can rearrange Links in your navigation in the same way you move pages around.

Summary

You've now learned everything there is to know about pages, items, and navigation, so you are fully equipped to create your site's content framework, ready for us to fill with content and functions in the next chapters. Now is the time for you to create all the core pages that you included in your Website Toolkit sitemap and arrange them in the right order.

Remember, you can store pages that you don't need in your **Not Linked** section, so it's a good idea to keep some of the demo pages that we created as part of the exercises in this chapter. You will then have something to refer to if you forget how your template handles certain page settings or types, such as custom header images or Indexes, even if you aren't using them on your real site right away.

> Create a Folder in your **Not Linked** section and label it as the name of your template. Store your unused demo pages there, so they are easy to find and refer to when you need them. You can also rename the pages to refer to the function or feature you want to reference, such as "Sample Index Page".

The next two chapters are where you will start to see your site really come to life. You will do most of the hands-on work in building your site here, so ensure that the content for your site is ready and available before proceeding.

5
Adding, Editing, and Arranging Content in Your Web Pages

In the last chapter, we created empty or sample pages and items to prepare your site framework for the main event: filling the site with real content and functions and arranging them on the page to create your desired page layouts. This chapter will show you how to add, remove, and edit content on your site and give you all of the core skills you will need to manage your page layouts. You will also gain a better understanding of the page and item properties that we introduced in the last chapter by adding and arranging the real content that you gathered in your Website Toolkit to result in finished web pages.

In this chapter, you will learn how to use three of the most powerful and creative tools that Squarespace offers: Squarespace **Blocks**, which allow you to insert a range of content and functions; the Squarespace **LayoutEngine**, which controls page layouts; and the **Aviary Image Editor**, which allows you to manipulate images directly within Squarespace without needing fancy software, such as Adobe Photoshop. So, make sure you have the content from your Website Toolkit handy, and get ready to learn the following:

- Understanding the different types of blocks and how to use them
- Adding and formatting text content on your website
- Adding images, cropping, and adjusting them using the Aviary Image Editor
- Adding links to other web pages and downloadable files
- Arranging blocks using LayoutEngine
- Using spacing blocks to fine-tune page layouts
- Using sidebars and footers to apply content to multiple pages

Understanding Blocks

Much like pages in a newspaper, web pages on Squarespace are made up of different rectangles, or blocks, of content. However, unlike a block in a newspaper, a Squarespace Block can actually contain much more than just text or images. Squarespace Blocks can contain any of the main types of web content, such as:

- Text formatted in a range of styles, such as headlines, subheaders, quotations, or body text

- Text hyperlinks or buttons that link to other web pages or files

- Images, such as photographs, illustrations or graphic design elements

- Multimedia content, such as video or audio, with a player embedded into the page, so visitors can see and hear without downloading files or leaving your site

However, Squarespace Blocks can also contain functions and not just content. For example, there are Squarespace Blocks that allow users to perform tasks on your website, such as:

- Using a search box to find things on your website

- Filling in a form

- Signing up for a newsletter

- Making a donation

- Buying a product

- Making a reservation at a restaurant

There are also blocks that can dynamically pull content from other places and display it on your page. For example, you can display:

- A list of all the categories that you have used in your blog

- An embedded slideshow of photos from a Gallery you created on your website

- A Google Map

- Your latest Twitter tweets or other social media updates

- Photos that have been posted on external photo-sharing sites, such as Instagram

Lastly, there are special blocks to add code or embed technical elements into your web pages to expand functions beyond the ones that Squarespace offers.

In this chapter, we'll use basic blocks to add the most common types of business website content—text, images, and links. Then, we'll explore the more advanced kinds of blocks in the next chapter.

Adding and removing blocks

All types of blocks are added to pages in the same way. Remember, you can add blocks to certain types of items as well. For example, you can add images, forms, or any other type of block to a blog post or event in exactly the same way as you would add a standard page.

Adding a block

Follow these steps to add a block to a page:

1. In the Preview screen, hover your mouse over the body area of the page to activate the Annotations, as shown here:

 Make sure you are hovering over the body area and not over another part of the page, such as the header or footer. Annotations appear over these areas as well—and you'll only confuse yourself if you click on the **Edit** button there instead of on the **Page Content** area.

2. Click on the **Edit** button next to **Page Content**. This will open the Content Editor screen: the side panel will close, and a wide floating window will appear above the Preview. This is where you can add and edit your content.

By default, every new page comes with one **Text Block** already inserted. This appears as **Write here...** instructional text, as shown in the following screenshot of the Content Editor window:

3. Hover your mouse over the **Write here...** instructional text (or whatever text may be in the page already), and you will notice two gray teardrop-shaped Insert Points appear on the left-hand side.

4. Hover your mouse over the bottom Insert Point. You will notice that the icon turns darker, and a dark horizontal line appears next to it, as shown:

The horizontal line indicates where the new block will appear. In this case, it will appear below the empty block with the placeholder `Write here...` text, and it will run across the full width of the page.

5. Click on the Insert Point to add a new block to this location. You will see a pop-up selection window appear next to the Insert Point. This allows you to select from the wide range of block types available, as shown here:

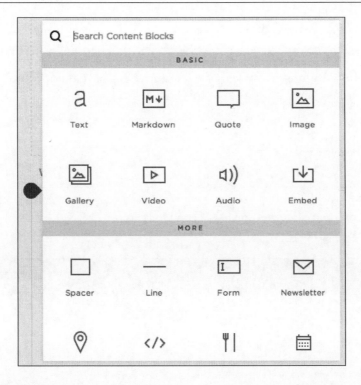

You will see that the blocks have been organized into different categories to make it easier for you to find the kind of block you want to use. The categories are:

- ° **Basic**: These are the most common types of standard content
- ° **More**: This is a general catch-all term for specialized blocks
- ° **Filters & Lists**: These are blocks that pull other content or properties from elsewhere on your site
- ° **Commerce**: These are blocks associated with making a transaction
- ° **Social**: These blocks display content from external social media websites

6. Click on the type of block that you wish to insert, and the system will add the element to that point in the page. For this exercise, select **Spacer**, as it is the most basic type of block. For non-text blocks, an overlay editor will open so you can add any necessary elements and/or configure the settings of the block.

Removing blocks

There are two different ways to remove blocks. The first method is as follows:

1. Hover your mouse near one of the outer edges of the block until your cursor turns into a hand, as shown in this screenshot:

2. Click on the pale gray border of the block to select it, and drag it down into the trash can icon.

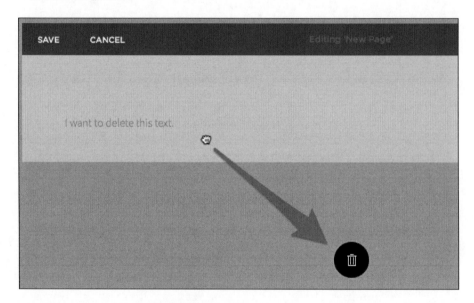

Here's the second way to remove blocks:

1. Click (for Text Blocks) or double-click on the block (for other types of blocks) to open the editor window.
2. Click on the **Remove** button or trash can icon in the editor window.

 Removing blocks is permanent, so be careful. Once you have removed a block, there is no way to get it back.

Adding basic content to your pages

As most web pages are composed of text and images, let's start by adding this kind of basic content to one of your empty pages. You should add a heading, some body text, and at least one image to the page, so you have a page full of content to use in the next step: arranging blocks to create custom page layouts.

The Content Editor window displays content exactly as it will appear on your web page, making it easy for you to see and understand how your finished page will look. This means you can control the layout of the page while you are filling it with content without needing to move outside of the Content Editor.

 Don't forget to click on the **Save** button at the top of the Content Editor whenever you add content to your page.

Adding and formatting text using Text Blocks

The most commonly used type of block is a **Text Block**. All new pages come with a single Text Block inserted by default. You can either type directly into this space, or you can copy and paste text content from other documents into a Text Block.

 Squarespace has a built-in spellchecker. Any unknown or misspelled words will show a red dotted line below them, and you can right-click on a word to correct it.

Text Blocks come with a range of formatting tools and controls that allow you to change the appearance of your text or apply visual styles that have been set by your template. To activate the Text Block formatting toolbar, click into the Text Block (or on the **Write here...** placeholder text) and you will see a toolbar appear above your cursor.

Let's go through all of the controls in the toolbar to learn what they do:

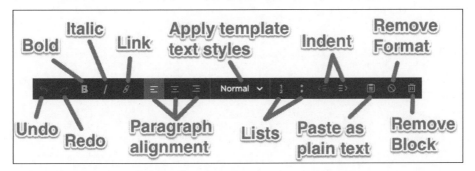

Here are the toolbar controls and their functions:

- **Undo**: Discard a change if you do not want to commit to it.

- **Redo**: Reapply a change if you have clicked on Undo.

- **Bold** and **Italic**: Apply these styles to the selected text.

- **Link**: Add a hyperlink (we'll cover this in more detail later in this chapter).

- **Alignment**: Align your paragraph to the left, center, or right.

- **Apply template text styles**: Use this drop-down menu to apply special styles, such as your template's heading or subheading styles to make your text larger and draw attention to it. Heading fonts, colors, and sizes are set by your template.

The heading styles Heading 1, 2, and 3 correspond to the HTML styles h1, h2, and h3. Search engines use h1, h2, and h3 as part of the formula that determines search engine ranking, so it's a good idea to use keywords that describe the page content in your headings. The h1 heading is also used as the text link on search engine results' pages, so ensure you use clear, concise, and engaging wording for all of your Heading 1 text.

You can also use this menu to apply your template's **Quote** or **Code** style to your text. Quote can be used for callout text that you want to draw attention to, such as a client testimonial or an important note. Some templates will indent the text, italicize it, and/or add a box or border around it. The Code style is usually only used by technical instruction websites to show pasted computer programming code in a different style from body text. However, you may find a creative use for it, such as showing recipe text on a cooking website or any other purpose that requires certain lines of text to stand out.

You can also add quotes to your pages using a **Quote Block** if you need to assign an author to the quote. Quote Blocks display the author name on a separate line and can be moved around the page easily.

- **Lists**: This formats your sentences as bulleted lists or numbered lists.

- **Indent**: This controls the indentation of your paragraph.

- **Paste as plain text**: You can use this to discard any formatting that may have been applied by an external program, such as Microsoft Word or Apple Pages, when copying or pasting text into your Text Block.

 Always use this whenever you are copying or pasting text from any other document. Most word processing programs add unnecessary hidden code when you paste, so using this function ensures you don't end up pasting unwanted code into your nice, clean Squarespace pages. Sometimes, this code can break your pages; other times, it can make pasted text look different from the rest of your pages, and sometimes, you won't see any effects, but it will make your pages load slower.

- **Remove Format**: This clears any styles you have applied to your text—such as bold, italics, or lists—and restores the text to normal paragraph style.

- **Remove Block**: This deletes the entire Text Block from your page.

 If you don't like the font, color, or style of text that has been set by your template, you can change it as part of the visual style adjustments we'll perform in *Chapter 8, Tailoring Your Site's Look and Feel*.

Adding images using Image Blocks

An **Image Block** allows you to upload and display a single image on your page.

 You can also add images using other methods such as Gallery Blocks or as feeds from photo-sharing sites, which will be covered in the next chapter.

When you add an Image Block to your page, the **Edit Image** overlay will open, as shown here:

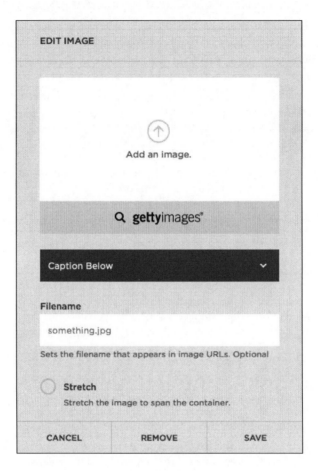

You will see the following settings in the **Edit Image** window:

- **Add an image**: Click here to browse to your image, or drag an image onto this space to upload the image from your computer.
- **gettyimages**: Click here to select an image from the Getty Images stock library. We'll cover this in more detail in the next part of this chapter.
- **Caption**: You can choose **Caption Below** to display a caption under the image, as an overlay on your image, or have the overlay appear when the mouse is hovered over the image. If you don't need a caption, you can choose **Do Not Display Caption**.
- **Filename**: The name of the image file is loaded here by default.

If your filenames look like DS139668.jpg, renaming the filename to something that matches your brand or page topic can add a little boost to your page in search engines.

- **Stretch**: You can use this to force an image to fill the width of the block. If you don't select this, the image will fill the block based on height only. Stretch is most useful when adding vertical images to horizontal spaces or horizontal images to vertical spaces.

 Use Stretch with caution: if you have small images, selecting this checkbox will make the image stretch beyond its original size, causing the image to appear blurred and look unprofessional.

- **Lightbox**: Select this if you want to show a smaller version of a large image in the page but allow users to click on the smaller version to open the large version in an overlay.
- **Clickthrough URL**: Use this if you want to make the image link to a web page or file when clicked on. We'll cover how to do this shortly.

 You can use **Lightbox** or **Clickthrough URL** but not both.

After you have added your image to the block and adjusted the settings, click on **Save** to close the edit window and return to the Content Editor.

Using stock images from Getty Images

The Getty Images stock library is integrated with Squarespace, which means that you can find and purchase stock photography and illustrations directly from the Squarespace interface, and the cost will be automatically charged to the credit card that you use for your Squarespace subscription billing. Each image costs $10, and when you make the purchase, the image will automatically be loaded into your website, and a high-resolution version will also be downloaded to your computer. The Getty Images function is integrated to all the areas of Squarespace where you can add images, which means that you can use them for header images, Galleries, or logos, in addition to standard Image Blocks.

To use a Getty Images image in an Image Block, follow these steps:

1. Insert a new Image Block, or hover over an existing one and click on the **Edit** Annotation.

2. In the **Edit Image** window, click on the **gettyimages** button. This will open the Getty Images browser, as shown here:

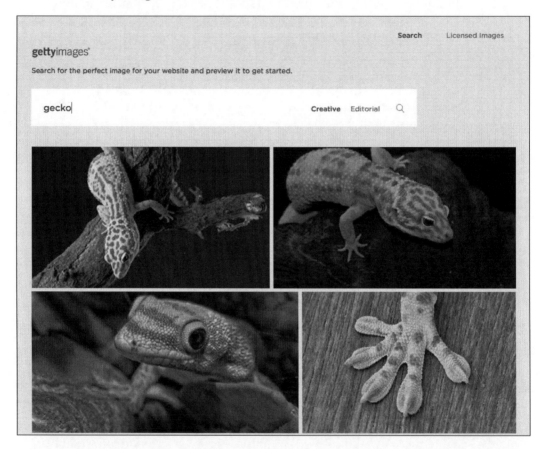

3. Use the search box to enter keywords for the image you want to find. Search results showing image thumbnails will load below the search box.

4. When you find one you like, click on the thumbnail to preview the image. This will load a low-resolution watermarked placeholder into the block to allow you to test it on your page.

5. If you like the image, you can license the image now or in the future using the **License** button that appears below the image thumbnail in the **Edit Image** window, as shown in the following screenshot:

6. Clicking on the **License** button will open a confirmation window where you can complete the purchase.

7. Once you have purchased the image, the low-res placeholder will be replaced by the actual image, and a high-resolution version of the image will also be downloaded to your computer.

 You can see all of your previous purchases and reuse a previously purchased image by clicking on the **Licensed Images** link above the search box in the Getty Images browser.

Arranging blocks on the page

Now that you have a few blocks on your page, it's a good time to introduce one of the most powerful and easy-to-use browser-based web design tools available on the Internet: the Squarespace LayoutEngine. LayoutEngine allows you to change the size and position of blocks simply by clicking, dragging, and dropping the blocks directly in the page itself.

When adding blocks, the default behavior is for all blocks to stretch to fit the full width of the page. This results in lots of horizontal blocks stacked vertically on top of one another. Using LayoutEngine, you can change the layout of pages so that blocks appear side by side in columns, have text wrapping around images or other types of blocks, or add spacing between blocks to create a more open and airy feeling on the page.

Moving a block to another position on the page

Follow these steps to move a block to another position:

1. Hover your mouse over the block, and you will see a pale gray border around the block.

2. Move your cursor towards an edge of the block until it changes into a hand icon, as shown here:

3. Click and hold down your mouse to pick up the block. It will appear grayed out, and the cursor icon will change into a closed hand.

4. While still holding down the mouse, slowly drag the block toward the position where you want to place it. As you get close to an area where you can place it, you will notice one of two things:

   ° A thick black horizontal or vertical line will appear to indicate that you can drop the block there to position it next to the other block. You can position blocks to the left, right, above, or below other blocks to create rows or columns of content. The following screenshot shows you the black line indicating that the photo can be dropped to the right of the text:

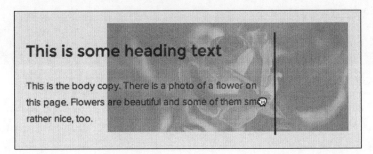

   ° A translucent dark gray box with a thick black border will appear to indicate that you can drop the block there to wrap the other block's text content around it. This is shown in the following screenshot:

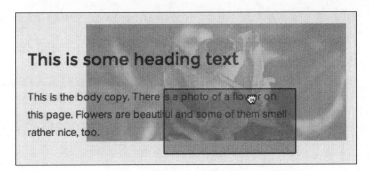

5. When you reach your desired placement, release the mouse to move the block to its new position.

6. After you have moved your content block, click on the **Save** button at the top of the page to save your new layout.

You can split a multi-paragraph text block into two horizontal slices by dragging another block onto the point where you want to divide it. Make sure the thick black indicator line runs all the way across the width of the Text Block before you drop the dividing block.

Canceling a move or other adjustment

If you move an item or adjust its size and decide that you don't like it, you can cancel the change and revert to the previously saved layout. After the move or adjustment, but before clicking on **Save**, click on the **Cancel** button in the top-right section of the screen, and the system will discard whatever changes you have made and restore the page to the last saved version.

Understanding fluid layouts and responsive design

Before going further, it's important to highlight that all Squarespace templates use a web design practice called **responsive design**, which means that the dimensions of the page will automatically scale to fit the type of device the visitor is using, whether it's a desktop computer with a large monitor, a laptop with a smaller screen, an HD TV, tablet, or smartphone. While this is a best practice in the industry and is great for usability, it does make things a little more complicated when it comes to page layouts and web design.

Responsive design uses a technique called **fluid layout** to ensure that pages and elements are sized relative to the size of the device screen. For example, if we have a page width of 100 percent, and a photo width of 50 percent, these proportions will stay the same regardless of screen size. On a large monitor, 50 percent of the width might be 800 pixels, whereas on a smartphone, it might be 180 pixels. However, in a fluid layout, the photo will always take up half the width of the page.

To keep text readable even on small screens, the font size is not usually scaled down in responsive design. This means that even though the relative size of images is maintained in proportion to the page width, your pages will not look exactly the same on different screen sizes, as text wrapping points and flow will be affected. To demonstrate, here are some screenshots showing the same page in different screen sizes. The first screenshot shows how the page would appear on a large desktop computer monitor:

THIS IS THE HEADING FOR THIS PAGE

Lorem ipsum dolor sit amet, consectetur adipiscing elit. Quisque imperdiet neque id dignissim vehicula. Integer in mauris odio. Suspendisse potenti. Ut facilisis dolor non justo lobortis, eu mattis est porttitor. Nulla vehicula luctus augue et sagittis. Quisque tincidunt elit ac dui tempus, vitae aliquet augue mollis. Pellentesque dolor orci, volutpat eget dui vel, posuere dictum nibh. Cras at egestas mi. Curabitur vehicula risus a dapibus lobortis. Aliquam at quam ultricies, egestas mauris ac, tristique mauris. Praesent fringilla, odio nec varius tristique, ipsum metus va

Lorem ipsum dolor sit amet, consectetur adipiscing elit. Quisque imperdiet neque id dignissim vehicula. Integer in mauris odio. Suspendisse potenti. Ut facilisis dolor non justo lobortis, eu mattis est porttitor. Nulla vehicula luctus augue et sagittis. Quisque tincidunt elit ac dui tempus, vitae aliquet augue mollis. Pellentesque dolor orci, volutpat eget dui vel, posuere dictum nibh. Cras at egestas mi. Curabitur vehicula risus a dapibus lobortis. Aliquam at quam ultricies, egestas mauris ac, tristique mauris. Praesent fringilla, odio nec varius tristique, ipsum metus va

This screenshot shows the same page as it would appear on a handheld tablet screen:

THIS IS THE HEADING FOR THIS PAGE

Lorem ipsum dolor sit amet, consectetur adipiscing elit. Quisque imperdiet neque id dignissim vehicula. Integer in mauris odio. Suspendisse potenti. Ut facilisis dolor non justo lobortis, eu mattis est porttitor. Nulla vehicula luctus augue et sagittis. Quisque tincidunt elit ac dui tempus, vitae aliquet augue mollis. Pellentesque dolor orci, volutpat eget dui vel, posuere dictum nibh. Cras at egestas mi. Curabitur vehicula risus a dapibus lobortis. Aliquam at quam ultricies, egestas mauris ac, tristique mauris. Praesent fringilla, odio nec varius tristique, ipsum metus va

Lorem ipsum dolor sit amet, consectetur adipiscing elit. Quisque imperdiet neque id dignissim vehicula. Integer in mauris odio. Suspendisse potenti. Ut facilisis dolor non justo lobortis, eu mattis est porttitor. Nulla vehicula luctus augue et sagittis. Quisque tincidunt elit ac dui tempus, vitae aliquet augue mollis. Pellentesque dolor orci, volutpat eget dui vel, posuere dictum nibh. Cras at egestas mi. Curabitur vehicula risus a dapibus lobortis. Aliquam at quam ultricies, egestas mauris ac, tristique mauris. Praesent fringilla, odio nec varius tristique, ipsum metus va

Finally, here is how the same page would appear on a smartphone screen:

THIS IS THE HEADING FOR THIS PAGE

Lorem ipsum dolor sit amet, consectetur adipiscing elit. Quisque imperdiet neque id dignissim vehicula. Integer in mauris odio. Suspendisse potenti. Ut facilisis dolor non justo lobortis, eu mattis est porttitor. Nulla vehicula luctus augue et sagittis. Quisque tincidunt elit ac dui tempus, vitae aliquet augue mollis. Pellentesque dolor orci, volutpat eget dui vel, posuere dictum nibh. Cras at egestas mi. Curabitur vehicula risus a dapibus lobortis. Aliquam at quam ultricies, egestas mauris ac, tristique mauris. Praesent fringilla, odio nec varius tristique, ipsum metus va

Therefore, when we adjust the sizes of blocks in this chapter, and when we adjust other design elements later, we will need to view and test things on a variety of different screen sizes.

If you use the Firefox browser, you can quickly switch between different screen sizes using the Mozilla Web Developer tools that come with the browser. This is a lot easier than manually dragging the right edge of your browser to simulate different screen sizes.

Responsive design, image sizes, and screen resolutions

Responsive design also makes things a bit tricky when it comes to recommended pixel dimensions for photos. As your images will be presented in a range of sizes, you need to ensure that your image dimensions are at least as large as the biggest size that will be shown on large or high-resolution monitors. Today, nearly 80 percent of website visitors on computers or web-enabled TVs have screen resolutions of 1366 pixels wide by 768 pixels tall, or greater. Therefore, a good rule of thumb is to use images around 1500 pixels wide if they will be shown fullscreen. You can adjust down from this accordingly for images that will only be shown at smaller sizes within the page.

If your own computer monitor is small or old, you may not be seeing your website as a majority of your visitors will. For example, some templates display a background color around the edge of the canvas only at larger sizes, while others will stretch to fill the space. If you don't have access to a high-resolution monitor or HD Smart TV, you can simulate a larger resolution within your small screen by pasting your website URL into www.quirktools.com/screenfly and using the icons to select a large monitor size.

Adjusting the size of blocks and columns

When moving blocks to appear side by side or wrapped, the system will set the size of each item to be 50 percent of the width of the page by default. However, you can adjust the width of a block or column to be wider or narrower than 50 percent.

Squarespace uses a hidden grid structure to control page layouts and ensure they look balanced, so you won't be able to adjust widths by a single pixel or percentage. As you are adjusting, you will notice that widths will automatically snap to fit the grid, keeping your pages tidy without you even having to think about it.

Adjusting the width of columns, adjacent blocks, or wrapping blocks

Follow these steps to adjust the width of columns, adjacent blocks, or wrapping blocks:

1. Hover your mouse over the border between the columns, the two adjacent blocks, or the edge of the block that has the other wrapped around it. Your cursor will change to a resize icon, as shown in this screenshot:

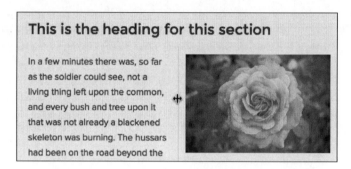

2. Click and drag to adjust the width of the blocks. Resizing one block will automatically adjust the other block to fill the space accordingly.

Using Spacer and Line Blocks to fine-tune layouts

There may be occasions where you want to have more space between columns or rows than what is allocated automatically by the system. In these instances, you can use **Spacer Blocks** or **Line Blocks** between other blocks. You'll find these blocks under the **More** category in the **Add Block** menu. Spacer Blocks can be used either horizontally or vertically to create space, but Line Blocks can only run horizontally. You can add, move, or adjust the width of these blocks in the same way as any other block, but Spacer Blocks have an added feature to allow you to control the height.

 Your template determines the color of the line in Line Blocks. Many templates allow you to adjust this color in Style Mode, which we'll cover in *Chapter 8, Tailoring Your Site's Look and Feel.*

Adjusting the height of a Spacer Block

To adjust the height of a Spacer Block, follow these steps:

1. Click on the Spacer Block to activate it. You will see a large gray dot appear near the bottom edge of the block.

2. Hover your mouse over the dot, and your cursor will change to a resize icon.

3. Click and drag the dot down or up to adjust the height of the block, as shown in the following screenshot:

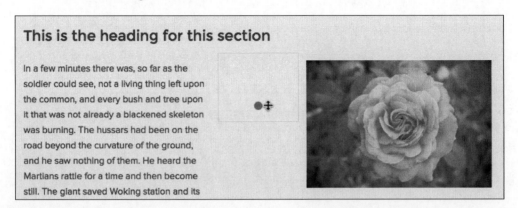

Adjusting images in Squarespace

We've learned how to adjust the size of images in relation to other elements on the page, but so far, the images themselves have remained intact, showing the full image. However, you can actually crop or zoom images so they only show a portion of the photo on the screen without having to leave the Squarespace interface. You can also apply effects to images using the built-in Aviary Image Editor, such as rotating, enhancing color, boosting contrast, whitening teeth, removing blemishes, or hundreds of other adjustments, which means you don't need fancy image editing software to perform even fairly advanced image adjustments.

Cropping and zooming images with LayoutEngine

If you only want to crop your image, you don't need to use the Aviary Image Editor: you can crop images using LayoutEngine in the Squarespace Content Editor.

To crop an image, you perform the same steps as those to adjust the height of a Spacer Block: just click and drag the dot to change the part of the image that is shown. As you drag the dot up or down, you will notice that:

- Dragging the dot up will chop off the top and bottom of your image
- Dragging the dot down will zoom in your image, cutting off the sides and making the image appear larger
- When dragging the dot very near the original dimensions of your image, you will feel and see the cursor pull/snap to the original size

Cropping an image in an Image Block in this manner does not remove parts from the original image; it merely adjusts the part of the image that will be shown in the Image Block on the page. You can always change your mind later.

Adjusting the Focal Point of images

You'll notice that all of the cropping and zooming of images is based on the center of the image. What if your image has elements near the edges that you want to show instead of weighting things towards the center? With Squarespace, you can influence which part of the image displays by adjusting the **Focal Point** of the image. The Focal Point identifies the most important part of the image to instruct the system to try to use this point as the basis for cropping or zooming. However, if your Image Block is an extreme shape, such as a long skinny rectangle, it may not be possible to fit all of your desired area into the cropped or zoomed image space.

Adjusting the Focal Point can also be useful for Gallery images, as certain templates display images in a square format or other formats that may not match the dimensions of your images. You can also adjust the Focal Point of any Thumbnail Images that you have added in Page Settings to select which part to show as the thumbnail or header banner.

To adjust an image's Focal Point, follow these steps:

1. Double-click on the image to open the **Edit Image** overlay window.

2. Hover your mouse over the image thumbnail, and you will see a translucent circle appear at the center of the thumbnail. This is the Focal Point.

3. Click and drag the circle until it sits on top of the part of the image you want to include, as shown in the following screenshot:

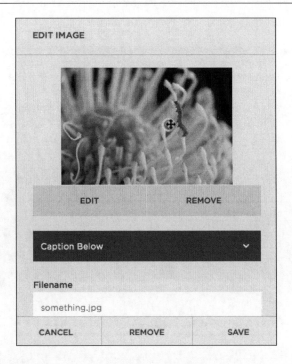

Using the Aviary Image Editor

You can also use the Aviary Image Editor to crop or zoom into your images as well as many more adjustments that are too numerous to list here. It's important to remember that all adjustments carried out in the Aviary Image Editor are permanent: there is no way to go back to a previous version of your image. Therefore, it's better to use LayoutEngine for cropping and zooming and reserve Aviary for other adjustments that you know you want to make permanently, such as rotating a portrait image that was taken sideways to display vertically.

 Because edits performed in the Aviary Image Editor are permanent, use it with caution and always keep a backup original version of the image on your computer just in case.

Here's how to edit an image with the Aviary Image Editor:

1. Double-click on the image to open the **Edit Image** overlay window.

2. Click on the **Edit** button below the image thumbnail. This will open the Aviary window, as shown in the following screenshot:

3. Select the type of adjustment you want to perform from the menu at the top.

4. Use the controls to perform the adjustment and click on **Apply**. The window will show you the effect of the adjustment on the image.

5. Perform any other adjustments in the same manner.

> You can go back to previous steps using the arrows in the bottom-left section of the editor window.

6. Once you have performed all desired adjustments, click on **Save** to commit the adjustments to the image permanently. The Aviary window will now close.

7. In the **Edit Image** window, click on **Save** to store the Aviary adjustments. The **Edit Image** window will now close.

8. In the Content Editor window, click on the **Save** button to refresh the page with the newly edited version of the image.

Adding content to sidebars or footers

Until this point, all of our content additions and edits have been performed on a single page. However, it's likely that you will want to have certain blocks of content appear on multiple or all pages, such as a copyright notice in your page footer or an *About the Author* text snippet in the sidebar of all blog posts.

You add content to footers or sidebars using the Content Editor in much the same way as adding the page content. However, there are a few restrictions. Certain templates only allow certain types of blocks in footers or sidebars, and some templates have restrictions on positioning elements as well — for example, it's unlikely that you will be able to wrap text around an image in a sidebar due to space limitations.

 If you are unable to get the system to accept an addition or repositioning move that you are trying to perform to a block in a sidebar or footer, it usually indicates that you are trying to perform something that is prohibited.

Adding or editing content in a footer

Follow these steps to add or edit content in a footer:

1. In the preview screen, scroll to the bottom of your page and hover over the footer area to activate the Annotations there, and click on the **Edit** button next to the **Footer Content** label, as shown in the following screenshot:

This will open the Content Editor window, just like earlier in this chapter when you learned how to add and edit blocks in the page body.

2. You will notice that Insert Points appear just like before, and you can click on an Insert Point to add a block, or click within an existing Text Block to edit it. You can move blocks in a footer in the same way as those in a page body.

Most templates have a footer, but not all of them do. Some templates hide the footer on certain page types, so if you can't see your footer, try looking at a standard page, or double-check whether your template offers one.

Adding or editing content in a sidebar

Not all templates have a sidebar, but if yours does, here's how you can add or edit content in your sidebar:

1. While in the **Pages** menu, navigate to a page that you know has a sidebar in your template, such as a Blog page. You should see the template's demo content preloaded into your sidebar.

2. Hover your mouse over the sidebar area to activate the Annotations, and click on the **Edit** button that appears at the top of the sidebar area.

Make sure you click on the correct Annotation. Other Annotations may be activated on the page, so don't get confused and click on anything other than the sidebar Annotations, as shown in the following screenshot:

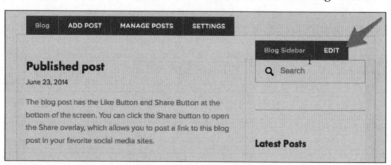

3. Once the Content Editor window opens, you can click on an Insert Point to add a block or click within an existing Text Block to edit it. You can move blocks in a sidebar in the same way as those in a page body.

Enabling a sidebar

If you do not see the sidebar, but you know that your template allows one, and you know you are on the correct page type (for example, a Blog post), then it's possible that your sidebar is not enabled. Depending on the template, you enable your sidebar in one of two ways. The first method is in the Style Editor, as follows:

1. First, ensure you are looking at a Blog page (or any page that can have a sidebar in your template). From the Home menu in the side panel, navigate to **Design | Style Editor**.

2. In the **Style Editor** menu, scroll down until you see a set of controls related to Blog Styles.

3. Find the control for the sidebar, and select the position you want. The following screenshot shows you an example of this:

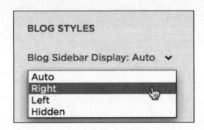

4. Click on **Save** to commit your changes.

If you don't see the sidebar control in the Style Editor, you may find it in the Blog or Page Settings instead, as described here:

1. First, ensure you are looking at the Blog page (or any page that can have a sidebar in your template), and then click on the **Settings** button in the Annotations or the cog icon in the **Pages** menu to open the **Settings** window.

2. Look for a menu item called **Page Layout** and select the sidebar position, as shown in the following screenshot:

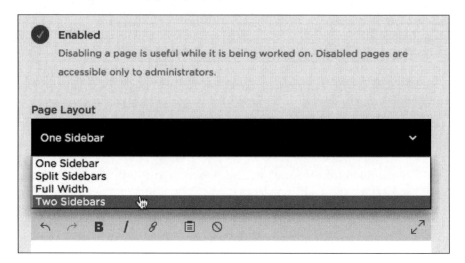

On smaller screens, many templates use fluid layout to stack the sidebar below the main content area instead of showing it on the left- or right-hand side. If you can't see your sidebar and are viewing the website on a tablet or another small/low-resolution screen, scroll down to the bottom of the page and you will most likely see your sidebar content there, just above the footer.

Adding links that point to web pages or files

The final type of basic content that we'll cover in this chapter is adding hyperlinks to your pages. You can use these links to point to external websites, other pages on your own website, or files that visitors can either view within the browser or download to their computers.

You can assign a link to any word or phrase in a Text Block, or you can assign a link to an image. You can also use a special type of block called a **Button** to make links really stand out and encourage users to click.

When creating links in any of these scenarios, you will be presented with three main options:

- **External**: You can paste or type the full web address of the external website you want the link to point to. You can also choose to have this website open in a new window to allow users to keep your site open instead of navigating away entirely. The following screenshot shows the **External** option:

- **Files**: You can either upload a file directly, or link to a file that you have already uploaded earlier. This screenshot shows the **Files** option:

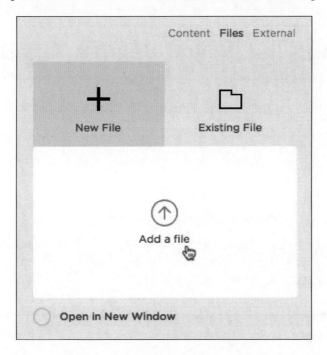

- **Content**: You can link to any page, category, or tag that you have created on your site. Linking to a category or tag will display a list of all items that have been labeled with that tag or category. Here's an example of the **Content** option:

Assigning a link to word(s) in a Text Block

Follow these steps to assign a link to a word or phrase in a Text Block:

1. Highlight the word(s), and then click on the link icon (two interlocked ovals) in the text editor menu.

2. Select the type of link you want to add, input the necessary settings, and then click anywhere outside the Edit Link window. This will close the Edit Link window, and you will see that the word is now a different color to indicate that the link has been applied.

3. Click on the **Save** button at the top of the page.

You can change or remove the link at any time by clicking on the word. A floating window will appear to show you what the link currently points to, along with the options to edit or remove the link. This is shown in the following screenshot:

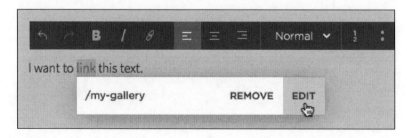

Assigning a link to an image

Here's how you can assign a link to an image:

1. Double-click on the image to open the **Edit Image** window.

2. Under **Clickthrough URL**, select the type of link that you want to add and input the necessary settings.

3. Click on **Save**.

Creating a Button on your page

You can create a Button on your page by following these steps:

1. In the Content Editor window, find the point where you want to insert the button on the page, and click on the Insert Point to open the Add Block menu.

2. Under the **Filters & Lists** category, choose **Button**.

3. Type the text that you want to show on the button, select the type of link, and select the button size and alignment you want. The following screenshot shows the **Edit Button** window:

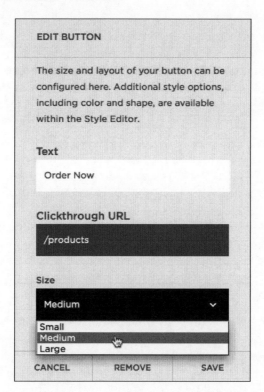

This is how the button appears on the page:

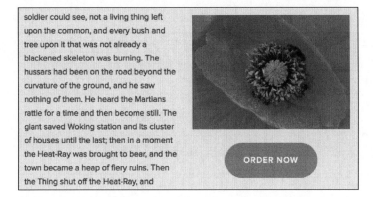

 In most templates, you can control the button color, style, and fonts using the Style Editor, which we will cover in *Chapter 8, Tailoring Your Site's Look and Feel*.

Summary

In this chapter, you have acquired all of the skills you need to add and edit basic web content, and you have learned how to move things around to create finished web pages with your desired page layout. Now is the time to add your real content from your Website Toolkit to all of the empty pages and items from the last chapter to flesh out your site with words and images.

 Visit www.square-help.com/inspiration if you'd like to see some examples of different page layouts to give you ideas for making your own pages. Here, you'll see how you can use LayoutEngine to create sophisticated layouts for a range of page types.

In the next two chapters, we will add functionality to your site, giving visitors the opportunity to interact with your business online. We will also add more advanced types of content, such as multimedia content or social media feeds, to really bring your website to life.

Remember, even if things such as colors, backgrounds, or fonts do not look exactly as you will want them to look on your final pages, you should go ahead and add all of your content now. It's easy to get distracted by these details and want to rush ahead to adjust the design instead. However, the more real content and functional elements you have in your pages, the easier it will be for you to see how the visual style adjustments we'll make later work with your website.

6
Using Blocks to Add Functionality, Rich Media, and Special Features

In the previous chapter, you learned about Squarespace Blocks and inserted some basic blocks into your web pages. In this chapter, you will learn how to use more advanced blocks to add interactivity to your website, pull in content dynamically from other places, and add helpful tools to your pages, making your website really come alive. We'll cover these in order, starting with the ones most commonly used on business websites.

Although the things that these blocks do are more advanced than basic blocks, using them is just as easy as using basic blocks, and you can adjust their size and move them around in exactly the same way. All blocks in this chapter are added the same way as the blocks in the previous chapter by clicking on the Insert Point icon when in the Content Editor.

In this chapter, we will cover:

- Inserting multimedia elements, such as audio, video, and photo slideshows
- Capturing customer data with Form and Newsletter Signup Blocks
- Adding navigational tools to your pages, such as search boxes and link blocks
- Highlighting internal website content in other places
- Pulling external content, such as maps or feeds, into your website dynamically
- Inserting an easy sales or donation call to action
- Displaying a formatted price list or menu on your site

Adding images – beyond the standard Image Block

Although you've already learned how to add single images to your pages using Image Blocks, there are other ways to add imagery to your website as well. You can add multiple images to a page in the form of a photo gallery, or you can add a feed of images from an external photo-sharing website and display them within your pages.

Gallery Blocks

You can use Gallery Blocks to display multiple images in a connected way. Gallery Blocks allow you to show a set of images in one of four different displays:

- **Grid**: This displays a table of image thumbnails that get enlarged when clicked on. The following screenshot gives you an example of a grid:

- **Slideshow**: This allows users to flick through images that fade or slide to reveal the next, with a strip of mini-thumbnails below the slideshow if required. Take a look at the following screenshot to see a slideshow display:

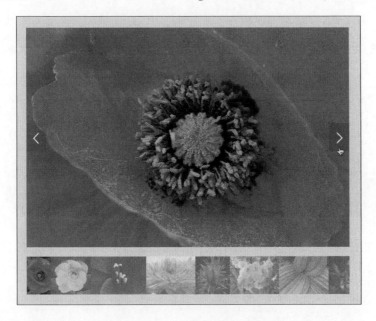

- **Slider**: This allows users to scroll through images in a horizontal strip. An example of a slider is shown in the following screenshot:

- **Stacked**: This displays large versions of images, stacked vertically with each one directly below the next. The following screenshot displays stacked images:

You can either reuse the images from a pre-existing Gallery Page, or you can add new images to your Gallery Block.

At this point, most people wonder what the difference between a Gallery Page and a standard page with a Gallery Block in it is and when to use each. It can certainly be a little confusing, so here's a summary of the key differences:

	Gallery Page	**Gallery Block**
Content on the page	In most templates, Gallery Pages do not display any information apart from the contents of the gallery itself. Gallery Pages are designed to remove distractions and allow the viewer to focus on the images.	Gallery Blocks can be inserted into any standard page, blog post, or event. Therefore, a Gallery Block is usually added to a page that already has other content. The gallery is usually meant to support or illustrate the topic of the page, or the text content of the page is meant to give context to the gallery images.
Style of display	The template dictates how a Gallery Page is displayed. It is usually either a grid or a slideshow, and you cannot have both within the same website. Sometimes, you can choose which view to use, but sometimes, the template only comes with one view. Once you have set the view and any settings associated with it, this applies to all Gallery Pages on your entire website.	Individual Gallery Blocks can be set to display images using any of the four views: slideshow, grid, slider, or stack. You can configure the settings of each Gallery Block individually, for example, choosing to show descriptions and navigation arrows on one Gallery Block but not on another. Therefore, Gallery Blocks are more flexible than Gallery Pages when it comes to the display style.
Size	Gallery Pages usually fill all of the available screen space with the gallery contents, making the images or grid as large as possible.	You can adjust the size and positioning of a Gallery Block in relation to other content on the page, just as you can adjust any other type of content block.
Reusability of images	Images added to a Gallery Page are available for use in Gallery Blocks on other pages, if you like. Whenever you update the Gallery Page, all of these Gallery Blocks will be automatically updated as well. It's usually best to upload your images to a Gallery Page if you think you may want to reuse the gallery elsewhere on your website. Refer to the following tip for further advice on this topic.	Images added to a Gallery Block are only assigned to that individual block. You cannot reuse galleries that you create as Gallery Blocks. If you are 100 percent certain that you will only ever want to display the gallery within one page, then you can safely upload them into a Gallery Block.

If there is any chance that you may want to display the same gallery in multiple places on your website, it's always best to use a Gallery Page as the place for you to upload your images even if you only want to use Gallery Blocks. You can use the master Gallery Page as an image storage facility and move it to the **Not Linked** area of your website, so it will not appear within your website's navigation. All the Gallery Blocks will still reference that Gallery Page and you will only ever need to maintain that one gallery.

You can also use this method if you prefer the way images are displayed in a Gallery Block over the grid or slideshow that comes with your template's Gallery Page design. This can be a real lifesaver if you love your template but don't like the way it displays galleries.

Adding a Gallery Block

To add a Gallery Block, perform the following steps:

1. In the Content Editor, click on the Insert Point where you want to insert the Gallery Block.

2. In the Add Block menu overlay, select the display style you want to use under the **Gallery** category. An **Edit Gallery** window will appear.

3. The **Edit Gallery** window will open on the **Content** tab, where you can either drag photos onto the **Upload Media** space, or select **Use Existing Gallery** and choose the existing Gallery Page you wish to use.

4. Once you have added your images, click on **Design** in the top right-hand corner to adjust the settings that apply to the display style you have chosen. The settings differ among the various display styles. Here's an example of the **Carousel** settings:

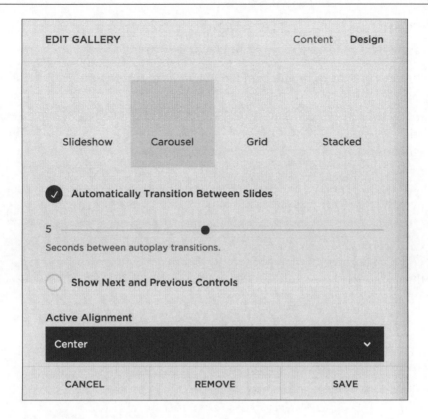

5. Click on **Save**.

If you decide you want to change the display of this Gallery Block, hover over it to activate the Annotations, and click on **Edit** to reopen the **Edit Gallery** window, where you can select a different display in the **Design** tab.

Adding galleries from external photo-sharing websites

You can also add image galleries from external photo-sharing sites, such as Flickr, Instagram, or 500px. These galleries will automatically pull in the latest photos that you have posted to the external site. You can choose to display these Gallery Blocks in any of the four display styles that you can use for normal Gallery Blocks.

Adding a gallery from Flickr, Instagram, or 500px

Follow these steps to add a gallery from Flickr, Instagram, or 500px:

1. In the Content Editor, click on the Insert Point where you want to insert the Gallery Block.

2. In the Add Block menu overlay, scroll down to the **Social Blocks** category, and choose the photo-sharing website you wish to use. An editing window will appear.

3. Unless you have already connected to the external website previously, you will need to connect your account to Squarespace. Click on **Add Account** to open a new browser window where you can log in to the photo-sharing website and authorize the connection to Squarespace.

4. Once connected, a message will appear in the editing window to tell you that you have a connected account. Now, click on **Choose an account** and select the username that you just connected. You should see the following screen:

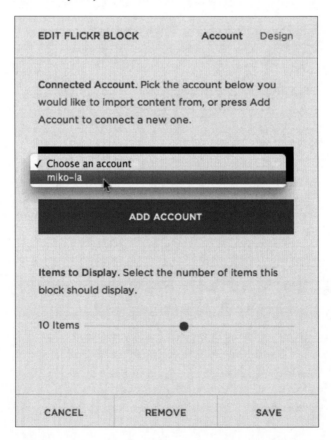

5. Adjust the number of items you wish to display in the gallery, then open the **Design** tab and adjust the settings.

 If you're using the Grid display, be sure to tick the **Lightbox** option, or else visitors will be taken away from your website and thrown onto the external photo website when they click on a thumbnail to view the larger image.

6. Click on **Save**.

Embedding video into your pages

With **Video Blocks**, Squarespace allows you to easily embed videos that are hosted on YouTube, Vimeo, Wistia, or Animoto. You don't even need to use the special **embed code** from the video website; all you need is the web address of the video. However, on many video sites, you can customize the colors of the player to make it match your website more closely when using their embed code. This can add polish to your website. To get the embed code and access the customization tools, look for a **Share** or **Embed** button on the video page on the external video website.

 You can't host videos on Squarespace, but it's free or very inexpensive to host videos on large video hosting websites. Businesses are advised to avoid YouTube and choose Vimeo or Wistia instead if they prefer not to have obtrusive advertisements in their videos. One of my clients found a competitor's advertisements showing on their YouTube videos, so beware.

When you add a Video Block, the editing window will load with the same settings as the ones that were loaded when adding a video to a gallery, which we covered in *Chapter 4, Creating Your Website Framework: Pages, Items, Collections, and Navigation*.

To add a Video Block, follow these steps:

1. In the Content Editor, click on the Insert Point where you want to insert the Video Block.

2. In the Add Block menu overlay, click on **Video** under the **Basic** category. The **Edit Video** window will appear, as shown in this screenshot:

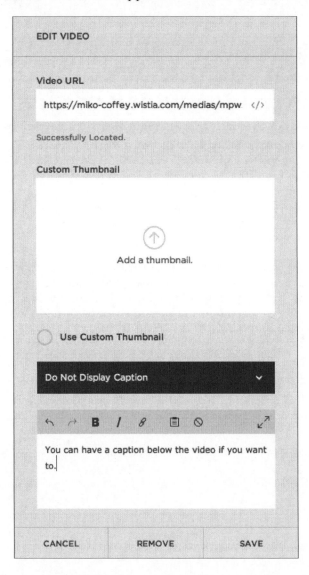

3. In the **Edit Video** window, enter the relevant settings, as follows:

    ◦ **URL**: Paste the web address of the video here or click on the **< / >** button to paste the embed code.

    ◦ **Custom Thumbnail**: You can choose to show an image in the page instead of a screen grab from the video itself. If you don't upload one, Squarespace will use the default screen grab from the video hosting website.

    ◦ **Caption**: You can choose whether to display this text or not. Squarespace will sometimes automatically pull in the caption or description text from the video hosting website, but you can adjust this manually if you prefer to display different text.

4. Click on **Save**.

Adding a Google Map to your site

If your business has one or more premises that customers may visit, it's a good idea to include a map on your Contact page. You can add a Google Map using a **Map Block** in the **More** category. Here's what a Map Block editing screen looks like:

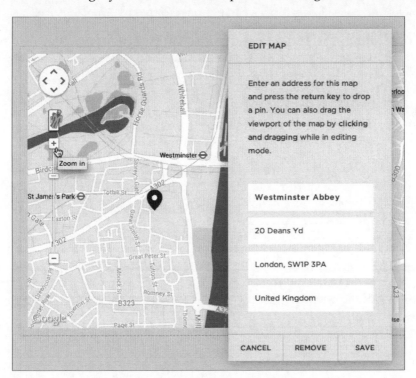

In the **Edit Map** window, enter the address of the location you want to show on the map.

> As you start typing the address, Squarespace uses Google Places to show autocomplete suggestions for the location you are entering. This can save typing when adding Map Blocks or setting locations on Event pages.

You can change the view of the map in the **Edit Map** window by dragging the map pin on the map preview to move to a different location. You can also use the Google Map tools to zoom in or out until you have the desired view of the map before saving.

Capturing data and handling enquiries on your website

You can use **Form Blocks** and **Newsletter Blocks** to allow website visitors to interact with your business and to capture data about your leads and customers. Both of these blocks are located in the **More** category in the Add Block menu.

Form Blocks and Newsletter Blocks can connect to two external services:

- **MailChimp**: This can be found at `www.mailchimp.com`. This is a popular email marketing tool to automatically subscribe contacts to your mailing list

- Google Docs (now Google Drive): This can be found at `https://drive.google.com/`. This is used to store all the form information in a spreadsheet

Form Blocks can also send an email to someone at your company every time someone completes the form, which enables immediate action to be taken.

It's a good idea to use a form for all electronic communication on your website rather than posting your email address as a link on your pages. Not only will a form ensure that the enquirer gives you all the information you need, it will also dramatically reduce the amount of spam you receive.

Another benefit of using a form on your Squarespace website is that if you store all responses in a Google Spreadsheet, it's easy for you to refer to all of your leads in one place or create charts and reports based on the information provided. This can be incredibly valuable to understand your customers and identify ways to grow or improve your business.

If you find yourself always asking for the same information when people contact you, consider whether you can add a field or two on your form to capture this information upfront in a more structured way.

Using forms

You can have as many forms on your website as you like, so you can create one for every purpose, from handling general questions to gathering customer feedback.

 Forms associated with credit cards, ordering products or services, or making donations will be created in a separate place as part of Squarespace Commerce. We'll cover this in *Chapter 7, Selling Online or Taking Donations with Squarespace Commerce.*

Squarespace offers a wide range of different field types that you can use on your form. There are specific preformatted fields, such as email address, date, or currency, and there are more general field types that can be used for a range of purposes, such as a free text box, drop-down menu of choices, set of radio buttons, or survey scale of ratings. You can also insert lines as section breaks into your forms to make them tidier and easier to use. The following is a screenshot of the **Add Form Field** window, showing all the different form elements you can add:

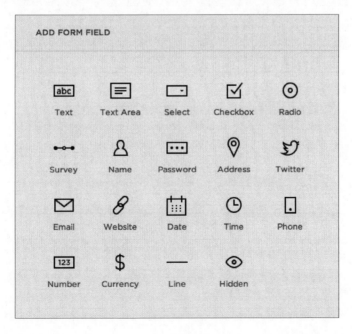

Adding a form to your page

When creating a form on your website using the Form Block, you will see that there are three main sections to fill in:

- **Build**: This is where you specify the name of your form and set up the form fields

- **Storage**: This is where you tell Squarespace where to put or send the information captured in the form

- **Advanced**: This is where you choose the words to display on the form's **Submit** button and set the message to show on the page when the form has been submitted

Using the Build section in the Form Editor

For all new forms, Squarespace will preload a set of default fields to the form: **Name**, **Email Address**, **Subject** (of the email), and **Message**. Here's a screenshot of the **Build** section of the **Edit Form** window with these default fields:

You can perform any of the following adjustments to your form in the **Build** section:

- Reorder the fields by clicking on the dotted icon on the left-hand side of the field and dragging to the desired position
- Delete a field by clicking on the trash can icon on the right-hand side
- Change the field label wording by clicking on the name of the field and typing your changes
- Edit the field settings, such as making the field required or adding instructions, by clicking on the **Edit** button
- Add a new field by clicking on the **+** button below the other fields

Setting the Storage preferences in the Form Editor

The **Storage** section can be accessed using the link in the top-right section of the **Edit Form** window. By default, Squarespace will set up the form to be emailed to the address associated with your Squarespace account. You can change this to another address or remove the **Email Address** field entirely if you are using another storage method.

If you use Google Docs or MailChimp, you can connect this form to your account and store the information there. In the **Storage** section, click on the Google Docs or MailChimp button, log in, and then choose the list or spreadsheet you want to use to store the data.

 If you are using MailChimp, you will need to create a new list. Squarespace will not be able to update an existing MailChimp list with the form data. You are also limited to 31 form fields when connecting to MailChimp.

Customizing the Advanced settings in the Form Editor

The link to the **Advanced** section is next to the **Storage** link in the top-right corner. Squarespace will automatically set the form's submit button to say **Submit**, but you can specify other wording here. You can also change the wording of the confirmation text that will be displayed after the submit button has been pressed and format that text or add a link to it using the simple formatting bar.

Using Newsletter Blocks

The Newsletter Block is a standardized and simplified version of a Form Block; it has only one or two fields and a smaller set of controls to make it easy to set up. By default, a Newsletter Block includes an email address field, but you can also add a name field if you like. You can also adjust the **Title**, **Description**, and **Disclaimer** fields displayed on the page and specify **Storage** and **Advanced** settings, just like on a Form Block. The following screenshot is how the **Edit Newsletter Block** window looks:

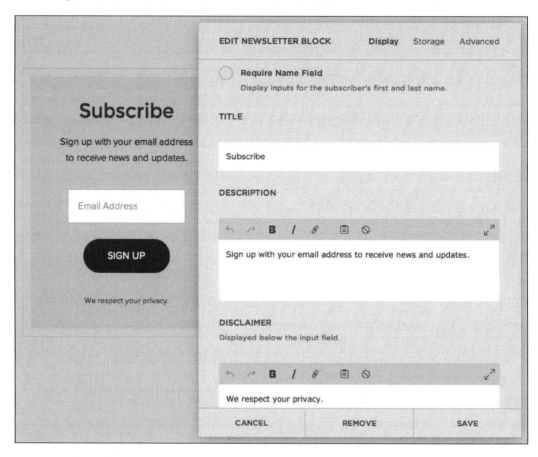

Using content blocks to improve internal navigation and highlight content

Most of the time, blocks are used to add content or functions to your page, but you can also use them to pull out content extracts or point visitors to other content on your website. You can use these kinds of blocks to highlight things that are important to your business and showcase them in high-visibility locations, such as your homepage or in a sidebar. For example, you could highlight your latest blog posts, display a list of all discounted products, or show a summary of all events happening within the next month. The really cool thing about these types of blocks is that they will automatically be updated anytime you update the source page, making it easier to manage your website and keep it feeling fresh.

Adding a search box

The most basic of these navigational blocks is the **Search Block**, which inserts a search box onto the page. Clicking on the search box opens an overlay where the visitor can type a word or phrase, and Squarespace will display an index of all pages or items that contain those search terms. A Search Block has no settings to customize; just add it and you're done.

> A search box can be useful even on a relatively small website because there are broadly two types of web users: searchers and navigators. Whereas navigators will go for menus first, searchers are naturally drawn to search boxes even if your navigation is clear and precise.

Displaying lists of tags, categories, authors, or dates

Another basic navigational block is a **List Block**. List Blocks allow you to display links to collections of items based on a shared characteristic. There are four types of List Blocks and they can be used on any type of container page. The types of List Blocks are as follows:

- **Category List**: This is sorted by weight, with the least used category at the top and most used at the bottom
- **Tag List**: This is sorted by weight, with the least used tag at the top and most used at the bottom

- **Author List**: This is sorted alphabetically based on the user who input the item (or the assigned user, if it has been adjusted)

- **Month List**: This is sorted in reverse chronological order for date-based items such as blog posts or events

 Squarespace does not provide a Blog archive page by default, so bloggers will be pleased to know that they can create a Blog archive using a Month List Block.

List Blocks are always shown in a single vertical column and there are no settings to configure. When you add a List Block, just choose the page you want to draw the list from. Here's an example of a Month List Block:

BLOG POSTS BY MONTH

May 2014

April 2014

March 2014

February 2014

January 2014

December 2013

November 2013

A List Block works in a way similar to a series of searches; each word in the list links to an index of all items that have that characteristic. For example, clicking on the word **cheese** in a Tag List will show you all blog posts that have been tagged with the `cheese` tag, and clicking on a month in a Month List will show you all blog posts that were published in that month, and so on.

Displaying a list of tags or categories as a cloud

A more creative way to display a list of tags or categories is to use a cloud display, which shows you the tags or categories in a block of words in different sizes rather than a vertical column. The words flow horizontally across the full width of the block and fill the space. The following screenshot demonstrates an example of a cloud display:

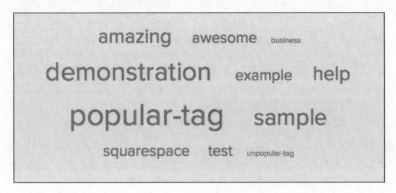

The block that you use to create a cloud is called a **Tag Cloud Block** even though you can choose to show tags or categories with this block. In a cloud, the font size of the word is determined by how often that tag or category has been used: the larger the word, the more frequently it has been used as a tag or category on items. When creating a Tag Cloud Block, you can set the number of tags or categories you want to show in your cloud. You can also choose to sort by the following:

- **A-Z**: This will display the words in alphabetical order
- **Weight**: This will show the most frequently used words at the top, moving down to the least frequently used at the bottom
- **Activity**: This will show the most recently used words at the top, moving down to the least recently used at the bottom

The **Edit Tag Cloud** window is shown in the following screenshot:

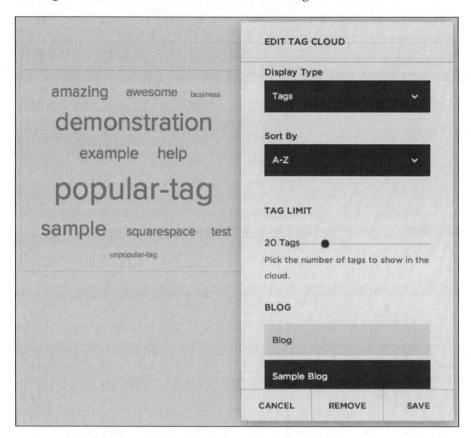

Displaying date-based lists in a calendar format

In some cases, a calendar may be a more user-friendly way to present a list of items based on dates rather than showing a list of months. A **Calendar Block** shows a small monthly calendar that website visitors can navigate using arrows to move forward and back. For each date that has one or more items associated with it, the date will appear highlighted, allowing the visitor to hover over the date to see the title and link to the full item. The hover overlay also shows the time associated with the item: either the start time for an event or the time when the item was published for nonevent items. Although this kind of display is most useful for Event Pages, you can also use a Calendar Block for Blog posts, and even Album tracks or Products — though I can't think of an instance when you'd want to use a calendar for these last two. The following figure shows you two views of the same Calendar Block: on the left, the date with an event associated appears highlighted, and the right shows how the event overlay appears when hovering over this date:

 The calendar is compact in size and you cannot stretch it to fill larger spaces, so it's best reserved for sidebars or columns. If you need a large calendar that fills the page, remember that you can choose Calendar as the Default Event View in the settings for an Events Page.

Using Content Link Blocks

A **Content Link Block** allows you to link to any type of page in a more visual way than just having a simple text link. Adding several Content Link Blocks and placing them side by side or in a column is a good way to draw attention to subpages within a folder or to cross-link to other areas of the website that you want visitors to see. The following screenshot displays three Content Link Blocks placed side by side at the bottom of a page (with a Text Block subheader):

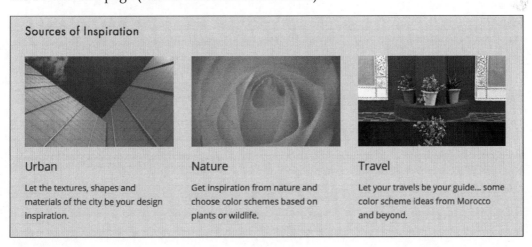

A Content Link Block will pull in and display the following items from the page you are linking to:

- The Page Title, as set in Page Settings
- The Page Description, if you have set one in Page Settings
- The page's Thumbnail Image, if you have set one in Page Settings

There are no settings to configure on a Content Link Block: the block will pull in all of these three items if they are set. Although there are no settings to control which of these three show, you could effectively turn off the Page Description or Thumbnail Image by simply leaving them blank in the Page Settings. Of course, you should only do this if you don't need to display that text or image elsewhere on your website.

If your template makes heavy use of Page Descriptions, which means you have lots of text in this field, then Content Link Blocks are not going to look very good on your website.

If your template uses page Thumbnail Images for other things, such as skinny rectangular header banner images, you may find that the image proportions needed to make the image fit there mean that the image looks bad in a Content Link Block that uses different proportions.

Using Summary Blocks – the most powerful of blocks

One of the most complex, flexible, and powerful blocks is the **Summary Block**. Summary Blocks can be used to show previews of up to 30 items from any type of Collection Page in any of four different designs, each of which can be customized. Summary Blocks can display titles, thumbnails, and certain **metadata** associated with items, and you can control the appearance and placement of each. Metadata is a subset of an item's properties, such as the published date, author, tags, categories, or location. The following screenshot shows a Blog Summary Block on a web page:

Latest from the blog

THIS IS A POST WITH THE EXCERPT SHOWING

May 2, 2014

This excerpt is where you can set a short summary to be shown in the blog container page, instead of the full post body.

POST WITH LOCATION ATTACHED

Apr 28, 2014

This is a Squarespace Blog post with a location attached to the post. Some templates show the location as a map link.

BLOG POST WITH EXCERPT AND THUMBNAIL

Mar 28, 2014

Here is another excerpt, which is showing instead of the full body text of the post. This post also has a thumbnail image associated with it.

POST WITH AN IMAGE AT THE TOP OF THE POST

Feb 26, 2014

This blog post has a full-width image at the top of the post. Sometimes this can mean lots of scrolling before you see content.

POST WITH A PROMOTED BLOCK

Jan 15, 2014

Not all templates use the Promoted Block feature. The ones that do, show the first image in a special way that makes it stand out.

POST WITH SMALL IMAGES IN IT

Dec 10, 2013

This post shows how you can have smaller images in the body text of a post, and flow the text around it.

Creative ways to use Summary Blocks

You can use Summary Blocks for many different purposes because they are versatile and can be configured in many ways.

Featuring and filtering content

The main use of Summary Blocks is to highlight featured content. Normally, a Summary Block is used to pull out a subset of items based on certain criteria, for example, the most recent blog posts or events. You can apply filters to Summary Blocks to only show items from certain categories or tags. To make things really interesting, you can combine categories and/or tags to create incredibly granular filters. This means you can do quite complex things, such as creating a *Related Stories* block at the bottom of every news item in your blog, making each one tailored to the topic of the article. You could do the same on a product page, adding the *People who bought this also bought…* label to cross-sell related products, similar to what you see on Amazon and other e-commerce sites.

Bypassing template design restrictions

You generally have more controls and options to work with on a Summary Block than you have on your template's container page design, which means that you can use these blocks to work around your template's limitations. For example, even if your template does not show certain metadata properties on the container page or item itself, you can show them in a Summary Block. In some cases, you could even fill an entire page with a Summary Block and use that page as your main page instead of the container page. For example, if you prefer one of the display options available within Summary Blocks to the Gallery Page display set by your template, you could use the Summary Block page in your main navigation (and leave the actual Gallery Page itself in the **Not Linked** area). If you are a photojournalist and want to show the date and location associated with photos, you could do this with a Summary Block. Or perhaps, you want to show your events in a grid, which is not possible without using a Summary Block.

 Visit www.square-help.com/inspiration to see examples of how Summary Blocks can be used creatively.

Summary Block design options

When you create a Summary Block, the next step after assigning the container page you want to use is to choose the design, which you will find in the **Layout** section of the **Edit Summary** window, accessed using the **Layout** link in the top-right corner of the window. The following screenshot shows the Layout section of the **Edit Summary** window:

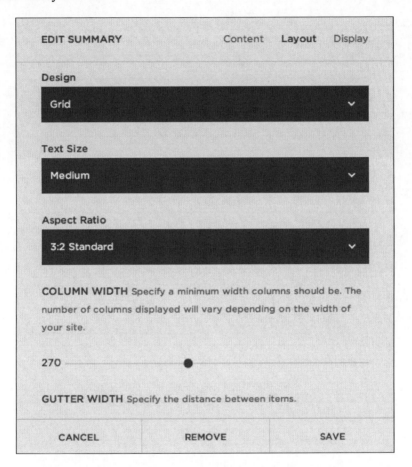

There are four different Summary Block designs, each with their own controls and settings that you can adjust in the **Layout** section.

Grid

A **Grid** design shows items in a table of equally sized and spaced cells. The cells are always the same size even if the contents of the cells are not. The following screenshot displays an example of the Grid design:

In the Grid design, you can adjust the following settings:

- **Text Size**: This shows the title and/or excerpt in a range of four preset sizes, from small to extra large.

- **Aspect Ratio**: This sets the thumbnail image dimensions from square to a range of rectangular shapes, including **Widescreen**.

- **Column Width**: This sets the pixel size of columns. Bear in mind the number of columns that your visitors see will depend on the size of their monitor.

- **Gutter Width**: This sets the spacing, in pixels, between items in the grid.

- **Text Alignment**: This sets the alignment as left, right, or center in relation to the grid cell.

- **Metadata Position**: This determines where the date, location, or other small metadata text will appear.

List

The **List** design displays items in a vertical column. The following screenshot demonstrates the List design:

THIS IS A POST WITH THE EXCERPT SHOWING

This excerpt is where you can set a short summary to be shown in the blog container page, instead of the full post body.

Read More →

POST WITH LOCATION ATTACHED

This is a Squarespace Blog post with a location attached to the post. Some templates show the location as a map link.

Read More →

BLOG POST WITH EXCERPT AND THUMBNAIL

Here is another excerpt, which is showing instead of the full body text of the post. This post also has a thumbnail image associated with it.

Read More →

POST WITH AN IMAGE AT THE TOP OF THE POST

This blog post has a full-width image at the top of the post. Sometimes this can mean lots of scrolling before you see content.

Read More →

In the List design, you can adjust **Text Size, Aspect Ratio, Text Alignment, Metadata Position,** as well as the following settings:

- **Image Size**: This sets how large the thumbnail image should be in relation to the space left for the text

- **Image Alignment**: This sets whether the thumbnail should appear on the left- or right-hand side of the text

Carousel

The **Carousel** design is like a mini slider; it displays one or more items on screen, with arrows to slide across to the next one(s). Take a look at the following screenshot to see what the Carousel design looks like:

In the Carousel design, you can adjust the **Text Size**, **Aspect Ratio**, **Text Alignment**, **Metadata Position** settings, as well as the following settings:

- **Header Text**: This allows you to specify the words that appear above the slider
- **Items Per Row**: This sets how many items should be visible at a time before clicking on the arrow to slide across

Wall

The **Wall** design creates an autoflowing tiled grid. Each cell of the grid is the same width, but the height adjusts to fit the height of the cell contents. This type of display is sometimes called **masonry**, or **mosaic grid**, because the cells are like tiles in a mosaic. The following screenshot is an example of the Wall display:

In the Wall design, the settings are exactly the same as those for the Grid design, except that you do not specify the aspect ratio of images. Instead, images always keep their original dimensions; this is what contributes to the mosaic effect.

 Although the mosaic grid is a design trend right now, it can look a bit messy, so the Wall display looks best with minimal (or no) text.

Summary Block filtering and display options

Once you have chosen the design for your Summary Block, the final step is to adjust the settings in the **Display** section. The **Display** section is where you set up your filters and specify which information to display, including the metadata. The exact set of options varies depending on the type of Collection Page you are using, but these are the main controls you can adjust:

- **Number of Items**: This sets the number of items that are displayed, from 1 to 30

- **Primary Information to Display**: This is a set of tickboxes that allow you to turn the display of the main information types on or off, such as **Title** and **Thumbnail**, and others depending on the type of container page

- **Primary Metadata** and **Secondary Metadata**: This allows you to choose whether to display one, two, or none of the types of metadata associated with your items

- **Category Filter** and **Tag Filter**: This allows you to enter the categories and/or tags you want to use for filtering; only items with these categories and/or tags will show up on the page

- **Featured Filter**: This is a simplified filtering option for Blog Pages to only show posts with the **Featured Post** checkbox checked

Inserting sales or donation blocks to make transactions fast and easy

You can insert a purchase or donation call to action anywhere on your website, making it easy for your customers to complete a transaction without needing to navigate to a Products Page or shop. You can use a **Product Block** or **Donation Block** if you are signed up to Squarespace Commerce. Or, if your products are available for sale on Amazon, you can use an **Amazon Block** to direct sales through that channel. All of these blocks can be found under the **Commerce** heading in the Add Block menu.

 Because you'll need to set up Squarespace Commerce first, we'll cover Product and Donation Blocks at the end of the next chapter after you're all set up.

Using Amazon Blocks

You can use an Amazon Block to pull in product information and a **Buy Button** for any product available on www.amazon.com or www.amazon.co.uk.

 If you want your Amazon Blocks to use www.amazon.co.uk, you will need to set United Kingdom as your location by going to **Settings | Language & Region**.

When you add an Amazon Block to your page, the first step is to find a product. You can search by typing the title, description, or **ASIN (Amazon Standard Identification Number)**, and then select the product from the search results. The **Edit Amazon Product** window is shown in the following screenshot:

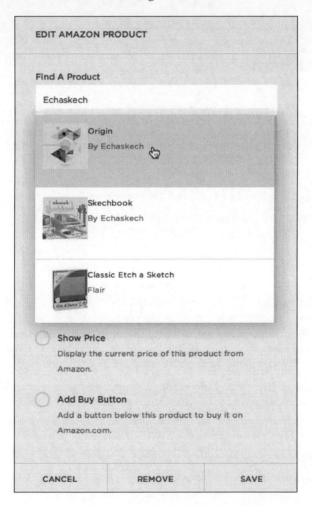

Then, choose the alignment and tick the boxes if you want to display the item title, author, price, and/or **Buy** Button. Here's how an Amazon Block looks on a web page:

Displaying a price list

Many service-based businesses want to display a list of prices for their services on their website. You could just use standard Text Blocks to do this, but it can be difficult to get the alignment right and make them look good. Fortunately, Squarespace has a special kind of block made just for this type of information. However, you might never know this because the block is called a **Menu Block**, and most people assume this is just for restaurants, especially because the icon shows a knife and fork. Although the Menu Block may have been originally designed for food and drink businesses, you can actually use it to display prices and information about any type of service. The cool thing about Menu Blocks is that they allow you to have different tabs for different menus or service types, so you can display a lot of prices neatly in one page, without making visitors scroll forever or jump around to different pages. An example of a Menu Block is shown in the following screenshot:

<u>SPA</u>　　SALON　　NAIL BAR

Massage

INDIAN HEAD MASSAGE $30

30 minutes, focusing on the head,
shoulders, neck and upper arms.

DEEP TISSUE $60

1 hour of firm strokes and
accupressure for maximum relief
of painful or locked muscles

SWEDISH MASSSAGE $50

1 hour of classic sports massage
to work out all the knots and
aches.

Facials

BEAUTY BRIGHTENER $25

30 minutes of facial
mini-massage, masque, toner and
deep moisturizer.

BEAUTY BLITZ $50

1 hour of luxurious treatment
includes massage, masque,
microdermabrasion, toner and
moisturizer.

Menu Block with three tabs of prices: Spa, Salon, and Nail Bar

Using Menu Blocks

When you add a Menu Block, it comes preloaded with a sample menu. You
may want to use this sample menu as a starting point and adjust the text to
your needs, because Menu Blocks require you to input text in a very specific
way. The punctuation and spacing used when inputting the menu text acts as
a kind of simplified code that determines the different tabs, item breaks, text style,
and columns. Squarespace has included a cheat sheet right inside the **Edit Menu**
window in the **Formatting Help** section.

Make sure you follow the menu formatting rules exactly,
or else your menu won't display correctly.

The **Edit Menu** window is shown in the following screenshot:

There is also a **Design** section where you can specify the style in the **Menu Style** option as a **Simple (Centred)** layout or a **Classic (Multi-column)** layout. You can also specify the currency to use for prices in the **Currency Symbol** option.

Adding audio to your website

Unlike video files, which must be hosted externally, you can upload audio files to Squarespace and embed them into your pages using an **Audio Block**. Squarespace has a built-in audio player that will allow visitors to play the audio within the page, as shown in the following screenshot:

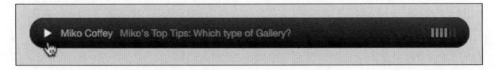

Alternately, if you use Soundcloud to host your audio files, you can also embed tracks, playlists, or profiles from Soundcloud. In addition, Squarespace supports the iTunes podcasting attributes, so you can use your blog for podcasting as well.

Using the Audio Block

Before you upload your audio file, first make sure that the file adheres to the following guidelines to ensure the best performance across all browsers and devices:

- **Format**: .mp3
- **File size**: Less than 160 MB
- **Bit depth**: 16 bits
- **Bitrate**: 128 Kbps max (96 Kbps recommended for the spoken word)
- **Channels**: Mono or stereo

 If your file is more than 160 MB, you can still embed the file but you will need to host it elsewhere. Refer to the *Link to an External File* section on http://help.squarespace.com/guides/using-the-audio-block for advice on how to do this.

When adding an Audio Block for normal use (not podcasting), all you need to do is click or drag the file onto the uploader area, fill in **Track Title** and **Track Author**, and then click on **Save**.

Additional settings for podcasting

If you are uploading a podcast episode in the Audio Block, you will also need to input the iTunes data in the **Podcasting** section before saving and closing. You can only enable podcasting for Audio Blocks added to blog posts, and you must also first ensure you have set up the **Syndication** settings in **Blog Settings** as well.

 Refer to http://help.squarespace.com/guides/podcasting-with-squarespace for step-by-step instructions on setting up your blog for podcasting and adding podcast episodes.

Using the Soundcloud Block

When adding a **Soundcloud Block** to embed audio, all you need to do is paste the URL of a Soundcloud track, playlist, or profile, and Squarespace will embed a Soundcloud player widget into your page, as shown in the following screenshot:

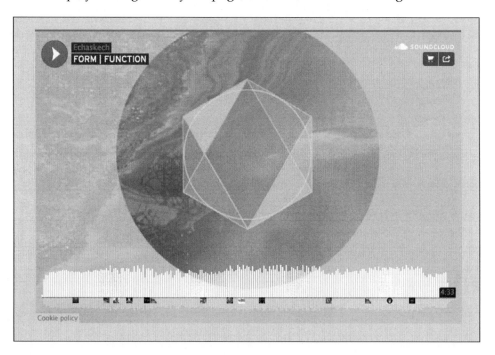

Alternately, if you prefer to use a customized version of the Soundcloud widget, you can use the embed code by clicking on the cog icon in the **Edit Soundcloud Embed** window.

Adding a Twitter feed

You can use a **Twitter Block** to pull in and display the latest tweets from your Twitter account. When adding a Twitter Block, you must first connect to your Twitter account, and then you can choose how many tweets to show and whether you want to display your avatar, username, and a **Follow** button. The **Edit Twitter Block** window is shown here:

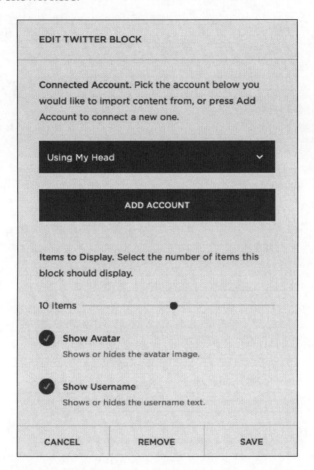

Chapter 9, Going Live with Your Website and Driving Traffic to It, includes more detailed information about connecting to Twitter and other social media accounts.

Other types of blocks

We've now covered the most commonly used blocks for business websites, but you may also want to make use of some of the following blocks. We won't go into the details of setting these up, because they are either very simple to use or they cover a specific niche that not many readers will need.

 If you need more information about these or any content blocks, you can refer to `http://help.squarespace.com/guides/what-are-blocks`.

Here are all other blocks that were not previously covered in the last two chapters:

- **Embed**: Use this to embed content or functionality from an external site, such as a Slideshare presentation, a Campaign Monitor sign-up form or any other third-party website that provides embed code.

- **Opentable**: This allows restaurants that subscribe to the `http://opentable.com` service to take reservations on their Squarespace websites.

- **Foursquare**: This shows your latest `http://foursquare.com` check-ins.

- **Social Links**: These display icons that link to your social media accounts (this uses the same icons as the ones many Squarespace templates show in the footer).

- **RSS**: This includes a link to your blog's RSS feed.

- **Markdown (Advanced)**: This uses Markdown Language to style text. This is only recommended for technical or advanced users.

- **Code (Advanced)**: This allows you to paste HTML, CSS, or JavaScript code into your web pages. We will cover Code Blocks in *Chapter 11, Moving beyond Standard Squarespace Tools*.

Summary

You've now learned how to add all of the Squarespace functions to your website, apart from e-commerce, which we'll tackle in the next chapter. You also learned about the many ways you can use blocks creatively to drive traffic to important parts of your website, to enhance your website's usability, or to add rich media. Hopefully, you have been adding these types of blocks to your pages as you moved through this chapter. If not, now is the time to do so.

If you will not be using Squarespace Commerce to sell products and services or take donations on your website, then our goal is for you to have all your pages as close to finished as possible at this point. You can then move on to *Chapter 8, Tailoring Your Site's Look and Feel*, where you will adjust the aesthetics of your website to match your brand and audience.

If you will be using Squarespace Commerce, you should still aim to finish building your nontransactional pages before moving on to the next chapter.

Remember, *Chapter 8, Tailoring Your Site's Look and Feel*, is where we will apply colors, fonts, and other visual style changes to your website, so for now, you should focus on getting your content blocks into the pages and adjusting their position. As you are doing this, make note of any particular elements that you think really need restyling, for example, headlines that are too large or the annoying use of *ALL CAPS*. You can then use these notes to ensure you address everything during the visual design process.

7
Selling Online or Taking Donations with Squarespace Commerce

Squarespace makes it easy to take donations or to sell goods, services, or digital products online using Squarespace Commerce. Your online shop will be fully integrated with your site, and you can manage transactions, track inventory, handle shipping, and communicate with your customers in the same place that you manage your website. Plus, the integration with the **Stripe payment gateway** makes credit card payments simple, both for you and for your customers. Even if you are an established trader who already sells through BigCartel, Shopify, or Etsy, you can import your products from these sites into your Squarespace shop with just a few clicks.

You'll learn all about Squarespace Commerce in this chapter, including handy features to help improve your shop and sales, such as managing discounts and promoting special offers.

In this chapter, we will cover:

- Setting up your Squarespace Commerce store, including taxes and shipping options
- Setting up Stripe to take credit card payments or using alternatives such as PayPal
- Creating products: physical goods, digital downloads, and services
- Importing products from other websites
- Taking donations on your Squarespace site
- Managing inventory

- Handling orders, including email notifications
- Setting up and announcing discounts or special offers
- Promoting products throughout your site using Commerce Blocks

Setting up your Squarespace Commerce store

No matter whether you want to sell products or services, or take donations on your website, you will need to set up your Squarespace Commerce store.

Prerequisites for Squarespace Commerce

There are a couple of prerequisites to Squarespace Commerce, so let's ensure you have them covered before we move on to setting up your store.

The physical location of your business

The main restriction of using Squarespace Commerce is the physical location of your business. In order to use Squarespace Commerce, you will need to use the Stripe payment gateway to process credit card transactions on your website. Stripe is currently fully supported for businesses located in Australia, UK, USA, Canada, or Ireland and is running in the Beta mode in 13 other countries. You can use the Squarespace/Stripe integration if you are located in any of those countries—though you might run into a few bugs if your country is still in running in the Beta mode. If you aren't located in any of these countries, then you won't be able to use Squarespace Commerce or set up a store.

Stripe is growing rapidly and expanding into new territories regularly—check https://stripe.com/global to see the list and status of all countries where Stripe is available.

You can take orders or donations from customers located anywhere in the world; your customers don't have to be located in a Stripe-supported country.

Even if you can't use Squarespace Commerce, you can still sell online or take donations on your Squarespace site using alternate methods. It won't be as seamless or easy as with Squarespace Commerce, but it is possible. Skip to the end of this chapter for more information on using alternate methods to sell or handle donations online.

The right Squarespace subscription plan

You will need to have the correct Squarespace subscription in order to sell products or services, as Squarespace places restrictions on the number of products you can offer based on your subscription plan.

 You can take donations on any subscription plan.

- If you are on the Personal plan, you can sell one type of product or service only. However, you can have as many **variants** of this product as you need. Variants are characteristics such as size, color, or flavor.

- If you are on the Professional plan, you can sell up to 20 different products or services.

- If you are on the Business plan, you can sell an unlimited number of different products or services.

Gathering your store content

Once you've confirmed that you will be able to use Stripe and that you are on the right level of subscription plan, you'll need to gather some essential materials to set up your store. Many of these are probably in your Website Toolkit, but others may require some research or advice from others. You may want to skim through this chapter to find the exact format or details of all of the elements you'll need to prepare, but here is a checklist to help you make sure you have everything.

To set up your store for donations or any type of product or service, you will need:

- **Policies and terms**: Ensure you have consulted a legal advisor regarding your legal requirements for your Terms of Service, Privacy Policy, and if necessary, Returns Policy.

- **Taxes**: You can set up different tax levels for different countries as well as local taxes at the state/province or local area level, if required. Consult a tax advisor to ensure you know your legal tax requirements, especially if you will be selling to other countries.

- **Email text**: Every time someone orders something or makes a donation on your site, they will receive an email notification. You can also set the system to send email notifications to you or another member of your company every time an order is placed or whenever the stock is running low.

- **Shipping costs** (optional): If you are selling physical products, you will need to consider how you will be shipping your products and what the costs for shipping different products to different places will be.

For every product or service, you will also need:

- **Product name**: Remember to use unique names for each product to avoid confusion.

- **Price(s):** You can set different prices for different variants of your products, if necessary. For example, you may sell a large jar of jam and a small jar of jam as two variants of a single product. Alternately, you could set them up as different products if that matches your business model better.

- **Product variants**: Ensure you have a list of all the different colors, sizes, or other variants you will be offering, along with any price variants that may accompany these.

- **Photos**: You'll need at least one photo per product. Even if you are selling a service or digital download, you should ideally source a stock photo or illustration that can accompany the product description, as the page will look much better with a photo.

- **Descriptive text**: This can be set up as a brief summary and longer description, if you like.

- **Stock levels** (optional): With Squarespace, you can specify a limited number of items or set the number to infinity if there are no limits on the number of products.

You may also need the following:

- **Downloadable files**: If you are selling downloadable files, ensure you have the files ready and named in a sensible manner.

- **Additional customer information**: Squarespace allows you to associate a form with a product or service to capture additional information from your customers, apart from the standard personal information captured as part of the checkout process. This is most useful for services where you may need to know certain things in order to carry out the service—for example, food allergies and the date of the wedding if you are a wedding cake company.

Configuring your store

You manage everything to do with your Squarespace store in the **Commerce** panel, which is accessible from the **Home** menu. When you open this panel, the first item in the Commerce menu is **Getting Started**. This guide shows you the four main stages of setting up your store. Although you can certainly do things using this guide in the order shown, it actually makes more sense to set things up in a slightly different order instead of using the **Getting Started** guide. It might seem counterintuitive, but doing it this way means you will see the correct currency, buttons, and shopping cart style from the start as well as be able to test things as you build.

If you get stuck at any time, you can quickly access the Squarespace help articles that are related to Commerce using the shortcut links below the main **Getting Started** steps.

You can remove the **Getting Started** menu item once your store is up and running by clicking on the **Dismiss This Guide** button at the top of the **Getting Started** panel.

Store Settings

The first area to address is the **Store Settings** panel, located at the bottom of the main Commerce menu. When you first open this panel, you will see an alert box that tells you to connect your store with Stripe, as shown in the following screenshot:

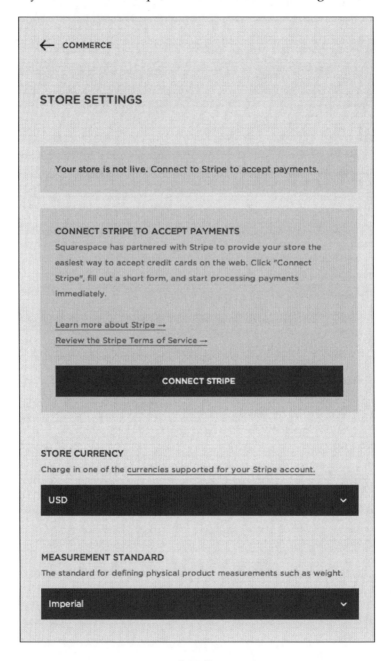

Connecting to Stripe

Follow these steps to connect your Squarespace website to the Stripe payment gateway:

1. Click on the **Connect Stripe** button. A new browser window will pop up, asking you to either create a Stripe account, or log in to an existing account.

    > If a pop-up window doesn't appear, ensure you have popups disabled on your browser.

2. If you have already signed up to Stripe, click on the login link and fill in your Stripe account details. If you don't have a Stripe account yet, complete the signup form to create one.

3. Once you have logged in to Stripe, the pop-up window will close, and the **Store Settings** screen will indicate that your Squarespace store is connected to Stripe. The message in the alert box will also change to indicate that your store is not live, as shown in the following screenshot:

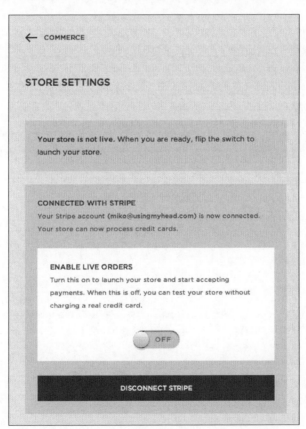

You will also notice a new **Enable Live Orders** box with an on/off switch. Ensure you leave this switch in the **OFF** position so we can safely test the purchasing process without making charges to real credit cards.

Below the **Connected With Stripe** box, you should also see that your **Store Currency** setting has been set to the currency you selected when setting up your Stripe account.

Other Store Settings

Now that your store is connected, you can move on to adjust the remaining Store Settings in this panel, as follows:

- **Measurement Standard**: Choose **Imperial** or **Metric** to set the method used to display measurements, such as the product weight, used to determine shipping costs.

- **Next Order Number**: Adjust the number if you prefer to start your order numbering system at something other than 00001. This is useful if you have already been trading or if you want to give customers the impression that you have.

- **Express Checkout**: If this is selected, customers will bypass the shopping cart and be taken straight to payment. This is not recommended unless you are selling only one product.

- **Shopping Cart Style**: Select this option if you intend to use a dark background on your pages to make the cart stand out more.

- **Newsletter**: You can connect to MailChimp if you want to give customers the option to sign up to your MailChimp newsletter list during checkout.

- **Checkout Page: Custom Form**: Select this if you want to collect additional information from customers on the checkout page in addition to the default contact and payment details required by Stripe and Squarespace.

- **Checkout Page: Store Policies**: Enter your **Return Policy**, **Terms of Service**, and **Privacy Policy** information that will appear as links in the footer of the checkout page.

 In most cases, it's a legal requirement for you to display these policies on your website, so ensure you have taken legal advice on the correct wording of these policies in your country.

Once you have adjusted these settings, make sure you click on the **Save** button before moving on.

Taxes

The next section of the **Commerce** menu that we'll set up is **Taxes**. Buckle up, because this one is a bit of a doozy.

Squarespace allows you to set up individual tax rates for every country, state/province, and local area where you will be selling goods/services or accepting donations. The kicker is that you must set up each individual location and rate manually: there are no default lists of countries and their tax rates built into Squarespace. This means that you will need to know the tax rules for every country where your customers live, and you'll need to spend time setting up taxes for each and every one of these, down to the local postal code level, in some cases. And, once you have set everything up, you'll need to ensure that the rates are updated whenever any rules are changed. Taxes are one of the main areas I hope Squarespace addresses in the future to standardize the rates and save all Squarespace Commerce users a lot of unnecessary work. However, in the meantime, it's up to you to manually set up and manage the tax rates you charge in your store.

You can find a list of all sales tax rates by country here:

- www.tradingeconomics.com/country-list/sales-tax-rate: this shows the country level in a handy reference table.
- www.ey.com/GL/en/Services/Tax/Global-tax-guide-archive: This link is good for a downloadable PDF with the latest sales tax rates for all countries, including local taxes and detailed information.

If you are a small business and the majority of your customers will be based in one or a few countries, you may want to consider only setting up taxes for those countries initially for the launch. You can then come back and fill in the rest post the launch, and/or you could insert a message on your product pages, asking residents of other countries to contact you before ordering.

You should always consult a tax advisor to ensure you are following the law. Taxes normally apply to all types of goods or services, even digital downloads, but exact rates may vary depending on the type of goods or services you are selling or where you and your customers are based.

Remember, donations may not be tax-exempt, and you may have tax requirements on *gifts* or *tips* that you set up as donations in Squarespace, especially if you are not a registered charity.

Setting up a new country tax rule

The first type of tax you'll need to set is at the country level. Even if your country does not charge national tax, you will need to set up the country before you can drill down to set up the taxes at regional levels.

To set up a country tax, follow these steps:

1. In the **Taxes** panel, click on the **Add Country** button. This will open the **Create Country Tax Rate** overlay window, as shown here:

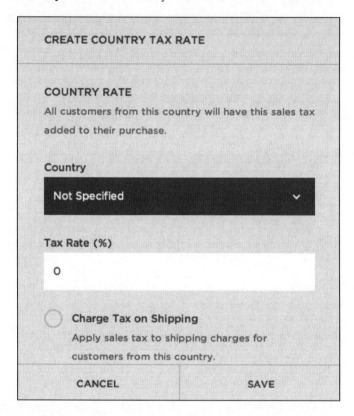

2. Select **Country** from the drop-down list, and type the correct number into the **Tax Rate (%)** box.

3. Tick the relevant box(es): **Charge Tax on Shipping** or **Charge Tax on Services** if you need to charge the respective taxes.

4. Click on **Save**.

Setting up a new state/province tax rule

First, ensure you have created a country tax rule for that country. If the country does not charge any tax at the country level, set the rate for the country as 0 percent. Next, follow these steps to set up the new state/province tax rule:

1. Hover your mouse over the name of the country in the **Taxes** screen, and you will notice a link that says **Add State** appears next to the country name, as shown in the following screenshot. Click on this link to open the overlay window.

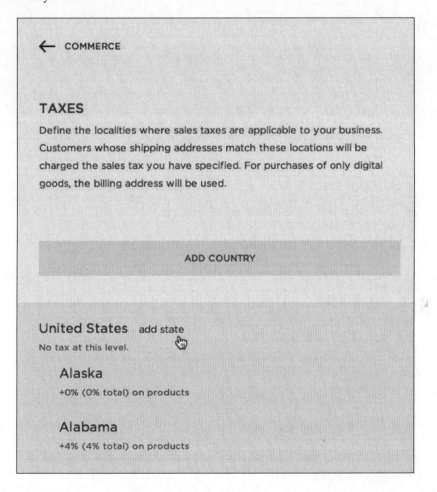

The **Add State** link will only appear for countries that have state/province sales taxes, such as Canada or USA.

2. Select the state/province from the drop-down list, and type the correct number into the **Tax Rate (%)** box.

3. A **Tax Name** box will show up if it's applicable for the country, for example, Canada. Enter the correct name for this tax.

4. Tick the relevant box(es): **Charge Tax on Shipping** or **Charge Tax on Services** if you need to charge the respective taxes. You may also see a **Show as Combined Rate** tickbox for some countries, such as Canada.

5. Click on **Save**.

Setting up a local area tax based on postal/zip codes

First, ensure you have created a state tax rule for that state/province. If the state does not charge any tax at the state level, set the rate for that state at 0 percent. Next, follow these steps to set up the new local area tax rule:

1. Hover your mouse over the name of the state in the **Taxes** screen, and you will notice a link that says **Add Local** appears next to the state name. Click on this link to open the **Create New Local Tax Rate** overlay window.

> The **Add Local** link will only appear for countries that have local areas sales taxes, such as USA.

2. Choose whether you want to set the tax rate based on **Single Zip Code** or on **Range of Zip Codes**.

3. Enter the zip code(s), and type the correct number into the **Tax Rate (%)** box.

4. Tick the relevant box(es) if you need to **Charge Tax on Shipping** or **Charge Tax on Services**.

5. Click on **Save**.

Email Settings

The next **Commerce** menu item to set up is **Email Settings**. Squarespace will automatically send an email to your customers or donors whenever a transaction is made. If you are selling physical goods or services that will be delivered later, Squarespace will also send an email to let your customer know that the item has been shipped or to confirm that the service has been completed. You can customize the text that appears in these emails. If you are selling items with limited stock levels, you can also set the system to send an automatic email to alert you when stocks are running low.

On the **Email Settings** screen, the first settings you should adjust are the **Customer Support Email** addresses for **Reply-To** and **From**, as shown in the following screenshot:

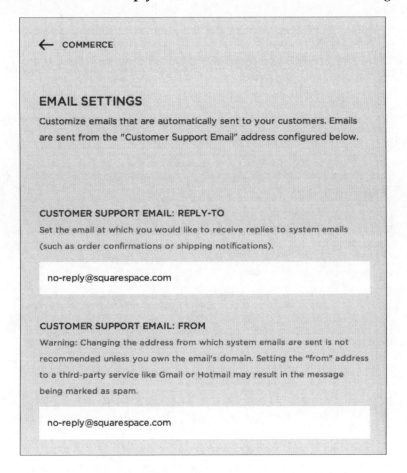

You'll very likely want to change these to an email address from your own company. The **From** email address is what will appear in the customer's inbox, and the **Reply-To** address is where any replies from the customer will be sent.

 If you don't change the **Reply-To** address, your customers will not be able to reply to any of the emails about their orders or donations. Be sure to use an address that will be monitored regularly.

Below these email settings, you will see the **Automatic Stock Level Alert Email** slider. You can adjust the slider to any number, from never up to 20 items.

The remaining **Email Settings** fields pertain to the appearance and words in the emails that are sent for various purposes: **Order Confirmed**, **Order Shipped**, and **Donation Thank You**. You can also set up an email **Header** and **Footer** that will display at the top/bottom of all emails. Squarespace automatically applies default text for all of these, and for some businesses, this will suffice. If you don't like what is set by default, you can change it, but be aware that you need to be very careful when making adjustments, and you may also need to use some basic HTML or Squarespace's bespoke code when doing so.

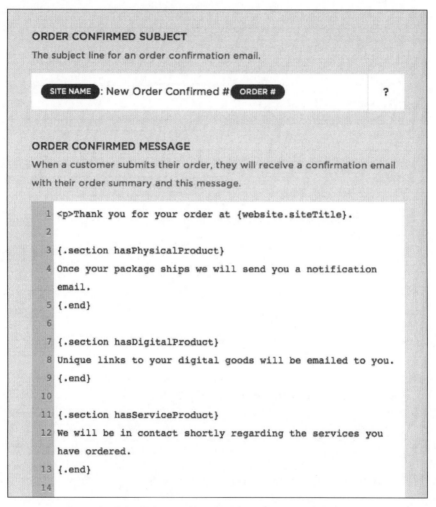

Example of the Order Confirmed Message box, with default code

Here's how to make safe adjustments to the emails:

- Never ever remove or adjust anything that appears within curly brackets {like this}. Squarespace's bespoke code uses these brackets to tell the system to insert information about the order into the email.

- Never use curly brackets {} in your text because it could confuse the system into thinking it's a special code.

- The Squarespace screen displays HTML code in different colors, so don't mess with anything that's not in black text unless you are confident that you know what you are doing.

- If you want to insert a return (a single line break), you will need to use the
 HTML code at the end of the line where you want the break to occur, like this:

```
Here is some text. <br/>
And here's the rest, on a new line, directly below.
```

- If you want to insert a double return (a paragraph break), you will need to surround your paragraph with the correct HTML code, like this:

```
<p>This will have a double-line space after.</p>

<p> This sentence will appear on a new line, with an empty
   line space above it.</p>
```

- If you know how to use HTML and CSS, you can apply this to make your emails match your brand colors or to display a logo within the email. However, all email-reading software displays things slightly differently, so you may need the help of an experienced HTML email designer if you want very precise control over your emails' appearance.

 Whenever you make a change to an email, it's a good idea to send yourself a test version of the message using the **Send Test Email to...** button that appears below the message box.

Shipping

If you are selling selling physical real-world products, the final step to configure your store in the **Commerce** menu is to set up **Shipping** to specify the delivery charges that apply to send your products to your customers. You can specify different rates and methods of shipping for different countries. You can also choose to calculate shipping based on the total weight, or you can charge based on the number of items and/or a flat fee per order.

Don't forget to factor in the cost of packaging to the shipping fee you charge. You may also want to consider adding a bit on top for your or your staff's time.

For each shipping option, you can set whether the option will be available to one or more specific countries. You can also set up a "rest of world" option, so you don't need to set up shipping for each and every country.

To set up a shipping option, follow these steps:

1. In the **Shipping** panel, click on the **Add Shipping Method** button to open the **Add Shipping Option** overlay window.

2. Choose whether you want to charge **Flat Rate** (per item and/or per order) or **Depending on Weight**.

If you are based in the USA and on a Business subscription plan, you can also choose **Carrier Calculated by USPS** to get real-time rates from the United States Postal Service.

3.   Enter your settings in the **Formula** section, as shown in the following example:

If you chose **Flat Rate**, keep these points in mind:

- Enter a name in **Option Name**. This will be shown to customers, so use a name that makes sense and describes the type of service—for example, **Next Day - Express**.

- If you want to charge a base fee for every order, enter this into **Per Order Fee**.

- If you want to charge based on the number of items, enter this into **Fee Per Item**.

 You can charge per order *and* per item or just one of these if you prefer.

If you chose **Depending on Weight**, keep these points in mind:

- ○ Enter a name in **Option Name**. This will be shown to customers, so use a name that makes sense and describes the type of service—for example, **Standard (3-5 Business Days)**.

- ○ Set **Weight Ranges**. For each **Weight** (range) value, set **Cost**. When you change the ending weight of a range, it causes the beginning rate of the next range to be .01 units higher. Use the **+** button to add a new range.

4. Click on the link in the top-right section to open the **Country Restrictions** section.

5. Choose whether you want to specify **Countries Allowed** or use this option to **Ship To the Rest of the World**, which will enable this shipping option for all countries that do not have any other shipping option associated. If specifying **Countries Allowed**, click on the **+** icon and start typing the country name. The system will autocomplete and find countries based on what you are typing; click on the country name to add it. The following screenshot shows you the country selection autocomplete function in action:

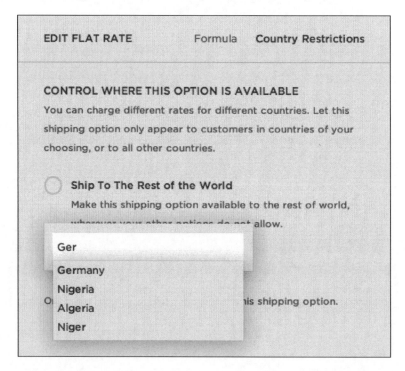

If you need to remove a country, hover over the country name and click on **X**, which appears next to the name.

6. Click on **Save**.

Repeat the steps for every country and shipping option you need to set up. You can have more than one shipping option per country—for example, an Express service and a Standard service.

Creating and managing products

Now that your store has been configured, it's time to add products to your website. You'll need a Products page to hold your product items, so if you have not already created one, now is the time to go into the Pages panel and create one.

 You can have multiple Products pages if you want to group some products together but separate them from others—for example, a page for men's clothing and another for women.

Refer to *Chapter 4, Creating Your Site Framework: Pages, Items, Collections, and Navigation* if you need a reminder of how to create a Products page.

Product types

Squarespace currently offers three different types of products that you can use in your Commerce store:

- **Physical**: These are real-world goods that require being shipped to the customer. Customers will need to select a shipping method, and you will need to manage the order and mark it as dispatched in the **Orders** section of your site.

- **Digital**: These are downloadable files, such as documents, photos, audio files, or *zipped* folders containing multiple files (`.zip`). Squarespace will send a secure link to the customer that they can use to download the file within 24 hours from the time of purchase. You do not need to manage digital orders, as they happen immediately and automatically.

[Always use common file formats that your customers will understand and be able to open.

Files must be less than 200 MB.]

- **Service**: Services must be rendered outside of Squarespace, and they do not have any shipping associated. You may want to mark the order as complete in the **Orders** section once the service has been rendered.

[We will cover **Orders** later in this chapter.]

Adding product items

You can add product items to your site in two different ways. You can do either of these:

- Add products directly to your Products page within the Pages panel
- Add products to any Products page from the **Inventory** section of the **Commerce** panel

We'll cover Inventory in more detail shortly, so let's start by adding products to a Products page.

Follow these steps to add a product to a Products page:

1. Click on the **Add Product** button. An overlay window will appear, showing you the different product types: **Physical**, **Digital**, and **Service**.

2. Select the type of product you want to add. This will open the **Edit Product** window to allow you to set the properties of the product. The exact properties will depend on the type of product you have selected, but the properties will always be split into multiple screens, accessible through the row of text links running across the top of the overlay window. You can see these links in the example screenshot displayed here:

3. Set up the product properties and content on the **Item** screen:

- ° **Product Name**: Use a short, descriptive, unique name for your product. The text you put here will be used in Page Title, as a text link in content blocks, and as part of the URL for the product item page.

- ° **Image(s):** Use the image uploader area to upload one or more images of your product.

 The first image will be used as the product Thumbnail Image, so make sure it's the most enticing image of your product or service. Some templates also use this Thumbnail Image as a banner image on the page, so ensure your image size is large enough to fit the space.

- ° **Categories and/or tags:** Categories are useful for grouping products together for display or promotional purposes. You can use categories to filter products in Summary Block, or you can apply **Coupons** to certain product categories, which we'll cover later in this chapter.

- ° **Pricing:** For physical or service products, you can set the price for each variant of the product or service you are selling. Clicking on the **Edit ->** link opens the **Pricing & Variants** screen for physical or service products or the **Pricing & Upload** screen for digital products. See step 4 for details of these settings.

- ° **Brief Description:** Enter a short description of the product here. You can use the simple formatting tools to style your text.

- ° **Product Status:** By default, this is set to **Not Listed,** which means that your product will not be shown in your live store yet. You can set the status to **Available** to make it live, or you can choose **Scheduled** and set a date and time in the future to make the product live.

4. Configure the **Pricing & Variants** screen for physical or service products or the **Pricing & Upload** screen for digital products.

   Pricing & Variants for physical or service products:

   - ° **SKU**: A unique identifier for each product variant (**SKU** is an abbreviation of **stock-keeping unit**). Squarespace will set a default SKU number, but you can enter your own if you prefer.

   - ° **Pricing**: Enter the **Price** value associated with this product variant. You can also set **Sale Price** and tick the **On Sale** box if you want to show the lower price and a *sale* banner on the item.

   - ° **Stock**: You can either enter the total number of units you have to sell, or you can tick the **Unlimited** box.

To add multiple product variants, click on the + icon below **SKU** to add a new row and create a new variant. If you need to add another type of property to your product variants, you can click on the + icon next to the last column to add a new column and create a new property. These two options are shown in the following screenshot:

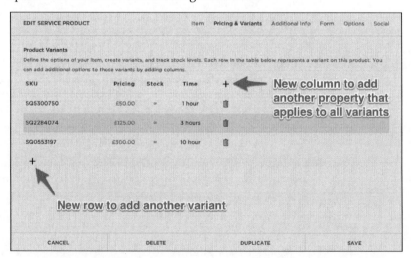

For physical products, you can also enter the following:

- ° **Weight**: Enter the weight of the item. This is especially important if you are using a weight-based shipping formula.
- ° **Dimensions**: Enter the dimensions of the product in length, width, and height.

 You may need to use the total dimensions including any packaging if you are linking to USPS to use their real-time shipping calculator.

Pricing & Upload for digital products:

- ° Use the **file uploader arrow** to upload the file
- ° Enter the price options for the digital product

5. If you wish, use the **Additional Info** screen to input further information about your product. You can use any type of Block in this area, and it will appear on the Product page below the photo and summary information. You can add and reposition Blocks in this area just like on a standard page.

 This is a great place to cross-promote similar products using a Summary Block or a Product Block, which we'll cover later in this chapter.

6. If you need to capture additional information from your customer as part of the checkout process, you can use the **Form** screen to add a form to the shopping cart:

- ° Click on **Create New Form** and enter your form fields, just like when creating a Form Block.
- ° You can reuse checkout forms on multiple products; every form you create within the **Form** screen can be selected from the **Form** screen of another product.

7. If you wish, change **Options** for the product:

   ○ **Thumbnail Image**: By default, Squarespace uses the first photo that you uploaded as the thumbnail. If you want to change this to a different image, you can change it here.

 Squarespace keeps the first image you ever uploaded as the thumbnail, *even if you subsequently delete or replace that photo* in the Item screen. This can be very confusing, so remember to check here in the **Options** section if you find that your site is showing an old or incorrect product thumbnail.

   ○ **Product URL**: By default, this is set to the product name, but you can adjust it manually if you prefer a different URL.

   ○ **Use Custom Add Button label**: Tick this box and enter the revised text that you want to display instead of the default **Add to Cart**

   ○ **Featured Product**: You can use a Summary Block to display products that have this box ticked. This is an alternative to filtering based on category.

8. If you wish, set the **Social** options for this product.

 You can use this section to automatically publish a product on your social media profiles. We'll cover this in *Chapter 9, Going Live with Your Website and Driving Traffic to It*.

9. Click on **Save** if you are finished entering products, or click on **Duplicate** if you want to save this product, and at the same time, create an identical product to use as a starting point to enter another similar product item.

Removing or rearranging products

You can delete or rearrange products in the same way as you manage Gallery or Album items, which we covered in *Chapter 4, Creating Your Site Framework: Pages, Items, Collections, and Navigation*. If you have multiple Products pages, you can also use these steps to move items from one Products page to another.

Importing products from Big Cartel, Etsy, or Shopify

If you already have a store on Big Cartel, Etsy, or Shopify, you can export your products from these sites and import them into your Squarespace store. While this is a nice feature, you should be aware that some third-party stores don't include all information in exported items due to the different ways their system handles things. For example, Big Cartel does not export the stock levels or variants, and Etsy cannot export digital downloads well. The process to export varies from store to store.

Imported products will be added to a new Products page, and this page will be added to your site in the **Not Linked** section. If you wish, you can move these products onto another Products page, following the steps to move items in *Chapter 4, Creating Your Site Framework: Pages, Items, Collections, and Navigation*.

Step-by-step instructions to import products can be found here:

- Shopify: `http://help.squarespace.com/guides/importing-products-from-shopify`
- Etsy: `http://help.squarespace.com/guides/importing-products-from-etsy`
- Big Cartel: `http://help.squarespace.com/guides/importing-products-from-big-cartel`

Managing products using Inventory

The **Inventory** area within the **Commerce** panel is the most convenient way to keep track of all products at a glance. **Inventory** displays summaries of all your products in a sortable list to allow you to have an overview of all products and their stock levels in one place. If you have multiple Products pages, all products will be shown mixed together in your **Inventory** panel. You can sort your Inventory by item name, price, or stock level. The following screenshot shows you the **Inventory** panel:

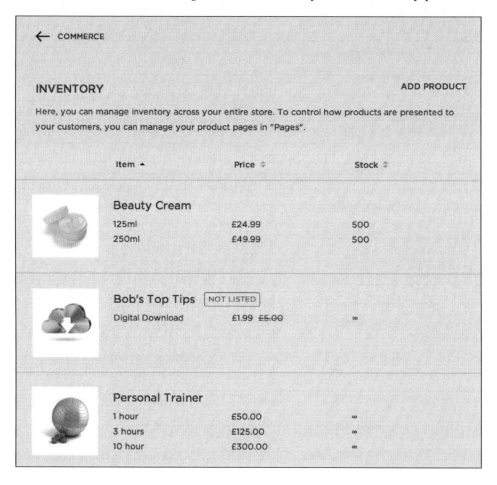

The **Inventory** panel shows you the following characteristics of your products:

- The Thumbnail Image
- The Product Name
- Stock levels for each variant
- Price(s) for each variant (both the normal price and sale price if the item is on sale)

Clicking on any of these will open the **Edit Product** overlay to allow you to edit the product properties without having to leave the **Inventory** area. This makes it easy for you to adjust stock levels or prices quickly.

> If you have forgotten to include critical information, have not yet listed, or have forgotten to save a Product, an alert will show on the item to draw your attention to it. An example is shown in the preceding screenshot.

You can also add new products directly from the **Inventory** panel instead of having to navigate to the **Products** panel. This can save time, especially if you need to add products to multiple different Products pages or if you are performing other store administration and maintenance. Use the **Add Product** button in the top-right corner to add a new product to any page, following the same procedure as the one outlined earlier in this chapter.

Testing your store

Once you have created your products and variants, now is the time to test how to add them to a shopping cart and check out. It's a good idea to test as many product variants as possible to ensure that you haven't accidentally made a typo or set up a variant incorrectly. Your store should still be in *test* mode, so you can safely add things to a shopping cart and go through the entire checkout process without worrying that real charges will be made to a credit card.

To make a test purchase, follow these steps:

1. Go into the fullscreen Preview mode or log out of the Squarespace administration if you prefer.

 Use a different browser if you want to keep your site open in the Site Manager in one place but test the purchase process as a normal user in another.

As your site is still password-protected, you may need to enter your password during the checkout process. This will not happen once we launch your site.

2. Visit your Products page(s) and add item(s) to your cart. A floating **Shopping Cart toolbar** will appear in the top-right corner of your screen.

3. Once you have added as many items as you like, click on the Shopping Cart icon to go to the **Shopping Cart** page. You may want to test removing some items or adjusting quantities while there.

4. Click on the **Checkout** button to open the Billing page. If you have connected a Stripe account but not yet flipped the *live* switch, the Billing page should display a **Store Not Live** message along the top of the screen to reassure you that you are still in *test* mode. This is shown in the following screenshot:

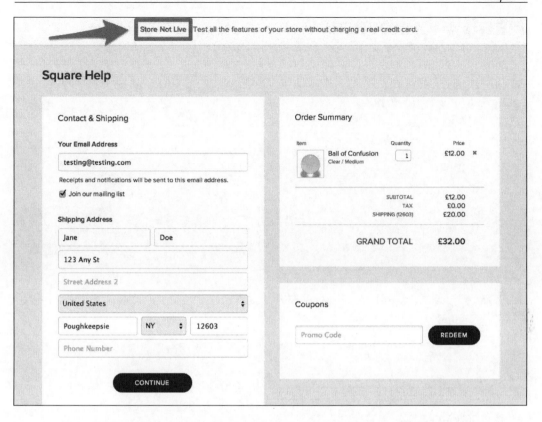

5. Enter information in the **Billing Info**—and if applicable, **Shipping Options**—section(s). Use a real email address that you have access to, so you can see the emails that are sent to customers.

6. When you get to the **Secure Payment** box, you should notice that Stripe has already prefilled the credit card with test numbers and dates. Click on **Order & Pay Now** to check out.

 If the credit card info is not prefilled, you can find the test card information at www.stripe.com/docs/testing.

Once your test order has gone through, you can check your email inbox to see the Order Confirmation email, and you can see your test order in the **Orders** part of your store, which we will cover next.

Handling orders

You manage all aspects of the orders placed on your site in the **Orders** area of the **Commerce** menu. Whenever an order is placed, it appears in the **Orders** panel as soon as the payment has been successfully processed. The **Orders** panel is shown in the following screenshot:

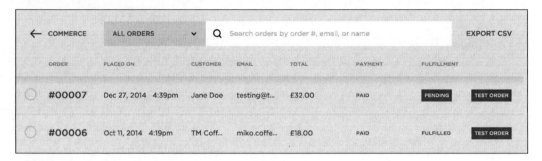

The **Orders** panel defaults to show **All Orders**. You can use the drop-down menu to filter the list, as follows:

- **Pending**: Orders for physical products or services appear here, ready for you to action or ship.

- **Completed**: Orders for physical products or services appear here once you have marked them as complete. Digital download orders appear here instantly.

- **Cancelled**: Any orders that have been marked as canceled will appear under this tab.

For each order, the following information is displayed in columns:

- The order number
- The date and time the order was placed
- The customer name and email address
- The total amount paid, payment status, and fulfillment status

If the order is a test order, it will display a **Test Order** label so you can distinguish test orders from real orders.

You can use the search box on the Orders panel to quickly find an order based on the order number, customer name, or customer email address.

You can use the **Export CSV** button in the top-right corner to export all orders from all three tabs as a spreadsheet for use in Microsoft Excel or another spreadsheet program.

Processing orders quickly or in bulk

The round checkbox on the left-hand side of the order can be used to quickly print invoices or change the order status from **Pending** to **Complete**, or vice versa. It can also be used to delete test orders.

Check the box on one or more orders, and you will see a floating toolbar appear at the bottom of the viewing and editing screen, as shown in the following screenshot:

You can check the box(es) and use the floating toolbar buttons for the following:

- **Select All**: Use this to quickly select all orders in the tab you are viewing
- **Print**: This will open a printer-friendly version of the order in a new browser tab and will also open the print dialog box for quick printing
- **Mark Completed/Mark Pending**: If you are in the **Pending** tab, this will change the order status to complete and move it into the **Completed** tab (or vice versa)
- **Delete Test Order**: Use this to clear out any test orders prior to going live.

Using Order Summary

To view order details or perform operations on an individual order, you can click anywhere on the order row to open the **Order Summary** window. The following screenshot shows you an example of **Order Summary**:

ORDER SUMMARY   **Order**   Notes   Email Notifications

BILLED TO: SHIPPING TO:

Jane Doe   Jane Doe
123 Any Street   123 Any Street
Anyplace   Anyplace
Towntown, 76305   Towntown, 76305
United Kingdom   United Kingdom
CC: XXXX-4242   USA
testing@123.com   Standard (2-5 Business Days)

ITEM	SKU	PRICE	QTY	SUBTOTAL
Flame Tulip	SQ1840158	£3.00	4	£12.00

Subtotal	£12.00
Sales Tax (20.00%)	£2.40
Shipping & Handling	£1.50
Grand Total	£15.90

CHARGE   ch_1044lq2bwWNsG19rBb1VCNxM   view in stripe →

CLOSE	PRINT	ISSUE REFUND	CANCEL ORDER	MARK COMPLETED

Order Summary shows you the full details of the order, including:

- The customer's full billing address and phone number
- Specific product information, including the SKU for every item ordered
- Any additional customer information captured as part of a form
- The breakdown of costs, including tax and shipping charges
- The unique ID of the Stripe payment, along with a link to view the order in the Stripe interface

Using the buttons and links at the top and bottom of the **Order Summary** window, you can also perform a variety of tasks on the order, as follows:

- **Print**: Use this to print the invoice.
- **Issue Refund**: You can refund all or part of the amount paid. Enter the amount you wish to refund, and the customer will receive an automatic email, alerting them about the refund. You will also be able to see the refunded amount in **Order Summary**, and the status will show **Refunded** on the **Orders** screen.
- **Mark Completed / Mark Pending**: This changes the status of the order and moves it to the relevant tab.
- **Cancel Order**: This will issue a full refund to the customer and move the order to the **Cancelled** tab.
- **Mark Fulfilled**: This changes the status of the order and allows you to send an email notification to the customer, including shipping information such as **Tracking Number**. You can specify the Tracking Number in the overlay window that appears after clicking on the **Mark Fulfilled** button.
- **Notes**: You can add a Private Note about the order, which will only be visible to you or your colleagues who have access to store administration. This can come in handy if you need to record any customer issues or communicate privately with others about an order.
- **Email Notifications**: You can resend an order confirmation or shipping notification email or use the **Send Message** area to quickly send an email to the customer about anything else without needing to open your email software.

Promoting products and offering discounts

We've now covered the basics of getting your store ready for selling, but there are several other tools in your Squarespace Commerce toolkit that can help you improve sales on your website.

Using Product Blocks to enable quick purchases from anywhere on your site

You can use a Product Block to insert summary information about a single product on any page, blog post, event, sidebar, or anywhere you can insert a Block. This is a great way to cross-promote products that relate to the topic of the page or give products an extra boost by highlighting them in prominent places. The best part is that you can also include the **Add to Cart** button, which means that customers can purchase with a single click without ever needing to navigate to your Products page(s). Here's an example of a Product Block on a standard page:

A PRODUCT BLOCK WITH TEXT WRAPPED AROUND IT

Lorem ipsum dolor sit amet, consectetur adipiscing elit. Vestibulum fermentum velit in purus pretium dapibus. Ut fermentum et nisi quis sodales. Etiam eget nulla consequat, semper massa sed, imperdiet ante. Aenean molestie auctor mattis. Nunc et lorem congue, semper neque quis, ornare lorem. Quisque eget vehicula felis. Curabitur nisi nisi, gravida dapibus ultrices quis, condimentum sit amet odio. Quisque vitae aliquam metus, in fringilla erat.

Flame Tulip
£3.00

Quantity:
1

ADD TO CART

Etiam id urna laoreet, pulvinar velit eget, venenatis diam. Mauris facilisis, purus non consectetur accumsan, arcu lacus euismod felis, vel tempor eros magna et neque. Duis lobortis ultrices enim nec venenatis. Morbi gravida vitae sapien at tincidunt. Phasellus sed purus lacus. Donec congue cursus quam. Nunc sed egestas diam. Maecenas vel sem quis nulla dignissim feugiat. Suspendisse potenti. Sed consequat eu massa sed accumsan.

Maecenas ac lorem et est iaculis viverra. Praesent porta suscipit rutrum. Sed lacinia, diam in blandit adipiscing, ligula justo sodales velit, sit amet vehicula lacus dolor vel

To add a Product Block, follow these steps:

1. Go to the page where you want to insert the block, open the Content Editor, and click on the Insert Point.
2. Under the **Commerce** category, click on **Product**.
3. Use the **Find A Product** box to search for a product by name.
4. Select the product you wish to feature from the search results. This will pull in the title and thumbnail of the product, as shown in the following screenshot:

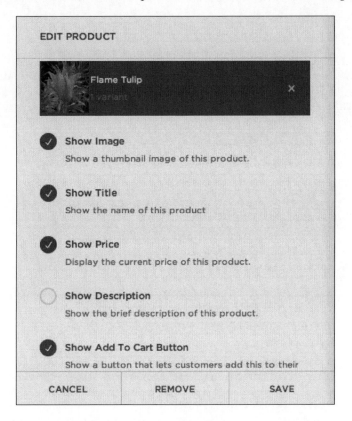

5. Check the relevant boxes to show the Thumbnail Image, Title, Price, Description, and/or the **Add to Cart** button.
6. Click on **Save**.

You can now move and resize this Block in the same way as other Blocks.

Using Summary Blocks to showcase featured products

In the last chapter, we discussed the flexible Summary Block and listed some ways you can use that type of block. One of the best uses of a Summary Block on an e-commerce site is for the cross-selling of products. Here are just a few ideas to help encourage purchases:

- Insert a *Bestsellers* carousel on your home page or in your footer that allows visitors to flick through and access your most popular products quickly.

- Display a row of related products in the **Additional Info** section of a product item page to increase add-on purchases.

- If your products have great photos, create a mosaic or grid to showcase companion products—for example, *This season's must-haves* or *Everything you need for the perfect BBQ*. Change this regularly with the season or other marketing schedule.

- Instill a sense of urgency by displaying a *Last chance to buy* Summary Block. Create a category and assign it to items with low stock levels, and then filter your Summary Block on this category.

- Fill up the empty space at the bottom of your blog sidebar with a list of featured products.

Offering and promoting discounts

We've already mentioned that you can set up sale prices on individual product variants, but you can also offer discounts that apply to all or certain types of orders on your site by creating **promo codes** that your customers can enter into the checkout page. You can create different promo codes for your different marketing channels to help track the effectiveness of your marketing efforts, or you can use promo codes to upsell by offering discounts on orders over a certain amount, for example.

You can also add an **Announcement Bar** that will show across the top of your website to display a promo code and draw attention to it.

Coupons

In Squarespace, discounts or promo codes are called **coupons**, so you create and manage all promo codes in the **Coupons** area of **Commerce** under Site Manager.

The **discount type** offered by a coupon can be one of the following:

- **Flat Discount**: This is a single amount, such as £5 or $2.50 off
- **Percentage Discount**: The discount is calculated as a percentage of the cost
- **Free Shipping**: There will be no shipping cost added to the order

Coupons also have different restrictions based on the **purchase type**. You can create coupons that apply to the following:

- **Any Order**: This will apply a discount to any order
- **Orders At Least**: This will apply the discount to orders over a specified amount
- **Products By Category**: This will apply the discount to a subset of products based on their category
- **Single Product**: The discount will only be applied to a specified product

A coupon is always comprised of the discount type plus the purchase type. For example:

- €7 off any order
- Free shipping on all orders over £50
- 15 percent off on all handbags

Coupons also have date limits, so they are only valid for a certain time period.

To create a Coupon, follow these steps:

1. In the Coupons panel within the **Commerce** menu, click on the **Add Coupon** button. This will open the **Create a Coupon** overlay.
2. Select the purchase type. This will move you to the next step.

3. Select the discount type. This will open the **Edit Coupon** screen, as shown in the following screenshot:

4. Enter the coupon settings:
    ○ **Coupon Name**: Use a unique, descriptive name. This will be visible to customers when they apply the promo code on the checkout page, so ensure you don't use internal jargon.
    ○ **Promo Code**: You can let Squarespace generate a random code for you, but it's nicer for your customers if you use a short, memorable code instead.
    ○ **Start Date / End Date**: Specify when you want the coupon to be valid.

Depending on the discount type and purchase type, you may also need to set:
    ○ **Flat Discount**: Enter the monetary amount that should be taken off the order value
    ○ **Minimum Price**: Specify the minimum subtotal that customers must have in their cart in order for the discount to be applied

- ° **Discount %:** If you have chosen to offer a percentage discount, enter it here
- ° **Categories**: Click on the name to select the category or categories of products
- ° **Find A Product**: If the coupon is only valid for a single product, use this box to search for it by name

5. Click on **Save**.

Once you have set up your coupon, your customers will be able to enter the promo code in the **Coupons** section on the checkout page to apply the discount, as shown in the following example:

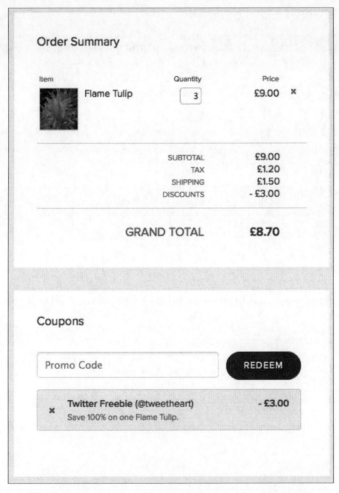

Checkout page showing the Twitter Freebie discount applied

The page will show you an alert and deny the discount if the coupon is not currently valid.

Using the Announcement Bar to highlight discount codes

Squarespace allows you to set up an Announcement Bar to draw attention to any short message you want visitors to see when they land on your site. The Announcement Bar is a thin strip that runs across the top of your website, with an **X** button that visitors can use to close the bar once they have read the message. Using the Announcement Bar to show customers the promo code for a coupon is a great way to encourage purchases. Here is an example of an Announcement Bar:

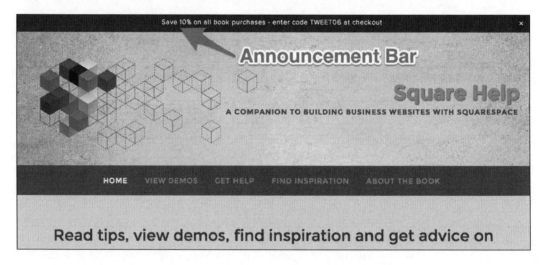

You can set up the Announcement Bar in the **Design** panel, which is accessible from the **Home** menu.

Follow these steps to set up an Announcement Bar:

1. In the Design menu, click on **Announcement Bar**.

2. Click on the drop-down menu to select **Enable Announcement Bar**. This will load additional items into the **Announcement Bar** panel, as shown in the following screenshot:

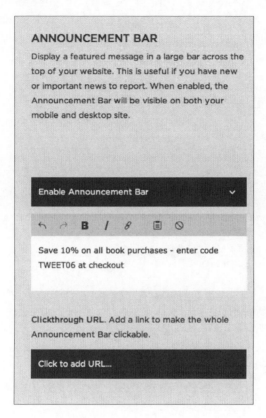

3. Type the text you want to display in the text box, and use simple formatting tools to style the text if you wish.

4. If you want to make the Announcement Bar a clickable link, enter **Clickthrough URL** for the page you want to link to.

Setting up and managing donations

You can use Squarespace Commerce to accept donations on your website if you are a nonprofit organization or if you would like to accept monetary gifts or tips online.

 Be extra careful if you will be taking donations as tips or gifts, because the law is very specific about how these terms are defined where tax is concerned.

Adding a Donation Block

You can add a **Donate** button to your site using a **Donation Block**. Donation Blocks can be added, moved, and resized in the same way as other content blocks and can be inserted anywhere a content block can go. The following screenshot shows you an example of a Donation Block:

To add a Donation Block, perform the following steps:

1. Navigate to the page you want, open the Content Editor, and click on the Insert Point where you'd like to place the block.

2. Scroll down to the **Commerce** category and click on **Donation**. The **Edit Donation** overlay window will open, as shown in the following screenshot:

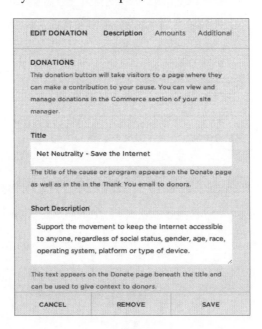

3. Enter information on the **Description** screen:

   ○ **Title**: This will appear in on the Donate page and in the Donation Thank You email for donors.

   ○ **Short Description**: This text appears on the Donate page to help provide context or further information to donors.

   ○ **Custom Button Label**: The default button text says **Donate**, but you can change this to any text you like.

   ○ **Button Alignment**: Choose whether the button should be aligned left, right, or centered in the space occupied by the content block.

4. If you wish, you can set up suggested contributions on the **Amounts** screen:

   ○ You can choose to use the default amounts or adjust them to other amounts.

   ○ For each amount, you may choose to use the optional **Label** property to provide context for what this donation will buy/support—for example, "Buys food for a family of 4 for a week".

   ○ Use the **+** icon to add additional amount levels and labels.

   ○ Donors can always choose one of these amounts or enter their own amount when donating.

5. If you wish, you can use the **Additional** screen to add any form fields that you would like donors to complete. For example, you can ask them to make the donation in the honor of someone or to choose a specific project to support. This information will appear in the Donation Thank You email and in the Squarespace Donation management area.

6. Click on **Save**.

Testing donations

You can test the donation process in the same way as the product purchase process is tested. Refer to the *Testing your store* section earlier in this chapter for details. The only process difference between a donation and a product is that donations bypass the shopping cart and take you straight to the Billing page.

Once your test donation has gone through, you can check your email inbox to see the Donation Thank You email, and you can see your test donation in the **Donations** part of your store, which we will cover next.

Viewing and exporting donations received

You can see details of all donations that have been made in the **Donations** panel in the **Commerce** menu. Whenever a donation is made, it appears in the **Donations** panel as soon as the payment has been processed successfully.

Clicking on an individual donation opens the **Contribution Summary** overlay, where you can see full details of the contribution, including any additional information you asked donors to complete. An example of this is shown in the following screenshot:

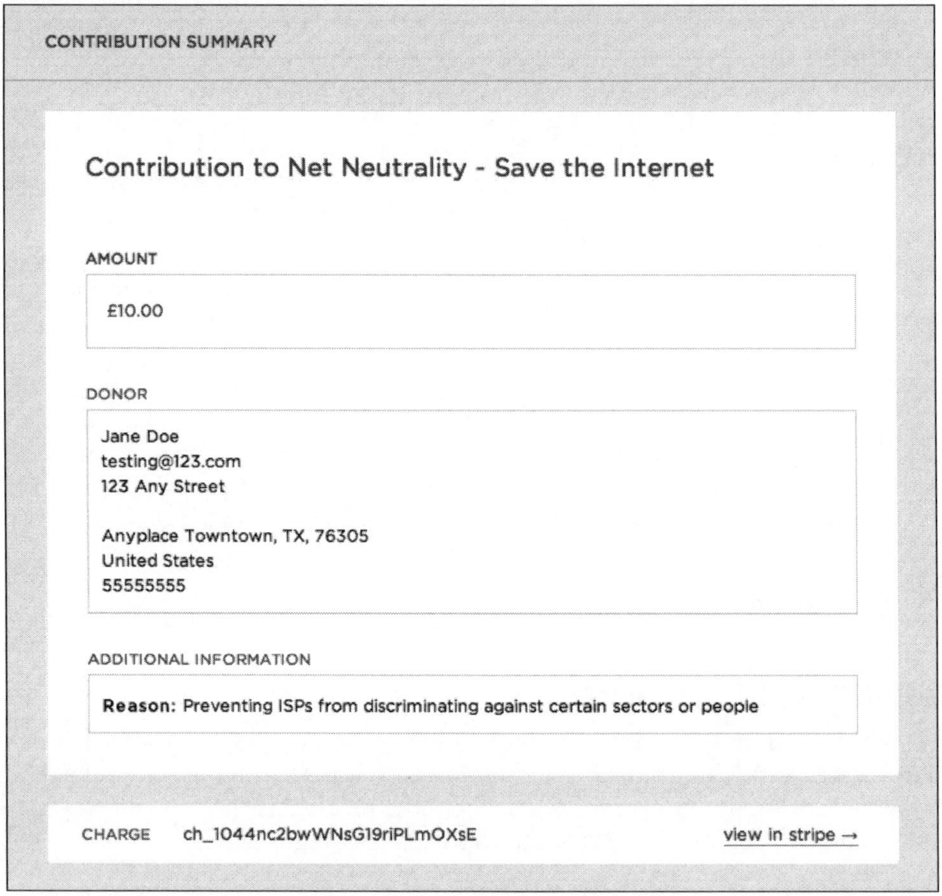

CONTRIBUTION SUMMARY

Contribution to Net Neutrality - Save the Internet

AMOUNT

£10.00

DONOR

Jane Doe
testing@123.com
123 Any Street

Anyplace Towntown, TX, 76305
United States
55555555

ADDITIONAL INFORMATION

Reason: Preventing ISPs from discriminating against certain sectors or people

CHARGE   ch_1044nc2bwWNsG19riPLmOXsE   view in stripe →

You can use the **Export CSV** button to export all the donation information as a spreadsheet for use in Microsoft Excel or another spreadsheet program.

Handling transactions without Squarespace Commerce

If, for any reason, you can't or don't want to use Stripe and Squarespace Commerce to manage transactions on your website, you can use third-party systems such as PayPal or JustGiving on your site instead. You will need to use an Embed Block to paste the code for your PayPal shopping cart button, or your JustGiving donation button, into any page that accepts blocks. You can use this method to insert code from any third-party service that offers embed codes to customers.

 Some third-party sites allow you to style the buttons to match your site's branding when generating the embed code.

This approach is a workaround, and it means the experience will not be as seamless for your customers, as they will need to visit the third-party site to complete their transaction. You will not be able to set up a proper *shop* on your site, but you can make standard pages look very similar to product pages, with a little effort in LayoutEngine.

 Using a template with an Index of pages is usually the best approach to replicate something similar to a shop. Visit www.square-help.com/inspiration for an example that uses PayPal instead of Stripe.

Summary

We've just covered all the skills you need to build and promote a beautiful online shop to showcase your products or services. Furthermore, working through this chapter means that you've now mastered *all* of Squarespace's primary building and content tools.

Once you have finished setting up your shop or donations, it's a good time to log out of the Squarespace administration mode and use the site password to see your website exactly as a normal visitor would. Take some time to move around the site, and see how the flow is working — or not. You may find it helpful to refer to your Website Toolkit and check whether your customers will be able to perform their primary objective(s) easily. You may also want to take this opportunity to ask a colleague to do the same. People are often distracted by design details, so doing it now, when you have not yet applied colors or other stylistic elements, can help them focus on the task rather than the appearance of the pages. Just be sure to set their expectations upfront, and explain that the visual design will come next.

As you move through the site, make note of any visual style adjustments you'd like to make, just as you did at the end of the last chapter. Your site should now be completely finished in terms of content and function, so you will be able to see how every single element of every page looks and will, therefore, be able to identify exactly what you'd like to adjust in the next chapter.

8
Tailoring Your Site's Look and Feel

It's finally time to apply the paint and furnishings to our building; this chapter will teach you how to use the Squarespace Style Editor to adjust the appearance of your website. You will probably find that this chapter is either your favorite part of the project or the bane of your life, depending on how you feel about working with visual design.

By this point, your website should be filled with content and have all the key functions set up. In theory, you can go live right now, and you'll have a fully operational website. Saving visual design choices until now was a deliberate decision, because you will quickly discover that there are infinite ways to customize your site's look and feel, even if you are using one of the more restrictive Squarespace templates. A lot of choice can be overwhelming, and confusion or frustration about not being able to get the visual design right is the number one reason why people abandon their sites unfinished or turn to professional help.

However, because your site is in good working order *before* you start playing with the aesthetic side of things, you will be able to launch your site even if you can't get things to look exactly the way you want them to. You (or a designer) can always come back and adjust things later. Furthermore, because you already have all of your content and functions in the pages, you will be able to make better style choices from the outset, reducing the time you need to spend on tweaking the look and feel.

So, put your creative head on, make sure that your idea boards are handy, and get ready to bring your site visually in line with your brand image. In this chapter, we will cover the following topics:

- Understanding the Squarespace template's customization options
- Using the Style Editor to apply aesthetic changes

- Choosing and applying fonts and font variants
- Adding a logo to your site header
- Choosing and applying colors, including transparency
- Choosing and applying background or header images
- Controlling the size, position, or visibility of template elements
- Saving, testing, and undoing style changes

Design is subjective: what you find appealing, someone else may find appalling. Remember to make aesthetic choices based on your website's target audience, rather than on your own taste, which may be quite different.

Keep your brand image in mind throughout this chapter. You may want to write your brand values or perception words on sticky notes and post them on your wall or desk to ensure that your aesthetic choices reflect the right image.

Understanding Squarespace template customization

As mentioned in *Chapter 3*, *Working with Squarespace Templates*, every Squarespace template allows some level of control over the appearance of various page elements, but the amount of control and which elements you can change varies from template to template. In most templates, you will usually be able to make the following kind of adjustments:

- **Color**: This allows you to change the color of text, backgrounds, or certain page areas, such as the navbar or page borders
- **Typography**: This allows you to select fonts, adjust text size, and apply text styles, such as uppercase (all caps)
- **Size**: This allows you to adjust the height or width and spacing between elements
- **Position**: This allows you choose whether to show or hide certain features and where to display them
- **Images**: This includes logos, background images, or header images

In this chapter, we will cover the steps needed to make each of these adjustments.

As you make adjustments, you may find it useful to note down certain style elements, such as font sizes and colors, to ensure consistency across your website. Therefore, you may want to open a simple text editor application, such as Notepad or Text Editor — or keep an actual paper notepad handy.

All standard aesthetic adjustments are made in the **Style Editor**, which is located within the **Design** area, accessed from the **Home** menu. The Style Editor panel displays a column of controls and settings, as shown in the following screenshot:

If you know how to use CSS, you can make advanced aesthetic changes by applying custom CSS code to your entire site or specific pages. We will cover this type of adjustment in *Chapter 11, Moving beyond Standard Squarespace Tools.*

Finding your way around the Style Editor

The number and nature of controls available in the Style Editor panel varies depending on the template. If your template allows a great deal of control, you will probably find that the template designer has split the elements into different categories to make it easier for you to find the one you want to adjust.

In most cases, aside from very restricted templates, the elements shown in the Style Editor panel will vary according to which type of page is loaded in the Preview screen. For example, if you are on a Blog page and you open the Style Editor, the elements shown will relate to blog post styles. If you are on a Gallery page, the elements will relate to the way the images are displayed in the Gallery. These page-specific elements are sometimes shown alongside more generic site-wide elements, such as the site header or body text style controls. The best way to ensure you adjust all elements for all page types is to start by loading a standard page in the Preview screen, and applying all the desired adjustments there. Then, work your way systematically through all the different page types that you have on your website, applying style adjustments to each. This methodical approach will ensure that you don't forget to adjust less common elements such as buttons.

If you are using a Cover Page, you will need to set all of the style elements for that page separately, as the Cover Page does not inherit any of the styles you set elsewhere within the Style Editor. The method for adjusting Cover Pages is different from all other page types. See the *Adjusting Cover Page styles* section later in this chapter for details.

The Style Editor disables all links in the page Preview screen, so you won't be able to navigate around your site while the Style Editor panel is open. Clicking on a link will simply filter the Style Editor list to show the controls that relate to the link element. To navigate to a different page, you will need to navigate back to the **Design** menu using the link at the top of the side panel.

In some cases, the Annotations may get in the way of accessing your navigation. If so, simply use the expansion arrow to enable fullscreen preview and disable Annotations. Then, navigate to the page you want to adjust and click on the expansion arrow again to expand the side panel.

Selecting an element for adjustment

There are two different ways to select an element for adjustment:

- **The panel method:** Click on the element name in the Style Editor panel to open the adjustment tool for that element.

- **The filter method:** In the Preview screen, click on an item that you want to change. For example, if you want to change the font style for the page heading text, click on any word that uses this style. This will filter the list in the Style Editor panel, so it only shows the controls that relate to this element. An example of this is shown in the following screenshot. Here, the heading on a standard page has been clicked, and you can see that the Style Editor panel shows only the controls that are related to headings.

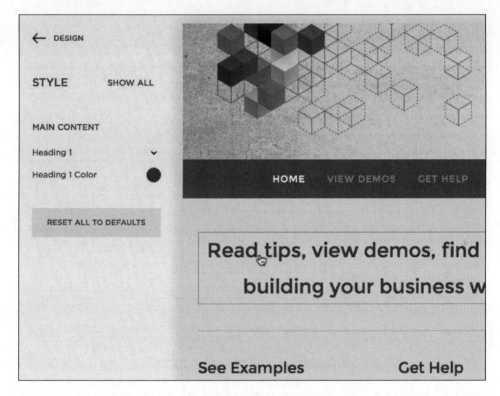

If you use the filter method, once you have made your adjustment, you will need to use the **Show All** link at the top of the Style Editor panel to disable the filter and reload all the style element controls.

Saving changes in the Style Editor

Whenever you make an adjustment to an element, the Preview screen will show the effect of the adjustment. This will allow you to see the changes in real time, on real content. Once you make a change in the Style Editor panel, the top of the panel will show two buttons:

- **Save**: This stores the adjustment and erases the memory of what it was before

> **Save** is permanent; you can't undo a change and revert to the previous setting after you have clicked on **Save**.
>
> Be careful not to accidentally close your browser window without saving your changes first. There will be no alert box and no way to recover those adjustments.

- **Cancel**: This reverts to the previous setting, before your adjustment

You can make adjustments to as many elements as you like before saving your changes. Any element that you have changed will display a small gray dot next to the name of the element to indicate that you have adjusted it, as shown in the following screenshot:

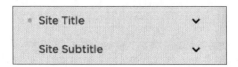

You can click on this dot to revert and discard that adjustment. However, if you are not confident with the design, you may want to consider adjusting only element one at a time, so you can use the **Cancel** button to revert that element's settings, without worrying about accidentally undoing others.

> **Cancel** will revert *all* the elements to their previous settings; you can't cancel one element and save changes to others at the same time. **Cancel** reverts all changes made since the last time you clicked on **Save**.

Testing your template customizations

What looks great on one page may not look as good on another page. For example, you may find that a particular text style looks great for short page headings, but doesn't work as well on long titles that run across multiple lines. It's a good idea to check the effects of your changes across multiple pages, ideally including a "worst case scenario" page.

Sometimes, a change you make to one element will also impact others. Certain element styles are based on the main element styles—for example, the footer or sidebar font may be based on the body text or heading font. Some templates may not allow you to adjust them individually.

Any time you make substantial changes to your website's look and feel, you should always test how the site looks on all kinds of devices, from smartphones, to tablets, to high-resolution computer screens. Although the Squarespace templates have been designed to look and function well across all sizes of screen and types of browser, your changes to the template may affect the appearance in an undesired way, especially on very large or very small screens.

When testing on different screen sizes, pay particular attention to any images you have used in your template customizations.

Some elements will be automatically resized or repositioned on small screens. This behavior is hardcoded into the template, and you won't be able to change it yourself without good knowledge of CSS code.

Resetting the template

If at any time you want to restore the template to the default settings for all elements, you can do so. Using the **Reset to Defaults** button at the bottom of the Style Editor column will erase all changes you have made, and set all styles back to the original styles shown in the template demo. You will lose all adjustments, so use with caution.

Switching templates with customizations applied

Sometimes, you may find your chosen template doesn't quite look how you want, even when customized, and you may be feeling you'd be better off with a different template. Squarespace stores all of your customizations to templates indefinitely, so you can safely switch to a different template at any time. You can then switch back to your first template and all of your saved customization work will still be there. You can customize as many templates as you want, switching back and forth whenever you like.

You can apply customizations to templates that you are previewing: you don't have to make a template live to work on its appearance. This means you can safely tinker with a different template in the background, without affecting your live site's appearance.

Working with fonts and typography

Fonts can make a huge difference in not only the readability and usability of your website, but they can also play a critical role in the *feel* or mood that your site conveys. Have a look at the following examples one by one and think about the emotive words or impressions that come to mind for each one:

Fonts (from top to down): Poiret One, Playfair Display, Alfa Slab One, Dancing Script.

Even subtle differences in fonts can change the feeling that is conveyed, as shown in the following examples:

Fonts (from top to down): Fjalla One, Francois One, Jockey One.

The top font gives a modern, reliable impression; the middle font seems friendly and approachable; and the bottom font feels masculine or technical. Fonts can make a huge difference to your business: just think about how much money has been spent by brands such as PayPal, eBay, or Microsoft on evolving their brand image through the years by adjusting their logos and the fonts used in their communications. Spend some time working with the fonts on your website to ensure you are conveying the right image to your target audience.

Choosing fonts

Selecting the right fonts for your site can make the difference between a site that feels polished and professional, and one that feels clunky and amateurish. Here are some things to bear in mind when choosing fonts for your website:

- A good rule of thumb is to use only two different fonts. Choose one font for headings, and a different one for body text. If you feel you need a third font, use this sparingly as an accent, such as the site title (logo) or navbar text.

- Ensure that the fonts you choose complement one another, and that they work together to convey your brand image.

- Avoid choosing fonts that are too close in appearance to one another: pages look best with some contrast between headings and body text.

- Keep your body text font simple and easy to read. Avoid overly stylized fonts here.

- You can use more dramatic or stylized fonts for headings, but be sure to test how your chosen font looks on your "worst case scenario" page, and remember that quirky fonts may not be appropriate for all audiences.

 Great advice on choosing and combining fonts can be found at www.smashingmagazine.com/2010/11/04/best-practices-of-combining-typefaces.

Using fonts on your website

Squarespace allows you to use any of 600+ Google fonts, as well as 60+ Adobe Typekit fonts, and the 15 standard fonts that come pre-installed on most computers. Your company may already have certain fonts that should be used according to your branding guidelines; however, unless those fonts are either included with Squarespace or other Adobe Typekit fonts, then you won't be able to apply them to text on your website. You may need to find similar fonts from the list that Squarespace offers. We'll go through some tips on how to do this a bit later in this chapter.

 Even if you can't use your company's font(s) to style the text on your website, you can still use images that have the font(s) applied within the image, such as a logo. Just remember that search engines cannot see text that is in an image, so use this technique only where absolutely necessary.

If your company fonts are Adobe Typekit fonts, and are not part of the set included free with Squarespace, you can purchase a license from Adobe and apply those fonts to your Squarespace site by going to **Design | Advanced**.

 Instructions for using Typekit fonts aside from the ones supplied through Squarespace can be found at http://help.squarespace. com/guides/using-typekit-with-squarespace.

Other typography settings

Choosing the font itself is only one part of **typography**, the art of arranging and styling text. In Squarespace, typography can also include adjusting the following attributes:

- **Size**: This is usually measured in pixels (px) or **em**, which is a decimal form of measurement used in web design
- **Weight**: This is measured from 100 to 900, where 100 is very thin and 900 is very heavy (400 is usually considered normal weight)
- **Style**: This includes styles such as bold, semi-bold, or italic
- **Letter spacing** (also called tracking or kerning): This is the spacing between individual letters
- **Line height** (also called leading): This is spacing between the lines of text
- **Text transformation**: This includes transformations such as uppercase, sentence case, or lowercase
- **Text decoration**: This includes underline or strikethrough

 Not all templates will allow you to adjust all of these settings, and some fonts only come in a limited range of weights or styles.

Applying typography changes to your template

Some templates have all typography elements grouped together in the Style Editor; others have type styles sprinkled throughout the list of elements. Some templates also have slightly different controls for typography than others, such as checkboxes instead of drop-down menus for font style. Although the controls and their location may vary from template to template, the overall process for applying typographic changes is the same.

To adjust a typographic element, follow these steps:

1. In the Preview screen, click on the text that you want to adjust. This will filter the list in the Style Editor panel.

2. In the Style Editor, click on the name of the element, such as **Headings Font** or **Body Text**. This will open the typography overlay window, as shown in the following screenshot:

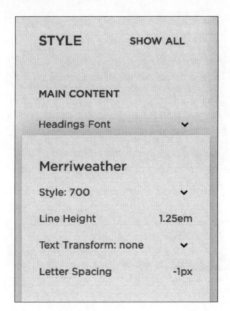

3. The first item shown in the typography overlay is the name of the font that is
    currently applied to the element. Click on the name to open the font selector.
    The font selector is shown in the following screenshot:

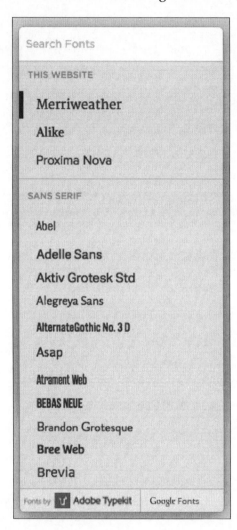

The font selector lists roughly 100 popular fonts, rather than all 700+ fonts available in Squarespace. It groups these popular fonts into sections to make it easier for you to find the fonts you need. The sections are **Sans Serif**, **Serif**, **Slab Serif**, **Display**, **Script**, **Mono** (monospace), and **More** (standard fonts). At the top of the list is a section called **This Website**, which shows you the fonts that are currently in use by the template. If you have applied any custom Adobe Typekit fonts, these will display at the top of the list, labeled **Custom Fonts**. Above the list is a search box that searches the entire set of available fonts, not just the popular ones shown in the font selector.

You will notice that the font currently in use by the element you are adjusting displays a black indicator bar in the left margin, in case you get lost or forget what it was.

In the font selector list, the name of the font is styled with that font applied, giving you some idea of what the font looks like.

4. Click on the name of the font you want to use. This will apply the font to the element, and you can see the change in the Preview screen.

5. Make any other adjustments to the other attributes that appear in the typography overlay:

   ◦ **Style**: Use the drop-down menu or checkboxes to change the font weight or style

   ◦ **Line Height** and **Letter Spacing**: Use the slider or click on the number to type your adjustment

1 em = the height of capital *A* in your font. The line height should be at least 1.2 em to ensure that the tails of letters such as *y* or *p* are not cut off or overlapping the line below.

You can type a negative number for **Letter Spacing** if you want to pull the letters closer together.

- ° **Text Transform** and **Text Decoration**: Use the drop-down menu to choose

[Because an underline is the traditional way to indicate links on a website, you should not use underlined text unless you are styling link text, such as buttons or navigation.]

6. If you do not see a **Size** slider in the typography overlay, the font size may be controlled separately in your template. Click outside the typography overlay to close it, and then click on the element size setting (usually located directly below the element name) and use the slider or type the number to adjust the font size.

[Be careful when using uppercase or sentence case to style things such as headings or page titles. Search engines ignore typographic styles applied in the Style Editor, so it's better to type things in the correct case, rather than typing all lowercase and relying on the Style Editor to fix the case later. If you type about us as your page title, that's what will appear in the search engine results, even if you have set the Style Editor to display **About Us**.]

Easier ways to find, compare, or match fonts

Although the font selector is fine when you have some idea of the font you want to use, it's not the most efficient way to find fonts. You could spend all day clicking on individual fonts within the font selector, but you would still only see a small portion of the fonts available. Plus, it's impossible to compare fonts easily in the Squarespace font selector.

Using Google or Adobe Typekit font-finders

Both Google and Adobe have online tools that allow you to easily search and filter fonts, make a shortlist of fonts, and compare multiple fonts side by side on the screen. You can even type your own sample text to preview how the fonts will look on specific words or phrases, such as your company name or strapline.

Google Fonts

The Google Fonts tool is accessible at `www.google.com/fonts`. The following screenshot shows the Google Fonts tool:

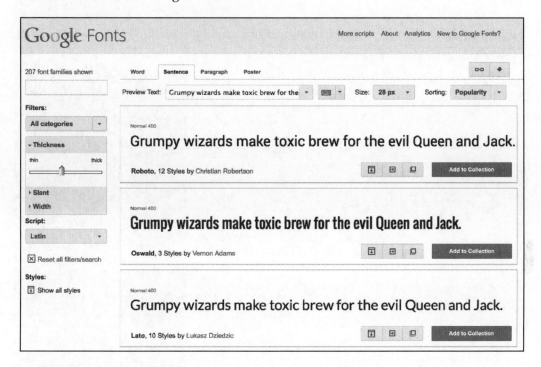

Follow these steps to search for fonts on the Google Fonts tool:

1. Use the filters on the left to narrow down the fonts shown.
2. Use the **Preview Text** box to paste your own text.
3. Use the **Add to Collection** button to save a font to your shortlist.
4. Use the **Review** button at the bottom to see your shortlist fonts side by side.

Adobe Typekit

The Adobe Typekit fonts tool is accessible at www.typekit.com/fonts. The following screenshot shows the Adobe Typekit fonts tool:

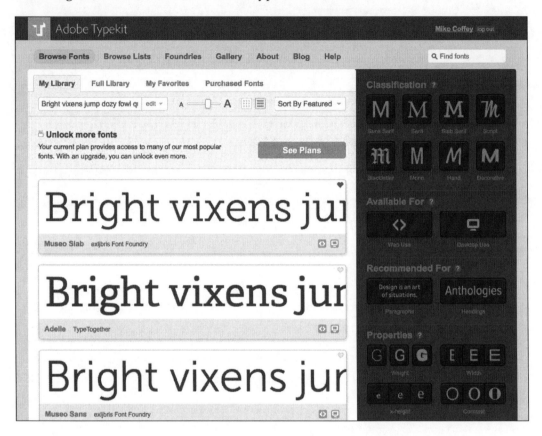

You'll need to sign up for a free trial account if you want to create a shortlist of favorite fonts to compare, but you can browse and preview fonts without an account. To use the Adobe Typekit fonts tool, follow these steps:

1. Use the mini toolbar above the fonts to change the preview: the drop-down menu selects the preview text, the slider controls size, and the list button switches to list view (a better view for choosing fonts).

2. The dark band on the right side contains filter buttons that you can use to narrow down the fonts shown.

3. If you are logged in, you can click on the **heart icon** above a font to save it to your favorites, then view your favorite fonts under the **My Favorites** tab.

You can use any Google font in Squarespace, but only a small portion of the Adobe Typekit fonts are included in Squarespace's font selector. Visit www.square-help.com/Squarespace-typekit-fonts to see the list of 60+ Adobe Typekit fonts that are included free of charge and built into Squarespace.

Finding fonts that are similar to other fonts

If your company font is not included in Squarespace, or if you know the name of a font that you like, and it's not included in Squarespace, you may want to find a similar font that *is* available in Squarespace.

You can use http://www.identifont.com/ to find fonts that look similar to the one you want, but bear in mind that the results will include fonts from a wide variety of sources, not just Google or Adobe Typekit. You'll need to cross-reference your Identifont results against those lists. However, it's a good place to start.

Adobe's Lists page— https://typekit.com/lists —is another place to look, not just for similar fonts, but also for ideas and inspiration.

Adding or creating a logo in Squarespace

Your website should currently be showing your company or brand name as text in the header, instead of a logo. You can either replace this text with a graphic logo, or you can choose to keep the text and restyle it using Style Editor, just as you would any page text. There are some benefits to using styled text as your branding, instead of an image-based logo:

- Search engines cannot see images, so they will not be able to tell that the image is your brand name. It's not a huge issue, but using text means that your pages will use your brand name in a prominent location in the code on every page, which can give your site a little boost in the rankings.
- It can be tricky to get the sizing just right on graphics or logos in Squarespace. You might need to use image-editing software to adjust your logo to the right dimensions, or to crop out unwanted empty space around the edges.

Pixlr Editor (http://apps.pixlr.com/editor/) is a fantastic free online image-editing tool that allows you to crop, resize, and save images without needing to download or install software.

- Graphic designers often save logo files on a white background, but the best type of file to use on a website is usually one with a transparent background. This is especially true if you are using a color other than white on your website in the area around the logo. You may need the help of a graphic designer if your logo does not have a transparent background.

Creating a text-based logo in Squarespace

If you are a new company, or you don't have a logo, consider using one of the Squarespace/Google fonts to create a text-based logo. Just select your site title in the Style Editor and choose any font. Feel free to use unusual or embellished fonts here.

There are hundreds of Google fonts that will suit any type of business, and you can even download them for free, so you can use them on your letterhead, business cards, or other communication materials.

 You can download Google fonts from http://www.google.com/fonts by first clicking on the **Add to Collection** button next to the font name. Then, click on the **Use** button in the gray bar at the bottom. On the next screen, click on the down arrow button at the top of the page to download a .zip file of your font(s).

Designing your own logo using Squarespace Logo

Squarespace now offers a simple logo design tool to enable small businesses or individuals to create basic logos themselves. It's called **Squarespace Logo**, and you can find it at http://squarespace.com/logo, or you can access it from within the Squarespace Design panel, as described in the following section. The service normally costs $10 per logo, but you get to create and download logos free with your Squarespace subscription. The logo will be available to you in full color, black, or white versions, as .png files on a transparent background. You can download the logo in sizes suitable for your website, as well as large sizes suitable for printing.

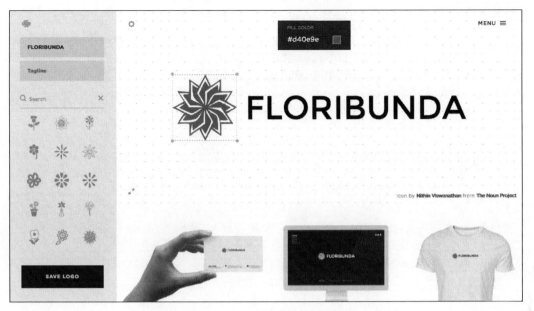

The design tool at Squarespace Logo

There are only a handful of fonts to choose from, but there are hundreds of shapes and symbols that you can use in your logo. However, the logo elements are limited to the brand name, one symbol, and a strapline/tagline—though you can position and color these however you like.

Although there are currently no limits on the number of logos you can make, you only get one chance to design each logo: you can't go back and edit it later, aside from adjusting the color. Therefore, it's best to make sure you are 100% happy before you save your logo. After you click on **Save**, you'll be able to log in with your Squarespace login details, and then you'll get an email with a link to download your saved logo in a range of sizes.

To get the right size for use on your website, use the drop-down menu to choose **Up to 500px** for most templates, **Up to 1000px** if you will be using a very large logo (such as the Aviator template homepage), or **Up to 2000px** if you will be using it as a full-width header image.

Adding an image-based logo to your site

Before uploading your logo, first ensure that you have the correct file type and dimensions. Most templates use a small logo as part of the header, so it's unlikely you will need an image greater than 250 pixels wide. However, some templates allow you resize the logo area, so you could use a larger image in those cases.

 To keep loading times down, it's best not to use an image that is many times larger than what you need.

Refer back to *Chapter 1, Setting Up for Success – Your Website Toolkit,* for information about file types and other formatting for logos.

You can add your logo in the **Logo & Title** panel of the **Design** menu. This is shown in the following screenshot:

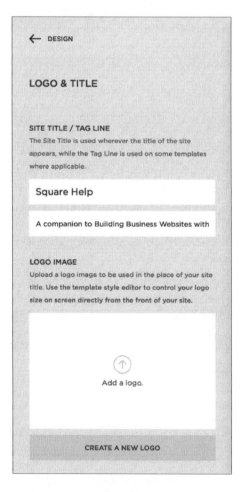

Look for the **Logo Image** area, and perform one of the following steps to upload or create a logo:

- Drag your logo file onto the image uploader area.
- Click on **Create a New Logo** to open the Squarespace Logo in a new browser window. Then, once you have finished, you can drag your newly created logo onto the image uploader area.

Adjusting logo size and positioning

If your logo does not appear the right size or position, you can sometimes make adjustments. Not all templates allow you to control the size or placement of the logo, but for those that do, you'll find the controls in the Style Editor. In the Preview screen, click on the logo and you will see controls that apply in the Style Editor panel. Some templates also allow you to choose the alignment or position of the logo in relation to the other header elements. This control is usually called Layout, Header Options, or something similar.

 Be careful not to resize the logo larger than the pixel dimensions of your logo image file. This will make the logo appear fuzzy or pixelated.

As mentioned earlier in this chapter, you may also need to crop or resize the logo image itself in order to get it to look the way you want on the website. Your logo file may have empty space around the logo graphic, which may prevent the logo from aligning with other page elements, as shown in the following example:

The space on the left of the logo is preventing alignment with the other page elements.

You can use the Aviary Image Editor to crop or resize logo images, just as you would any other kind of image. Simply hover over the logo thumbnail when you're in the **Logo & Title** panel, and click on the pencil icon as usual. However, if your logo is a dark color and/or on a transparent background, you may find it hard to see what you are doing because the Aviary Image Editor's editing window is very dark gray, and doesn't show the edges of files with transparent backgrounds. This is shown in the following example:

Logo with transparent background in Squarespace's Aviary Image Editor

You may find it easier to edit your logo image in Pixlr Editor, which shows transparency as a checkered grid background and shows the edges of the file, as shown in the following example:

Same logo in Pixlr Editor

 If resizing images in Aviary or Pixlr, never enlarge the image to a greater number of pixels than the original.

Adjusting your website's color scheme

Color can play a critical role in conveying your brand image to your target audience. In your Website Toolkit, you may already have one or more brand colors that you can use on your website. However, you may need to source additional colors or create a new color scheme from scratch. With an infinite number of colors to choose from, and an infinite number of color combinations, you could spend months trying to find the right ones to use. Fortunately, there are plenty of tools to help.

Before you dive into the wonderful world of color, here are some tips to help you focus and use color wisely on your website:

- A good place to start is with one **dominant color**, which will form the background of your pages, a **primary accent color**, for things such as page headings, navbar, or dividing lines, and a **secondary accent color** for link text or buttons.

- Because your dominant color will occupy the most space on the screen, it's usually best to avoid vibrant colors here, as they can be jarring. You should also consider how your website's image content will look with your dominant color.

- Ensure there is plenty of contrast between the color you choose for your main links and the color you use for other text or page elements. Important links and buttons should stand out. It's usually best to reserve a color for links alone, to prevent site visitors being confused by clicking on other things that are the same color, thinking they are links.

- To keep your body text readable, it's advisable to stick with shades of gray, or a very muted, muddy color if gray simply doesn't work with your other colors.

- If you are using pure white as your dominant color, you will find your pages are easier to read if you use a very dark gray instead of black for text. The same goes for using very pale gray for text on a pure black background.

Tools and resources for choosing colors

If you have saved some websites as color inspiration in your idea boards, or if you have a logo or other image that contains colors you'd like to use, you can identify the exact colors with a **color picker** tool. The color picker will supply the color's hex code that you can use in the Style Editor to apply color to your page elements. Refer back to *Chapter 1, Setting Up for Success – Your Website Toolkit,* if you need a reminder of what hex code is.

Copy and paste the color's hex code into a text document for easy reference, as you'll likely need to paste it into multiple places in the Style Editor. Don't forget to label your hex codes so you can easily tell which color is which.

Color picker tools

If you want to find out the colors used on a web page, you can install a color picker plugin for Firefox or Chrome browser that will allow you to click on any part of the web page to find out the color's hex code.

ColorZilla (`http://colorzilla.com/`) is the most popular free browser plugin for Chrome or Firefox, and is the one I recommend.

 There are plenty of other color picker plugins, but be careful when installing other plugins, because some have been known to install adware or malware too. You can also find color picker apps for your smartphone or tablet in the app store.

Plugins for Firefox are called **add-ons**, and can be found at `https://addons.mozilla.org/en-US/firefox/`.

Plugins for Chrome are called **extensions**, and can be found at `https://chrome.google.com/webstore/category/extensions`.

If you want to find colors from a logo, graphic, or photograph, the easiest way is to use the Colorpicker Tool in Pixlr Editor:

1. At `http://apps.pixlr.com/editor/`, choose **Open image from computer**. Browse to find the image on your computer.

2. Once the image opens in the editor, select the **eyedropper tool** from the toolbar on the left.

3. Click on the eyedropper on the point of the image that you want to use. This will sample the color and load it into the **main color** box at the bottom of the toolbar.

4. Click on the main color box to open the color selector overlay. You'll find the color's hex code in the box with a # character next to it, as shown in the following screenshot:

Resources for color schemes and color inspiration

If you are in need of color scheme inspiration, or you want to find colors that complement others that you already have, there are plenty of resources online to help you.

*   **ColourLovers** (http://www.colourlovers.com/) has a range of tools:

    o   http://www.colourlovers.com/palettes: Browse color palettes or search for palettes that contain a certain color by hex code

- ○ `http://www.colourlovers.com/palettes/add`: Create your own palette from scratch
  - ○ `http://www.colourlovers.com/colors`: Browse popular colors or search for a color range

- **ColorSchemer** (`http://colorschemer.com/schemes/`): Browse schemes, or search for schemes by key word or hex code
- **Adobe Kuler** (`http://kuler.adobe.com/`): Use **Explore** to browse or search for palettes by hex code or keyword or use **Create** to make your own schemes using different modes of color theory

Controlling the color and opacity of page elements

Now that you know the codes for the colors you want to use, you're ready to adjust the colors of elements in your Squarespace website. In the Style Editor, every page element with a color that you can control displays a dot of color next to it. Clicking on that dot opens the **color selector overlay**, as shown in the following screenshot:

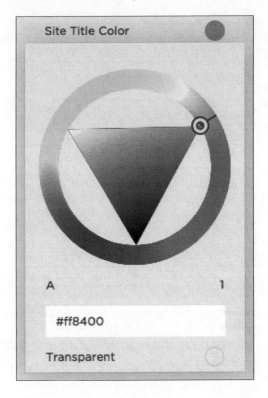

The color selector overlay has the following four elements:

- **Color wheel**: The inner triangle points to a dark line in the outer ring, indicating the overall hue of the color. The white ring inside the triangle indicates the exact shade of the color that is applied.
- **Opacity slider**: The slider allows you to make the element translucent by dragging along the scale from A (completely transparent) to 1 (completely opaque).
- **Color code box**: This indicates the hex code if the element is completely opaque, or the **RGBa value**, which is used for elements with any level of translucency.
- **Transparent checkbox**: This box allows you to hide the element by making it completely transparent. The box will automatically check if you drag the opacity slider all the way to the left.

 Checking the **Transparent** box will make the element invisible, but the space occupied by the element will still be there. This may result in unwanted spaces on the page.

To adjust the color of an element, you can either paste the hex code into the color code box or use the color wheel. If using the color wheel, you can:

- Drag the dark line around the outer ring to choose a different hue
- Drag the inner ring or click anywhere in the triangle to change the color's shade or value
- Choose a shade of gray by dragging the inner ring right up to the edge of the triangle that goes from white to black.

 If you want to use a specific color's hex code, *and* make that element translucent, always paste the hex code first, and then slide the opacity slider.

Using background or header images

Color is not the only way to introduce visual interest to your template: you can also use textures, patterns, or images in the background of the page or canvas. Using a subtle background texture or pattern can really help make your site feel more alive, but be careful not to overdo it with anything too distracting. Some templates also allow you to use a texture, pattern, or image in the header (banner) area.

Om template, with a banner image and subtle background texture

Squarespace has settings that can repeat (or **tile**) a pattern or texture vertically and horizontally so that it fills the entire space of the screen. If you choose this approach, make sure you use an image that is designed for **seamless** tiling/repeating. The edges of these images match up and blend smoothly, so you'll see a continuous texture rather than a bunch of square blocks. Some of my favorite resources for textures and patterns are:

- **SubtlePatterns** (`http://subtlepatterns.com/`): This contains hundreds of free seamless patterns

- **DeviantArt** (`http://deviantart.com/`): Search for `seamless, texture` to find thousands of textures, many of which you can use free of charge (check the individual image page for rules/restrictions, as they vary)

- **ColourLovers** (`http://www.colourlovers.com/seamless`): This allows you to design your own pattern

Some templates allow you to set a background image that fills the entire screen, with the page content floating in a box or column above it.

Same content as the previous example, but in the Aviator template with a fullscreen background image.

Others, such as Bedford or Marquee, use large full-width banner images, with text or buttons floating on top. In cases like these, evocative photographs can look better than simple textures, but you'll need to be careful to ensure your photograph isn't too busy and doesn't compete with the page content.

 Some templates allow you to apply a translucent color overlay to background or banner images. This can be a great way to subdue a photograph and/or make creative use of an accent color.

Here are a couple of my favorite places to find photography suitable for backgrounds or banners:

- **Unsplash** (`https://unsplash.com/grid`): This contains hundreds of beautiful photographs, free for you to use however you like
- **Creative Market** (`https://creativemarket.com/`): The items here are not free, but most cost only a few dollars

Creative Market is also a great place to find seamless textures or patterns, too: use the **Graphics** menu to choose **Patterns** or **Textures**.

Follow these steps to add an image, pattern, or texture to the background or header:

1. In the Style Editor panel, locate the element you wish to change, such as Site Background Image or Banner Image.

 Elements that can have images show an icon that looks like mountains on a gray background, as shown here:

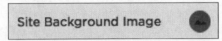

2. Click on the element to open the image settings overlay, as shown in the following screenshot:

3. Drag the image you want to use onto the image uploader arrow or use the Getty Images browser to locate a suitable stock image to purchase.

4. Once the image has loaded, you can adjust the following settings to ensure the image or pattern displays the way you want:

   ○ **Position**: This sets where the image should be positioned in relation to the screen or header space.

   ○ **Size**: Choose **auto** for seamless tiles or certain photographs, **cover** if you want the image to stretch to fill the space, or **contain** if you want the image to be cropped to fit the space.

   ○ **Repeat**: Choose **none** for photographs or non-tiling textures, **repeat** if you want the texture to tile across and down to fill the screen, **repeat-x** if you only want the image to repeat horizontally, or **repeat-y** if you only want the image to repeat vertically.

   ○ **Fix position**: If you want the background to remain static in one position, while the rest of the page scrolls, check this box.

 After adding an image to the header or background, always check how it looks on multiple screen sizes. You may need to adjust the position, size, or other settings to ensure it looks good on every type of device.

Other ways to adjust header or banner images

You may not be able to find a space to upload your header or banner image in the Style Editor, even though your template definitely allows for one. Some template designers have chosen not to include this in the Style Editor, so you will have to set the image on a page-by-page basis in the Pages menu, using **Thumbnail Image** under **Page Settings**. Just bear in mind that there may be other settings in the Style Editor that affect the appearance of this image, such as Banner Overlay or Banner Height.

In certain templates, you can set an overall default banner image in the Style Editor, and then override this image with a different one on a page-by-page basis using **Thumbnail Image** under **Page Settings**. In this case, whatever settings you have applied to the default image, such as repeat or position, will apply to the images that you set on other pages.

Adjusting an element's size, position, visibility, or other options

Once you've added your logo, set the text sizes, and possibly added a banner or background image, you'll be able to tell if your pages feel crowded, empty, or top/bottom-heavy. You can fix these problems by adjusting the width or height of elements, the **spacing** between or **padding** around elements, or the location of certain things on the page. You may also be able to turn on or off certain elements, depending on the template you're using.

Follow these steps to adjust the width, height, padding, or spacing of an element:

1. With the Style Editor panel open, click on the element or the part of the page you want to adjust in the preview screen.

2. Drag the slider, or click on the number and type the new value. The slider and value is shown in the following screenshot:

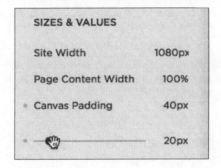

 You may want to consider installing the Chrome extension/Firefox add-on called **MeasureIt**, or similar page ruler plugin. This will allow you to measure the size of things on your website by dragging a box around whatever you want to measure, and MeasureIt will display the exact pixel dimensions.

Controlling element visibility and other options

Some templates allow you to turn on or off certain elements, such as a sidebar or page title, or to position elements in relation to others, such as aligning the logo to the left or right of the page.

In most templates, you'll find these settings in the Style Editor, and some template designers have made it even easier by grouping all of these elements together.

 In certain cases, you won't find your sidebar settings in the Style Editor; instead, you'll find these controls in the Pages menu, under Page Settings | Layout.

Adjusting Cover Page styles

The adjustments that we've discussed in the Style Editor panel will apply to all pages on your website aside from Cover Pages. Cover Pages are special and their elements must be set and adjusted independently. The types of controls and the methods for adjusting them are the same as those described in the earlier part of this chapter; the only difference is that the style settings for a Cover Page can be accessed in the following two different ways:

- In the Pages menu, click on the name of the Cover Page to open the **Cover Page** panel. You can now adjust the style elements using the **Style** button at the bottom, or add a logo using the **Branding & Text** button.

- Navigate to the Cover Page and then open the Style Editor panel. This will open the same set of controls as you would access through the Cover Page panel's Style button. However, you will not be able to access the logo settings for the Cover Page from here. You will need to use the previous method to add/edit a Cover Page logo, using the **Branding & Text** button.

 If you are using more than one Cover Page, you will need to set the style elements for each Cover Page individually.

Summary

By now, your website should be looking pretty fantastic. If you're not happy with it yet and are feeling the need for some design inspiration, you can visit `www.square-help.com/inspiration` for ideas.

In this chapter, we've covered all of the ways you can adjust the aesthetics of your website so that it matches your brand image and resonates with your target audience. Hopefully, you've been able to adjust everything so that it looks exactly the way you want it to look, but you may have found that your template doesn't allow you to adjust everything to your liking or you've reached the limits of your visual design skills. If this is the case, you may need to bring in some professional help or try using some more advanced techniques yourself. We'll cover both of these options in *Chapter 11, Moving beyond Standard Squarespace Tools*, but remember that a website is an ever-evolving thing. It's not like a printed brochure, where you slave away until it's absolutely perfect, then send it off to print, never to be adjusted again. Websites are never really "finished", because a good website will always be refreshed with new content or new features over time. Consider whether what you have now is good enough to launch, to keep your project deadlines on target. It's usually better to go live and promote your company with something that's 90 percent there, than to delay for that extra 10 percent.

In the next chapter, we'll go through all of the steps you need to launch your site successfully. Before you move on to this final stage, take a moment to pat yourself on the back and reflect on all that you have achieved so far. It's also a good time to tie up any loose ends or missing content that you might be waiting on from others. Ensure that you, your colleagues, and your Squarespace site are ready for the final stretch before the finish line.

9
Going Live with Your Website and Driving Traffic to It

By now, your website should be more or less finished, and ready to go live. It's OK if you don't have absolutely everything in perfect order yet: you can disable some less important pages if they're not quite ready, as long as your main pages are ready to face the public. In this chapter, we'll configure your final site settings, run through all of the pre-flight checks that need to take place before launch, and set up social media accounts and sharing buttons that can help drive traffic to your site once it's live. When all is looking tip-top, we'll finally configure the account and domain settings to launch your shiny new website into the world.

We will cover:

- Connecting to social media accounts
- Enabling social sharing and Pinterest pinning
- Adjusting the final pre-launch details
- Testing, testing, and more testing
- Setting up a custom domain name, including moving from an existing website to your Squarespace site
- Making your website live to the public
- Making your site visible to search engines
- Using your blog and social media to drive traffic to your site

Connecting to social media accounts

Connecting your social media accounts to Squarespace will not only enable your site to display **social icons** that link to your profile on those sites, but it can also allow you to promote your Squarespace website content on those sites, too. When you go live with your new website, it's likely that you will want to announce this in all of your social media profiles, such as Facebook, Twitter, or LinkedIn. Moving forward, you will probably want to do the same whenever you publish a new post or news item in your Squarespace blog. Luckily, Squarespace can automatically publish to certain social media accounts for you, so you don't have to do it manually. What's more, if you have a brand/business or fan page on Facebook, you can even display some of your Squarespace website's pages or galleries as tabs in your Facebook page.

Earlier in *Chapter 6, Using Blocks to Add Functionality, Rich Media, and Special Features*, we looked at ways to automatically pull in content from external sites into content blocks, such as Flickr photos or tweets from Twitter. In this chapter, we'll connect to social accounts to push content out from Squarespace to social sites.

Pushing and pulling content is not the only way social media can work for you: you can also use **Share Buttons** to allow site visitors to easily promote your content on their social networks, increasing your site's visibility and reach.

The following are the different social networking sites you can connect to Squarespace, and the different functions you can enable through this connection:

Site	Social Icon	Share Button	Push Content	Pull In Content	Other
Facebook	Yes	Yes	Yes		Show page/Gallery on Facebook page
Twitter	Yes	Yes	Yes	Yes	
Google +	Yes	Yes			
LinkedIn	Yes	Yes	Yes		
Pinterest	Yes	Yes			Show Pin it icon on images (only in Collection pages with images)
Instagram	Yes			Yes	
Tumblr	Yes	Yes	Yes		
YouTube	Yes				Manually add videos using a Video Block

Site	Social Icon	Share Button	Push Content	Pull In Content	Other
Vimeo	Yes				Manually add videos using a Video Block
Foursquare	Yes			Yes	
Flickr	Yes			Yes	
500px	Yes			Yes	
SmugMug	Yes				Import SmugMug Galleries
Dribble	Yes				
StumbleUpon		Yes			
Reddit		Yes			
GitHub	Yes				
SoundCloud	Yes			Yes	
Spotify	Yes				Embed a song player
iTunes	Yes				Connect to track, app, e-book, or podcast on your site
Google Play	Yes				Connect to track, app, and more on your site
Dropbox					Publish images uploaded to Dropbox in a Gallery page

Before we launch your site, we'll set up your social account connections and Share Buttons, as you'll want to see how they look and work before you go live with your website. Later in this chapter, we'll configure the more advanced social settings that can help promote your website once it's live.

Setting up Connected Accounts

For all accounts that have social icons, you will need to connect your social media account to Squarespace in the **Connected Accounts** panel of **Settings | Social**, as shown in the following screenshot:

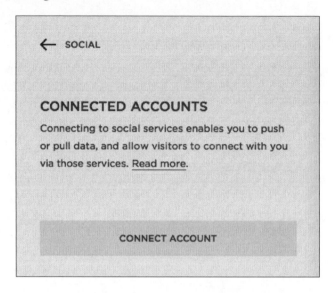

 If you added a Twitter, Flickr, or other social content block to any of your pages earlier, you will see those accounts have already been connected.

To connect a social media account, follow these steps:

1. Click on the **Connect Account** button. This will open the **Add Account** overlay window, as shown in the following screenshot:

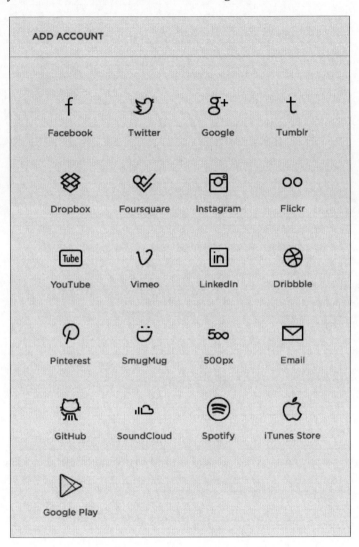

2. Click on the icon that corresponds to the account you wish to add. A pop-up window will open, asking you to enter your login credentials for that website. The following screenshot shows the Twitter authorization screen:

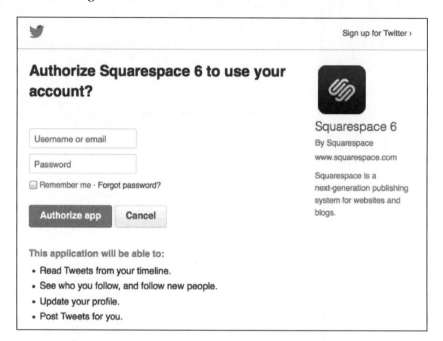

 If you can't see the pop-up window, ensure you have turned off any pop-up blockers used by your browser. If you are currently logged into the social media site and you have previously authorized it, Squarespace may bypass the pop-up window and automatically enable the connection.

3. Enter your username and password for the account. Depending on the specific site you are connecting to, you may need to enter additional details or authorize additional access on another screen.

4. Once the connection between the social site and Squarespace has gone through successfully, the popup will close, and you will see the connection listed on the **Connected Accounts** page, as shown in the following screenshot:

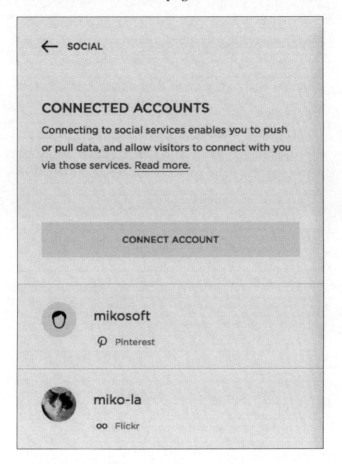

Although it's not a social media site, you can also connect to **Dropbox** using these same steps. Connecting to Dropbox allows you add images to certain folders in your Dropbox and publish them to Gallery pages. Find out more about this feature at `http://help.squarespace.com/guides/connecting-dropbox-with-squarespace`.

You can also use these steps to add an **email icon** that will allow visitors to send an email using their email software. As mentioned in *Chapter 4*, *Creating Your Site Framework: Pages, Items, Collections, and Navigation*, be wary of using this unless you are prepared to deal with spam.

Displaying social icons

As discussed earlier in this book, most templates will display social icons for all Connected Accounts, usually in the footer or header of your site, as shown in the following screenshot:

If you have not yet seen how your template handles social icons, take a moment now to look in the preview screen for the icons for the social sites you connected just now. You may also want to go into the Style Editor to adjust the appearance of your social icons, if necessary.

Using a Social Links block

If your template does not include social icons as part of the template itself, or if you would like to display them somewhere other than where they show on your template, you can also add social icons using a **Social Links** Block. You can add a Social Links block anywhere that a Block can go, but most people choose to add it to the footer or sidebar. The Social Links Block has configuration options that control the appearance of the icons, as shown in the following screenshot:

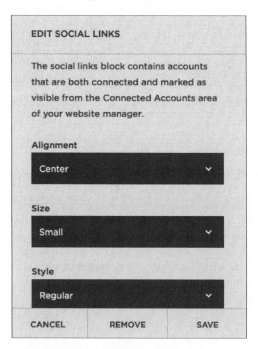

The Social Links icon configuration options are:

- **Style**: Choose round, square, or icon only (without a shape around it).
- **Size**: Choose small, medium, or large.
- **Alignment**: Choose aligned left, right, or centered in the space.
- **Color**: Choose black, white, or standard. Standard uses the brand colors of the social sites, resulting in colorful icons. The following screenshot shows standard colored icons in a sidebar:

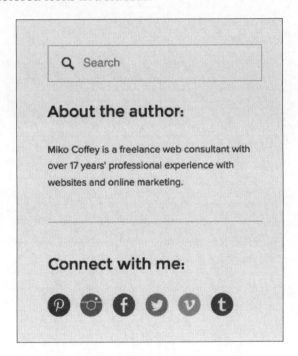

Showing or hiding individual social icons

Some templates allow you to turn off the systematic social icons entirely using an option in Style Editor, but there may be instances when you want to connect to a particular social account, but not display its icon. You can enable or disable social icons individually in the Connected Accounts panel of **Settings | Social**.

Follow these steps to show or hide the icon for a Connected Account:

1. In **Connected Accounts**, click on the name of the account you wish to change. This will open the Settings overlay for that account's connection.

2. Check/uncheck the box next to **Show Social Icon** to turn on/off the icon's display.

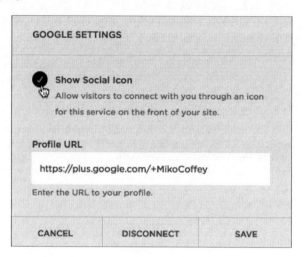

 Your screen may show additional items depending on which social account you are adjusting.

3. Click on **Save**.

Enabling social sharing on your website

Word of mouth is a good way to attract new potential customers, so if you'd like to allow your website visitors to easily promote your website to their friends, you should turn on the Squarespace **Share Buttons**. The Share Button appears at the bottom of each blog post, as indicated in the following screenshot:

Clicking on the condensed button or link will open an overlay with links to popular social networks, as shown in the following screenshot:

If you'd like to encourage Pinterest users to pin images from your site, you can also enable a **Pinterest Pin-It Button** that will appear as a small icon whenever someone hovers over an image on your blog or web pages.

 Social sharing is great for search engine optimization, so you should definitely make it as easy as possible for people to link to your website through their social accounts. The more links you have pointing to your site, the better.

You can enable the social network Share Buttons and/or the Pinterest Pin-It Button in the **Share Buttons** panel of **Settings | Social**. Simply check/uncheck the box next to each social network name to turn on/off the button for that website, as shown in the following screenshot:

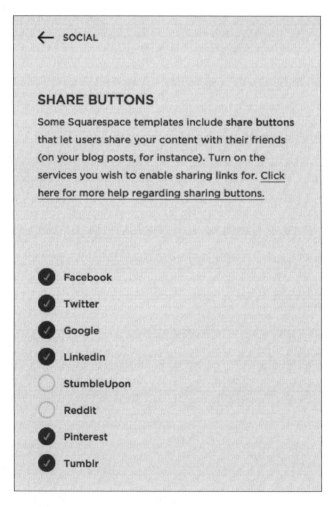

Below the set of checkboxes, you will see that the Pinterest Pin-It Button is set to **Disabled** by default, but you can choose **Enabled for Blogs** or **Enabled for Blogs and Pages**. Once you enable it, the panel will open a preview example image, and show the additional button options you can configure, as shown in the following screenshot:

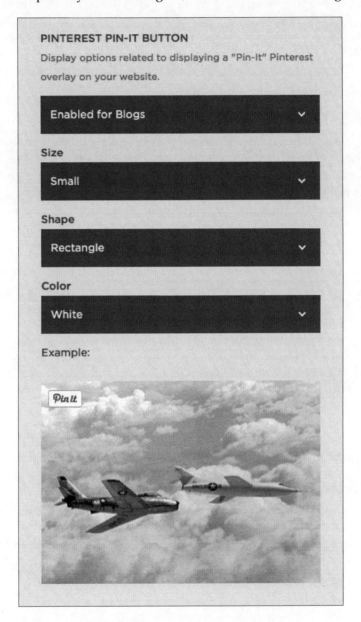

Adjusting the final details in your site settings

In this part of the chapter, we will go through a few final adjustments to your site's settings that you may want to perform before you test your website for launch. We'll only cover the most commonly used settings, so if you have specialized needs, you may want to refer to `http://help.squarespace.com/ guides/?category=Settings` for further information on all settings.

Adding a Browser Icon (Favicon)

You can add a custom icon that will display in the browser window next to the page name, or in the Bookmarks area if someone marks one of your pages as a favorite. This is called a **Browser Icon** or **Favicon**, and you can upload an image to use for your Squarespace site in the **Logo & Title** panel, accessed through the **Design** menu. An example of a custom browser icon is shown in the following screenshot:

Your icon image file should be square format, and the icon should be on a transparent background, unless you want a colored square to show around it. If you need to create or convert an image to an icon, try `http://converticon.com/`.

Squarespace displays its own icon when you are logged in, so you will need to log out in order to see your custom icon.

Using Google Analytics with your Squarespace site

Squarespace includes basic website analysis tools built into the system, so you don't need to use any external measurement tools if you only need standard reporting. However, if you prefer to use a more advanced tool, you can add your **Google Analytics Account Number** to track your site using Google Analytics. You'll find this setting in **Settings** | **Advanced** | **External Services**.

We will cover how to use Squarespace analytics in the next chapter.

Adjusting SEO settings: description, title, and URL formats

In the **Settings** | **SEO** panel, Squarespace allows you to specify the default description that appears in search engine results below your website's URL, as well as adjusting the format of your page titles in the browser window, and the way your item and collection URLs are constructed. When you open the **SEO** panel, the first thing you should do is set the **Search Engine Description:** use up to 155 characters of enticing, descriptive text.

Next, you'll notice that there are default settings pre-loaded in the various **Title Format** boxes, and you'll also see a **?** icon on the far right of each field. Hovering over this icon will bring up the **variable** formatting help menu, showing special codes (variables) that you can use to insert certain text, such as the collection or item title, into the field. This is illustrated in the following screenshot:

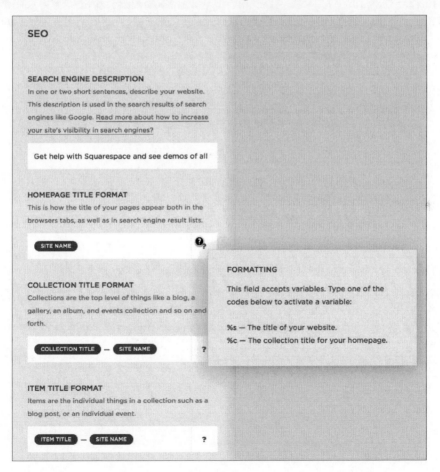

These variables are like **shortcodes** (or shortcuts) that the Squarespace system uses to pull in data and display it in certain places. For example, instead of having to type out the full name of your site, typing %s will insert the Site Name. You'll learn about other variables later in this chapter.

Consider adjusting **Homepage Title Format** to include some enticing words, as this will be shown as the link to your website on search engine results pages. Here are some examples:

- Standard format (Site Name only): *Using My Head*
- Better format: *Using My Head – London Squarespace design and support*

Configuring blog settings

If you have a Blog page in your site, you may want to adjust some of the settings found in the **Settings | Blogging** panel. Here, you can set the **Post URL Format**, enable **Simple Liking**, and set how your site will handle comments. Simple Liking is similar to the Facebook *like* feature: it's a quick and simple way for visitors to indicate the value of a post, without having to login or post a full comment.

The **Like** button usually appears near the **Share** button on a blog post, and displays a heart icon. The following is an example of the Like button:

By default, Squarespace allows comments on all blog posts, so if you don't want people to be able to comment on your posts, you can disable comments in **Comments Settings**, where you can also adjust a range of settings that control how comments appear, whether they will be moderated, and whether others can flag inappropriate comments. Each of these settings is accompanied by explanatory text, and each person's needs will be different, so we won't go into the detail of each setting here. However, I do recommend that you consider selecting **Require Approval** to avoid comment spam.

We will cover how to manage and respond to comments in the next chapter.

Testing your site before launch

Before you make your website visible to the public, it's important to thoroughly test that everything is looking and working as it should. This includes not only the things you can see on your pages, but also the settings and functions that may not be immediately visible. To help ensure you don't miss anything, this part of the chapter can be used as a checklist of items to review and test before you go live.

Verify that your site works at all sizes

Check the display of *every page* on multiple screen sizes and device types. If you are using multiple column layout, or a sidebar, make sure that the page still makes sense on smaller screens where the columns may shift to a stacked view with vertical scrolling. Pay special attention to other layouts that may adjust on smaller screens, such as Gallery grids, too.

 Remember to test any pages that are enabled but in your **Not Linked** section (if you have them), not just the pages in your main navigation.

Fine-tune your site and page elements with SEO in mind

Remember that Page Titles, Page Descriptions, URLs, and headings (H1, H2, H3) are used by search engines, and will be displayed in the search results pages. Make sure that *every* page is using these elements correctly, and that none of the hidden settings such as Page Description is left empty.

Thoroughly test all of your site functions

If you are using forms or comments, submit a few test entries. If you are using Squarespace Commerce, make sure you have tested *all* elements of your store: making purchases (including multi-product orders), managing orders, using different shipping options, sending customer emails, giving refunds, cancelling orders, and ensuring that every product variant is listed correctly. You should also test any embedded functions, such as a newsletter sign-up form from an external website.

Ensure your media files look the way they should

If you are using photo galleries with a lightbox overlay or caption on hover, click/hover on *every* image to make sure the overlay is displaying correctly. If you have any videos or audio files embedded, *play them all the way through* to look out for glitches.

Look out for broken links

Click on *all* of the links on your website: in your navigation, within the text, social icons, and any other links to pages, websites, or downloadable files. If you are linking to external websites, make sure you are doing so in a consistent manner: either always open these types of links in a new window or never open them in a new window.

Double-check your tags and categories

If you are using tags and/or categories on your container pages, open *every* item in the container and double-check that the correct tags/categories have been assigned.

Verify that your social blocks are automatically pulling in fresh content

Whenever you add a Twitter, 500px, Flickr, Foursquare, or Instagram content block to your site, the system normally defaults to the correct setting to ensure that all the content being pulled in from the external site is automatically refreshed whenever you add new content there. However, if you notice that your social block is not displaying your latest tweets, check-ins, or photos, there are a couple of things you can do.

First, open the account settings in **Settings | Social | Connected Accounts**, and ensure that the **Download Data** box is checked, as shown in the following screenshot:

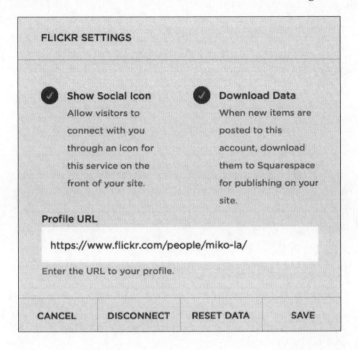

The Download Data option ensures that your Squarespace block is synchronized with the social site. If you are still having problems, try using the **Reset Data** button at the bottom of the settings overlay.

Making your website live to the public

You're finally ready to flip the switch to make your website live to the public. The process for doing this depends on whether you have an existing website that you need to turn off, or whether your Squarespace site is your first/only website for your company. We'll cover both of these now.

We're assuming you have already set up billing on your account. If you have not yet done so, and are still on a trial account, refer back to the *Setting up your subscription plan and billing* section in *Chapter 2, Getting Started with Squarespace*.

Removing the site-wide password protection

The first step to going live is the same, regardless of your situation: you need to remove the password protection that we set up in *Chapter 2, Getting Started with Squarespace*, to make your site visible on its Squarespace URL. To do this, go to **Settings | Security** and simply delete the password (shown by a series of dots), and click on **Save**.

> You may want to log out and/or try visiting the site in a different browser to ensure that the password protection has been removed.

That's it: technically, you have just published your website. However, it's unlikely that you'll want to use the Squarespace URL (`http://your-company.squarespace.com`) as the web address for your site, so the next step is to enable your custom domain name.

Setting up a custom domain

There are three ways to use a custom domain with your Squarespace site:

- Register a new domain through Squarespace (free if you pay your subscription annually)
- Link up your Squarespace site with an existing domain that you purchased elsewhere
- Transfer your existing Squarespace 5 domain name

You can set up any of these options in the **Domains** panel of the **Settings** menu, as shown in the following screenshot:

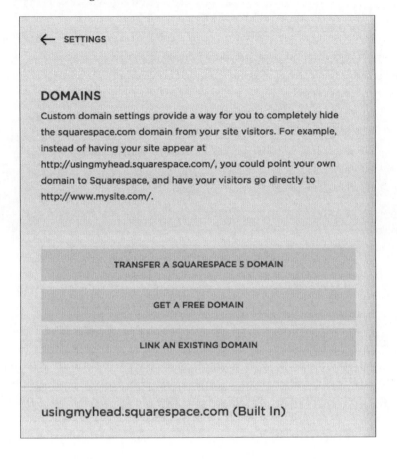

Registering a new domain through Squarespace

If you have set up your billing to pay annually, you will see a **Get a Free Domain** button. You can register one free domain per account.

Even if you already have another domain name that you want to use for your website, you may want to use this free domain name to purchase another variant. For example, if you own yourcompany.co.uk, you could use your free Squarespace domain to get yourcompany.com, too.

This is particularly useful if you already own a country-specific domain such as .co.uk because it's common for people to try .com if they don't know your web address.

Follow the given steps to register your free domain name:

1. Click on the **Get a Free Domain** button. This will open the **Register Domain** overlay.

2. Enter the domain name you wish to register, and choose the **extension** using the drop-down menu. You can choose .com, .org, .net, .biz, .info, or .mobi format. If the domain you choose is not available, try again with a different wording or extension.

3. Click on the **Add** button. This will open a confirmation message.

4. Click on the **Register** button. This will close the overlay and you will see the domain name in the **Domains** screen.

It can take up to 72 hours for new domains to start working. You'll notice an alert message next to your domain if it's not working yet.

Using an existing domain name

If you already own a domain name that you would like to point to your Squarespace site, you can do this through **domain mapping**, but you'll need access to the domain management tools offered by your domain provider, and it can be a little technical.

If you use this domain for other services, such as email, you may want to consult technical support from your domain provider unless you are confident adjusting DNS settings.

If you are using this domain with an existing website, ensure you have read and performed the steps in the following *Moving from an existing website to Squarespace* section *before* you map the domain.

To make the process easier, Squarespace have created a detailed step-by-step guide to help you map your domain to your Squarespace site. They have even created videos and instructions with screenshot walkthroughs for some of the most popular domain providers, such as GoDaddy, Bluehost, and 1&1. You can find all of this on the Squarespace Help site at http://help.squarespace.com/guides/mapping-a-domain-general-instructions.

It can take up to 72 hours for the domain mapping to go through.

If you have purchased web hosting through your domain supplier to host your old/existing website, once you transfer your domain to Squarespace, you'll no longer need the hosting. You can then cancel the web hosting to get rid of your old website, and just continue paying for the domain name each year.

Moving from an existing website to Squarespace

This is very important, so please read the following section carefully. If you are using this domain name with another website hosted elsewhere, changing the mapping will turn off the existing site. Unless you have copied your old site's structure exactly when creating your new Squarespace site by using all of the exact same page URLs, people may see a **404 – Page Not Found** error when trying to access URLs from your old site. Furthermore, if you had a good search engine ranking for certain pages on your old site, you could lose this ranking when you move to the new site unless you take action before the move.

You can avoid these problems by implementing **URL mappings** in Squarespace. URL mappings are like *Change of Address* instructions that the post office uses whenever you move to a different house. The type of URL mapping you should use is called a **301 redirect**, which is a permanent change of address.

Before you change your domain mapping to point to your Squarespace site, you should go through your existing site and write down the **relative URLs** for all of the existing pages. A relative URL is the part of the URL without the domain name on the front, for example /mypage/ is the relative URL for www.mysite.com/mypage/.

For each page, you should identify the new page on your website where you want the 301 redirect code to point, and write the relative URLs for the new pages next to the old pages. A spreadsheet might come in handy for this.

If the two relative URLs are exactly the same, you don't need to worry about creating a 301 redirect for that page.

The final step is to set up the mappings in the **URL Mappings** panel of **Advanced** panel under **Settings**. In the code box on this screen, you should type your URL mappings, one per line, using the following code format:

```
/original-page/ -> /new-page/ 301
```

If you need help, there is a link to the Squarespace
help page preceding the code box.

Once you click on **Save**, this will ensure that all traffic to the old page, including
search engines, will find the new page successfully.

Transferring a Squarespace 5 domain

If you have a domain name that is already managed by Squarespace through an
existing Squarespace 5 account, you can transfer it to your new Squarespace 7 account.
Once you transfer the domain, you can cancel your Squarespace 5 account to close
down your old Squarespace website.

To transfer your domain from your Squarespace 5 site to your Squarespace 7 site
follow these steps:

1. Click on the **Transfer a Squarespace 5 Domain** button. This will open the
   domain overlay window.

2. Enter the domain name you wish to transfer.

3. Enter the login details for your Squarespace 5 account.

4. Click on the **Transfer Domain** button. This will close the overlay and you
   will see the domain name in the **Domains** screen.

Using custom email addresses with your custom domain

Squarespace has partnered with Google Apps to allow you to create and use email
addresses that match your custom domain name. Google Apps costs $5 per month
per email address, and your subscription gives you access to other Google Apps
features such as Google Calendar and Google Drive. Squarespace has an extensive
help guide on setting up and using Google Apps with your custom domain at
`http://help.squarespace.com/guides/google-apps-and-squarespace`.

You can also find out more about the Google Apps features at `https://www.`
`google.com/work/apps/business/`.

Make sure you have disabled the site-wide password before you
sign up with Google Apps, or else the Google domain verification
process becomes quite complicated.

Managing your domain and URLs

Whenever you map, register, or transfer a custom domain to your Squarespace 7 site, the system will automatically make that domain your **primary domain**. You can map as many domains as you want to your Squarespace site, but all other custom domains will automatically redirect to your primary domain. The primary domain will be the web address that shows in the browser bar. You can change which domain is your primary domain in the **Settings | Domains** panel, by the clicking on the **Make Primary** button under the domain name.

Your Squarespace URL will always be active, even if you use a custom domain. For this reason, it's important to be careful when copying/pasting URLs from your Squarespace site, especially while logged in.

 If sending links in an email or pasting them elsewhere, make sure you are viewing/copying while on the primary domain.

If you are creating links to other pages within a Squarespace page, it's always best to use the built-in **content finder** in the link tool in the text editor toolbar, rather than pasting URLs. The following screenshot shows the link tool content finder:

When you click on **Content** and browse to find to the page you want, the link tool uses relative URLs to ensure that your links will not be affected by changes to the primary domain. Notice that the relative URL is shown in the following screenshot:

The link tool has used the relative URL /blog, rather than the full URL www.mysite.com/blog

Sometimes, you won't be able to use the link tool's content finder — for example, if linking to a specific blog post or product page. If this is the case, you'll need to paste the URL into the **External** field, even though you're linking to an internal page. Be sure to use the *relative URL only*, rather than copying/pasting the entire URL into the link box. An example is shown as follows:

Driving traffic to your website

Now that your website is live, you'll need to take action to ensure that the site is visible to search engines. If you use Facebook, Twitter, or other social media, you can also use these sites to drive traffic to your Squarespace website, as mentioned earlier when setting up your Connected Accounts.

Making your website visible to Google and other search engines

Google, Bing, Yahoo, or any other search engine will not be able to magically sense that you have a new website. If you are using a brand new domain, you will need to tell these search engines that your new site exists.

 If you are using an existing domain that is already visible to search engines, bear in mind it can take a little while for the search engines to index the new content on your new site, so you may see some results for your old pages for a while after launching the new site.

The absolute best way to make your site visible to all search engines is to get an existing website to link to yours. This will alert all search engines that there's a new website out there, and if the site linking to you is also in your industry, then you'll get a little extra boost in the rankings, too.

Another easy way to show search engines that your website exists is by linking to it through Twitter or other social media website. We won't be able to cover all of the ins and outs of how search engines work; that's a whole other book entirely. However, as a rule, the more links from relevant and/or popular websites you can get, the better (within reason— there are penalties for spamming search engines!). Include a link in your email signature, on your social media profile pages, in a status update, whenever you write a review or comment on another website— these are just a few simple ways to build links to your site.

Lastly, you can also submit your website to the major search engines directly. There is no guarantee that this will speed up the process of having your site indexed, but it certainly can't hurt. Here's where you can submit your website (you may be required to create an account first):

- **Google**: `https://www.google.com/webmasters/tools/submit-url`
- **Bing**: `http://www.bing.com/toolbox/submit-site-url`
- **Yahoo**: `http://search.yahoo.com/info/submit.html`

Using social media to drive traffic to your site

Squarespace has several built-in tools that can make promoting your website through social media really easy. To use these tools, make sure you have connected your accounts, as described earlier in this chapter.

Automatically promoting news or blog posts

If you have a blog on your Squarespace site, now is the perfect time to write a new post announcing your new website, and to use Squarespace's automatic **push option** to post a link to this announcement on your social media profiles.

You can enable the push option if you want to automatically promote posts from your Squarespace blog on your Facebook, Twitter, LinkedIn, and/or Tumblr accounts. The push option allows you to decide, on a post-by-post basis, on an account-by-account basis, whether to publish a link to that post on Facebook, LinkedIn, or Twitter, or to publish the entire post onto Tumblr. You can also set the **default posting format**, which determines the structure of what is posted on your social site. You'll always want to include the URL link, but you can also set up default text that should accompany the link—for example, "Check out my latest blog post"— as well as include the post title and/or author as part of the tweet/Facebook status update.

It's a good idea to set something very general for your default text, if anything. You will be able to override the default and use more specific words when posting each blog post.

You don't need to set a default posting format for Tumblr, because Squarespace will automatically publish the entire post as a new post in your Tumblog.

Enabling the push option

You can enable the push option and set the default posting format in the **Connected Accounts** panel of **Social** panel under **Settings**. Follow the given steps to enable the push option for Facebook, Twitter, LinkedIn, or Tumblr:

1. In **Connected Accounts**, click on the account name to open the settings overlay. An example of the LinkedIn overlay is shown in the following screenshot:

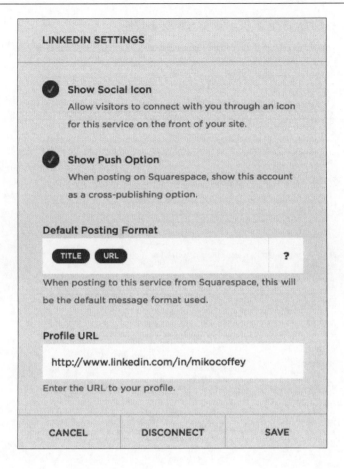

2. Check the **Show Push Option** box.

3. If desired/applicable, set the **Default Posting Format**. You can hover over the **?** icon for information on the variable codes to use to display the author, title, or URL.

4. If pushing to Facebook, you can also adjust the following settings:

    ° **Push Target**: If you have multiple Facebook pages, select the page you want to push to

    ° **Impersonate Page**: Check this box to post to the timeline as the page itself (recommended)

5. Click on **Save**.

Pushing a blog post to a social site

Once you have enabled the push option, you will be able to choose whether to push each blog post to each of the social sites you have set up for pushing.

Follow these steps to push a post to a social site:

1. After writing or editing a post in the **Edit Post** overlay, click on the **Social** link at the top right to open the **Social** screen. The Social screen is shown in the following screenshot:

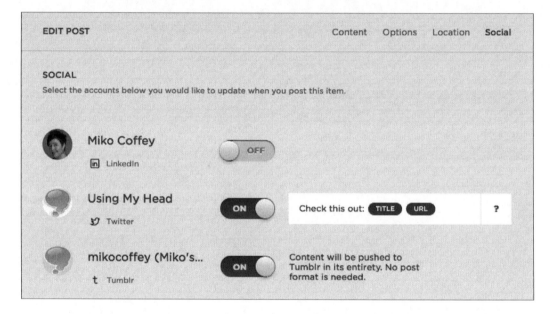

2. Use the toggle to turn on the account(s) you'd like to promote this post on.
3. If desired/applicable, you can adjust the wording/format of the post from the default. You can use variables for the author, title, and/or URL, if you wish.

4. Click on **Save** (if editing an old post or draft) or **Save and Publish** (if publishing a new post). This will publish the post *immediately* to your selected social site(s). The following screenshot shows an example of how the pushed post appears on Twitter:

 Only use this method once your website is live. If you are still preparing your website for launch, you can either schedule your post(s) to automatically publish and push on a future date, or save it as a draft and publish/push it manually later.

Displaying a Squarespace page or Gallery in your Facebook page

If you are on the Professional or Business subscription plan, you can display a page and/or Gallery from your Squarespace website as a tab in your Facebook brand/business or fan page.

 If you don't yet have a Facebook page for your business, you can sign up for one at https://www.facebook.com/about/pages?_rdr.

You can set up Facebook page promotion in the **Facebook Page** panel of **Settings | Social** as shown in the following screenshot:

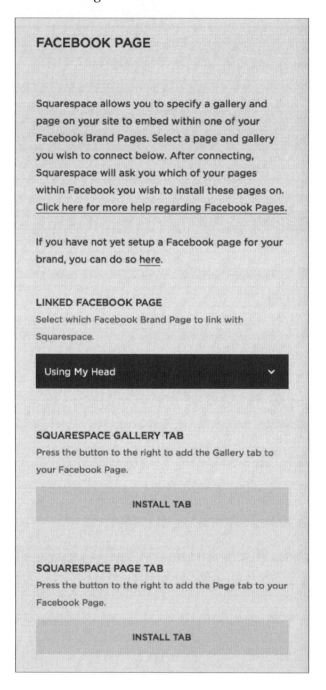

Follow these steps to display a page or Gallery on your Facebook page:

1. Under **Linked Facebook Page**, select the Facebook page where you want to install your tab.

2. If you want to install a Gallery as a tab on your Facebook page, click on the **Install Tab** button under **Squarespace Gallery Tab** (or click on the button under **Squarespace Page Tab** to install a page). This will open two new fields on the screen, as shown in the following screenshot:

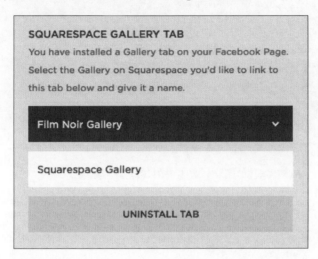

- ○ Use the drop-down menu to choose which Gallery/page you want to display
- ○ Type the words you want to appear as the Facebook tab name in the text box

3. Once you click on **Save**, your tab will be visible on your Facebook page, as shown in the following example:

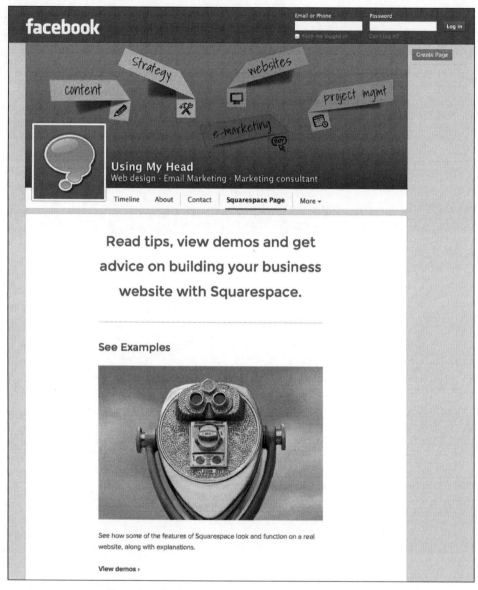

Homepage from www.square-help.com as a Facebook tab

On your Facebook page, if you can't see your tab or you want to change the order of your tabs, click on the **More** drop-down menu at the end of the row of tabs.

The styling of your page/Gallery may look slightly different on Facebook than it does on your Squarespace website.

Summary

Congratulations! You have successfully launched your new website, and you've taken the first steps toward marketing your website and bringing customers to it. In the next chapter, you'll learn how to use Squarespace tools for managing your site from this point onward. There are some useful tools that may come in handy during the early days of your new website (as well as later on), so you may want to dive straight into the next chapter as soon as possible, to take advantage of these now.

However, now is also the perfect time to get moving on promoting your website through as many channels as possible. If you have colleagues who can help with marketing or PR, make sure you are working closely with them to publicize your new site's launch. Then, move into the next chapter to find out how you can monitor the success of your promotional activities.

10

Managing Your Squarespace Website

You've successfully launched your new website, but there's no time to sit back and rest on your laurels. If you have a blog and are allowing comments, you'll need to learn how to manage them. You're probably curious to know whether people are visiting your site, and if so, what they're doing while there. You may also want to give access to other members of your company, so they can help you manage your site moving forward. We'll cover all of this in this chapter, as well as introduce the Squarespace mobile apps that can help you and your colleagues manage and monitor your website on the go. Plus, you'll also learn how you can use floating bars to improve access for your mobile customers or to highlight important information.

We will cover the following topics:

- Using Squarespace Analytics to monitor site activity
- Managing comments on your blog
- Adding contributors to help you manage, publish, or monitor your website
- Highlighting important messages, such as **EU Cookie Law** notification
- Making it easier for mobile site visitors to reach you
- Using Squarespace mobile apps

Monitoring visitors and activity on your website

There's no point in building a website if it's not being visited and, more importantly, delivering the right information and functionality to your visitors. Monitoring the activity on your website can help you understand why and how people are finding and using your site, and also help you make informed decisions about changes that you might want to make in future.

You can carry out basic monitoring and analysis using **Squarespace Metrics**, which is Squarespace's own built-in statistical reporting tool. You can find out things like:

- The number of visitors your site receives, on an hourly, daily, weekly, or monthly basis
- The number of pages viewed, and the relative popularity of each page
- The words that people typed into search engines to find your website
- Which websites are linking to yours, and how much traffic those links generate

You can access Squarespace Metrics in the **Metrics** panel, accessible from the Home menu.

Some businesses find that the statistics reported by Squarespace Metrics are not detailed enough for their needs. If you require more sophisticated reporting, you will need to use a third-party tool such as **Google Analytics** (see http://www.google.com/analytics). You can easily add Google Analytics tracking to your Squarespace site by pasting your Google Analytics Account Number into the **External Services** panel that you can access from **Settings | Advanced**.

Understanding your website traffic

When you enter the Metrics area, the first set of statistics that loads into the viewing and editing screen is the **Traffic Overview** screen. The top part of the **Overview** panel is a graph showing three metrics charted over time, as shown in the following screenshot:

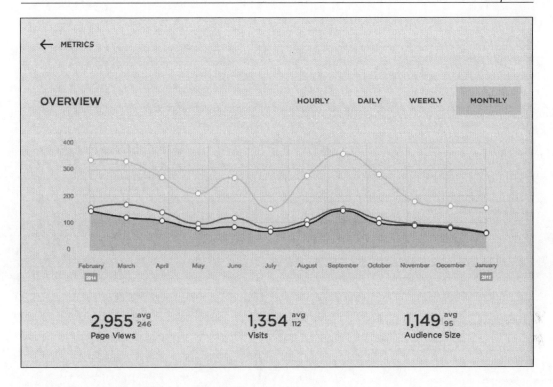

The lines in the graph show the following metrics:

- The darkest lower line shows the number of unique visitors, called your **Audience Size**
- The mid-gray middle line shows **Visits**

> Audience Size refers to the number of people visiting your site. Usually, one person equates to one visit, but sometimes a person will visit more than once during that time, or a visit will start during one time period and end in the next. This explains why Visits may be a different number than Audience Size.

- The palest top line shows the number of **Page Views**, which is the number of pages that were viewed by your visitors during that time period

Above the graph, there are four options you can use to change the time period shown in the graph:

- **Hourly**: Shows the last 24 hours
- **Daily**: Shows the last 30 days
- **Weekly**: Shows the last 13 weeks
- **Monthly**: Shows the last 12 months

 Monitoring the peaks and troughs of your site over time can help you determine when is the best time of the day or week to make changes (when the traffic is the lowest), or to see the effects of any marketing campaigns (hopefully reflected by traffic peaks).

The graph is followed by a table that shows **Page Views**, **Visits**, and **Audience Size** broken down numerically for the period of time you are observing, as shown in the following screenshot:

	Page Views	Visits	Audience Size
Jan 11	53	18	18
Jan 04	75	32	30
Dec 28	38	21	21
Dec 21	19	13	13
Dec 14	38	20	18
Dec 07	55	20	19
Nov 30	37	22	20
Nov 23	43	23	23

If you'd like to see a breakdown of the visitor numbers by mobile device versus desktop computer, you can find this information in the **Mobile Usage** panel in the **Metrics** menu.

Finding out where your visitors came from

One of the most valuable reports can be found in the **Referrers** panel of the **Metrics** menu. This report shows you the websites that your visitors used in order to find your site, so you can see how much traffic is being generated through search engines or links on external websites. The **Referrers** panel is shown in the following screenshot:

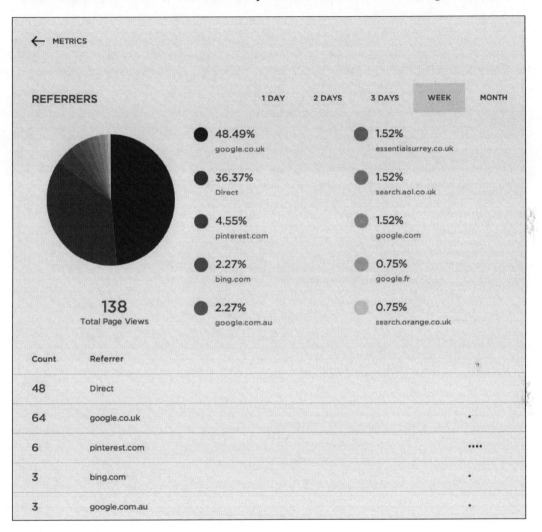

The top part of the screen shows a pie chart with the top 10 referring sites, and several options to allow you to change the period of time being reported on (1–3 days, 1 week, and 1 month). Below the pie chart, you'll find a breakdown of all referring sites, not just the top 10. The small dots on the right of the referring site address tell you how many pages on that website are driving traffic to your site. Clicking on the address of the referring site will reveal the URLs of the pages that are linking to your site. An example is shown in the following screenshot:

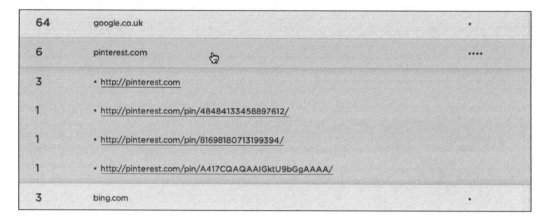

You can click on these URLs to visit the pages that are linking to you.

Learning how visitors search for you

Another useful report is the **Search Queries** report, as shown in the following screenshot:

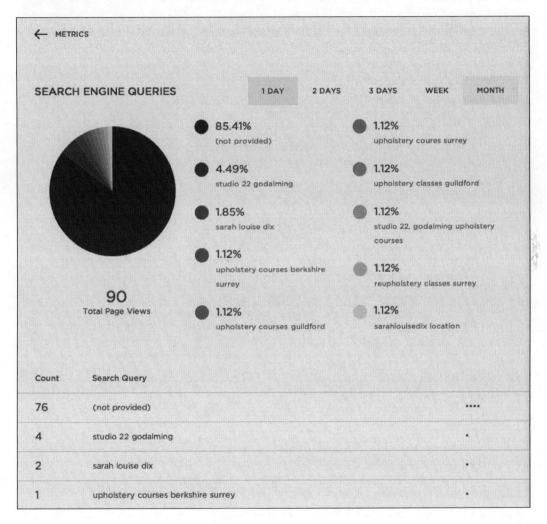

The screen for **Search Engine Queries** looks very similar to the **Referrers** report, except it shows the **keywords** that were typed into the search engines, instead of the referring sites. This shows you the exact words and phrases that visitors used to find your site to a certain degree. In nearly all cases, the search query at the top of your list will say **(not provided)**. This is because Google (and others) have implemented secure searching that prevents tracking for any searches performed via `https://` (instead of plain `http://`), and an increasing number of searches are performed this way. In the worst-case scenario, you may see no search queries at all aside from **(not provided)**. There is nothing you can do within Squarespace to discover what these hidden **(not provided)** terms are, but if it's important to you, you can try some advanced techniques in **Google Webmaster Tools**, **Google Analytics**, or a paid search through **Google Adwords**. Have a look at the following for more advice:

- `www.notprovidedcount.com/what-is-not-provided/`
- `https://blog.kissmetrics.com/unlock-keyword-not-provided`

Recently, Google have announced that they are looking into ways to make this information visible again, so it's worth keeping an eye on `http://searchenginewatch.com/` for breaking news in this area.

 You can use search query information to better understand which keywords are performing well for you on search engines and, if you find that obvious important words are missing, which words you need to improve by boosting the quality content related to that area on your website (and external links to it).

Finding out what's popular on your website

The final report that you'll find most useful is the **Popular Content** report, as shown in the following screenshot:

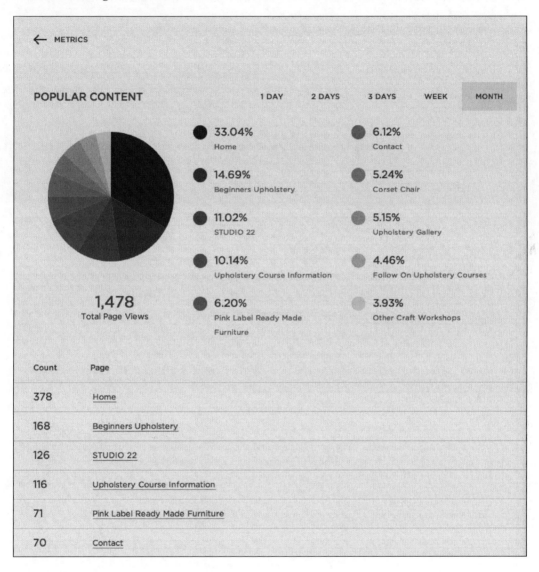

This report shows you a comparative breakdown of your web pages based on the number of views over a certain time period. Like the previous two reports, the information is presented in a pie chart showing the top 10 most popular pages, with a detailed list of all pages that were viewed in a table below the chart.

Popular content can help you to:

- Identify problems with your navigation or links, if the pages you want to be popular are not showing up.

- Determine the types of articles to write on your blog in future, based on popular topics or themes.

- Analyze your pages, comparing popular ones to unpopular ones, looking for patterns (such as larger images, shorter content, or other features).

- Find out which products or services are the most appealing to your customers. This may not match your actual sales— and if not, think about why initial interest isn't converting to sales.

Other metrics reports

If you have a blog on your site, you can find out how many people are subscribing to your blog's RSS feed in the **Subscribers** panel in the **Metrics** menu.

If you are really curious about your site visitors and what pages were viewed during individual visits, from the **Metrics** menu, you can access the **Detailed Activity** report to drill down to see individual visits by **IP address** (the unique identifier for an Internet connection). Clicking on the IP address will reveal further information about that visitor, such as the country, browser, and more.

Some people try to use the **Detailed Activity** report to see the geographic breakdown of visitors, or the paths that users are taking through their website, but Google Analytics is a much better tool for this kind of reporting.

Managing comments on your blog

If you have a blog on your website, allowing visitors to comment on your posts is a great way to engage with people who are interested in what you have to say. However, allowing comments can also potentially leave you vulnerable to comment spam, or give an open platform to unhappy customers, competitors, or just plain nasty people to air their grievances. The benefits of visitor engagement usually far outweigh the negatives, but you may want to consider enabling **moderation** on your comments, meaning the comments will not be published until you or one of your colleagues approve them. You can also allow comments to be **flagged** by other site visitors, which will alert you to any comments that they find offensive or inappropriate. If you did not already configure your comments settings in the last chapter, you can do this or adjust them by visiting **Settings | Blogging | Comments Settings**.

All comment management takes place in the **Comments** panel, accessed from the Home menu. The **Comments** panel is shown in the following screenshot:

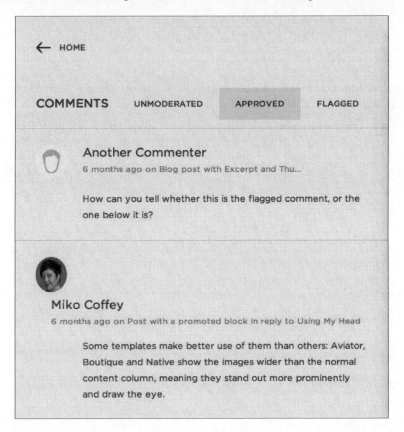

The **Comments** panel has three tabs for administration:

- **Unmoderated**: This includes the comments that are awaiting approval
- **Approved**: This includes the comments that have been approved and are displayed on your site
- **Flagged**: This includes the comments that have been flagged as inappropriate or offensive, and require your review

Approving comments

If you have enabled the Approval Required setting in **Settings | Blogging | Comments Settings**, all comments made by anyone other than site **Contributors** or **Trusted Commenters** will be held in the **Unmoderated** area until someone either approves or removes them.

 You will learn about Contributors and Trusted Commenters in the next part of this chapter.

To approve a single comment, hover your mouse over the comment, and click on the check icon that appears on the top-right corner, as shown in the following screenshot:

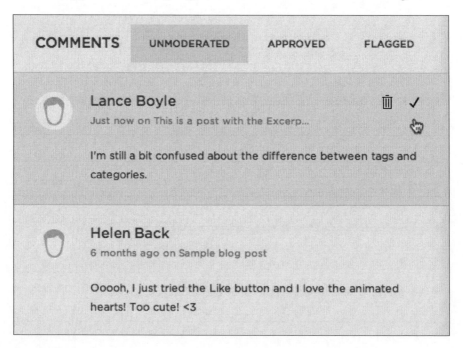

The comment will be immediately published to that blog post page. To approve multiple comments at once, click on the comments to select them. This will display a floating toolbar at the bottom of the screen, with buttons allowing you to **Approve**, **Delete**, **Deselect**, or **Select All** comments, as shown in the following screenshot:

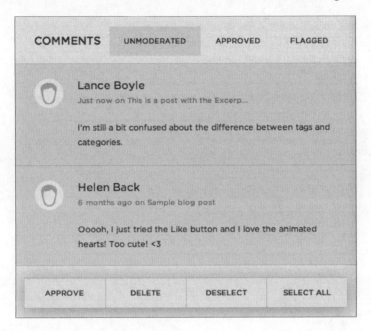

Replying to comments

You can reply to approved comments in two ways:

- On the blog post page, hover over the comment and click on the **Reply** icon to open a comment box, as shown in the following screenshot:

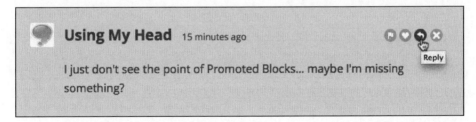

- In the **Comments** panel, hover over the comment and click on the speech bubble icon to open a comment reply box, as shown in the following screenshot:

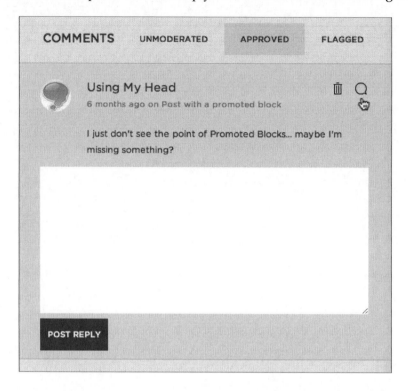

In either case, type your reply into the box, click on **Post Reply**, and your response will be published onto the blog page (nested below the original comment if you have enabled **Threaded Comments** in **Settings | Blogging | Comments Settings**).

Deleting comments

You can delete comments individually or in bulk, following the same steps used for approving comments: the only difference is that you use the trash can icon (when hovering over a single comment) or the **Delete** button (when selecting items for deletion). When deleting comments, you have two options that appear in a popup after you click on the **Delete** button/icon. The options are:

- **Delete**: This will simply remove the comment(s) from your site
- **Delete & Report Spam**: This will remove the comment(s) and also report the commenter to Squarespace

Handling flagged comments

It is up to you to decide how to handle a comment that has been flagged. You can:

- Delete the comment, following the steps detailed in the previous section
- Reply to the comment, following the steps detailed in earlier in this chapter
- Leave the comment on your site and remove the flagged status, by clicking on the **Clear Flags** button at the top of the **Flagged** section of the **Comments** panel, as shown in the following screenshot:

 The **Clear Flags** button will remove flags from all flagged comments; you cannot remove flags from comments individually.

Giving other people access to edit, monitor, or administer your website

Unless you're a sole trader or freelancer, you'll probably want to share the workload of managing your website, blog, or online shop with others. Squarespace has a role-based permission system that will allow you to give other people access to specific areas and functions. Each person who is granted access is called a contributor, and you can control access levels by assigning any of the following **Contributor Permissions**:

- **Administrator**: Full access to everything; the same level as you (the Account Owner)
- **Content Editor**: Edit or create new content or pages, but cannot change site settings
- **Billing**: Update credit card information in Billing
- **Reporting**: Access website statistics in Metrics

- **Comment Moderator**: Write, approve, and manage comments on your blog
- **Trusted Commenter**: Bypass comment moderation
- **Store Manager**: Receive store notifications, manage orders, manage Products, and edit existing page content (but not create new pages)

You can assign one or more of these permissions to each contributor. You can invite contributors and manage their permissions through **Settings** | **Permissions**. The Permissions panel is shown in the following screenshot:

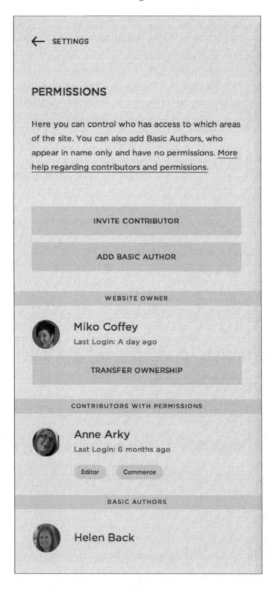

If you'd like to attribute content to someone, but don't want or need to give him/her access to create or edit content in the Squarespace system, you can create a **Basic Author**. Basic Authors can't log into the system, but you or any Content Editor can assign content to them.

Adding a Contributor

Contributors are added by inviting them by email through the Squarespace system. To add a Contributor, perform the following steps:

1. In the **Permissions** screen, click on the **Invite** button. This will open the **Invite Contributor** overlay window, as shown in the following screenshot:

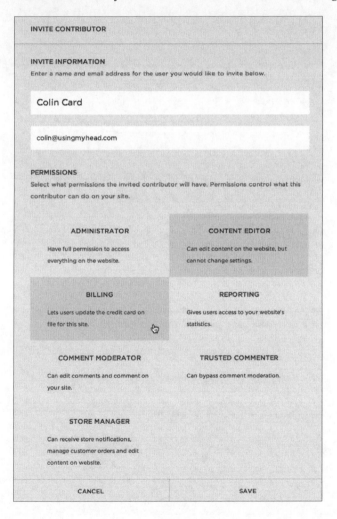

2. Enter the name and email address of the person you'd like to invite.

3. Select one or more permissions that you would like to assign.

4. Click on **Save**. An alert box will appear indicating that the message has been sent, and the invited person will appear on the Permissions page under **Invites Sent**.

Modifying, canceling, or resending a contributor's invitation

If you need to cancel an invitation or change permissions before someone accepts the invitation—or if the person didn't receive the email—you can open the invitation in Squarespace by clicking on the person's name under **Invites Sent**. This will open the **Modify Invitation** overlay, as shown in the following screenshot:

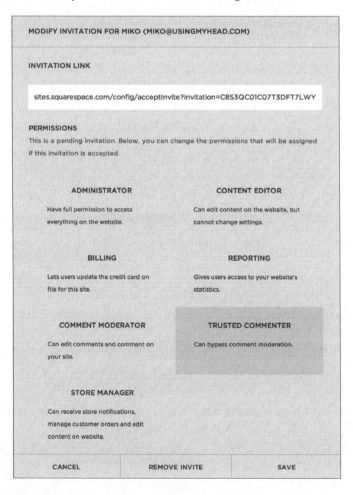

Here, you can perform any of the following actions:

- Copy the invitation link and paste it into an email in your normal email account to send the invitation link to someone who lost or didn't receive the email from Squarespace

- Adjust permissions and click on **Save**

- Cancel an invitation by clicking on **Remove Invite** to "uninvite" the person, disabling the link that was sent in the email from Squarespace

Modifying or removing a contributor's permissions

You can add or remove permissions for a contributor, or revoke all permissions and remove access from the system, by clicking on the person's name under **Contributors with Permissions**. This will open the **Modify Permissions** overlay, which looks very similar to the **Invite Contributor** and **Modify Invitation** overlays.

In this overlay, you can:

- Click on a permission to add or remove it, then click on **Save**
- Click on **Remove Access** to revoke all permissions

If you want to remove a contributor from the system entirely, you'll first need to remove access, which will move the person's account on the **Permissions** screen to appear under **Contributors Without Permissions**.

You can then remove the contributor's account using the following steps:

1. Click on the person's name to open the **Modify Permissions** overlay.
2. Click on **Remove Contributor**. This will open the **Remove Contributor** overlay.

3. You need to reassign the removed author's content to another author using the drop-down menu, as shown in the following screenshot:

4. Click on **Transfer And Remove** to complete the removal process.

Recommendations for all content editors

As an administrator, you can control each contributor's permissions, but you won't be able to adjust his/her profile information. Each user controls his/her own profile, which can be edited by clicking on the user icon at the bottom of the Home menu, and then selecting **edit profile**, as shown in the following screenshot:

In addition to the name and email address required for creating an account, Squarespace user profiles can also include a photo, bio, social media links, and more. The **Profile** overlay is shown in the following screenshot:

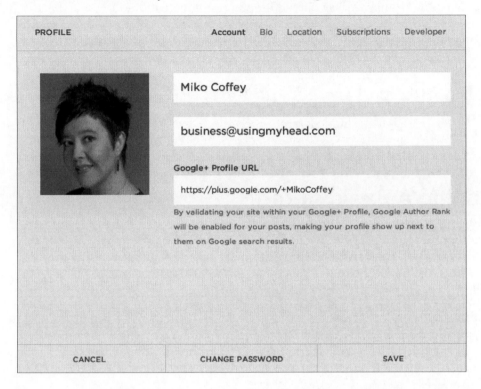

At the time of writing, Squarespace does not have a built-in method for displaying this information on your website—though it's looking likely that they will provide this in future. At the moment, some templates display the blog post author's name, which then links to a list of all posts that s/he has written. Therefore, although it's not critical that editors fill in all of the profile information, there is one profile field that is important to use whenever possible: the **Google+ Profile URL** field.

 If you want to display editor/author bio information in an **About the author** box automatically at the bottom of each blog post now, rather than waiting for a built-in solution, you can try adding some custom code to do so. We'll cover custom coding in the next chapter.

Google uses something called **Google Author Rank** to help determine the authenticity and authority of content, which forms part of the algorithm for ranking search results. By including your **Google+ Profile URL** in your Squarespace profile, Google Author Rank will be enabled for any content attributed to you. This can help boost your site's Google ranking, especially if your authors/editors have a solid (online) reputation in your industry. It's, therefore, a good idea to encourage all content editors and authors to include their **Google+ Profile URL** whenever possible.

To create a Google+ Profile, see `https://plus.google.com`
For more information about Google Author Rank, see `http://gplusgeek.com/authorship-authority-rank/`.

Adding a Basic Author

If you have guest authors, or need to manage content on the behalf of someone else (for example, posting to the blog for a busy CEO), using a Basic Author account is ideal. You can create and populate a profile for a Basic Author, and then attribute any of the following container page items to this author: Blog posts, Gallery images/videos, Events, or Album tracks.

Like any other Squarespace user account, a Basic Author profile can include a photo, bio, social media links, and location—even though none of this will show on your site, as mentioned in the preceding section. Therefore, we'll focus on setting up your Basic Authors with the minimum recommended information to keep things simple.

To add a Basic Author, follow these steps:

1. In the **Permissions** panel, click on **Add Basic Author**. This will open the **Add Basic Author** overlay, which looks pretty much the same as the **Profile** overlay, just with fewer tabs along the top (**Account**, **Bio**, and **Location**).

2. In the **Your Name** box, enter the name exactly as you would like it to appear publicly on your website.

3. If the person has a Google+ Profile, enter the URL into the **Google+ Profile URL** box to enable Google Author Rank for all attributed content.

4. Click on **Save**.

The author will now appear as an option in the Author menu when editing/creating content in your Blog, Gallery, Events, or Album. The following screenshot shows how you can change the author when in the **Options** tab of the **Edit Post** overlay on a blog post:

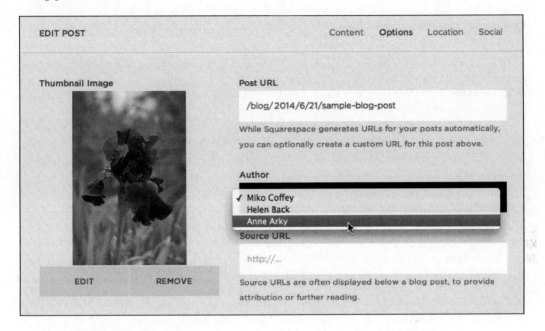

Using floating bars on your website

Floating bars are small strips of information that you can set to float on top of your Squarespace website. There are currently three kinds of floating bars available within Squarespace. They are as follows:

- **Squarespace Badge**: This displays a Squarespace logo on your site
- **Announcement Bar**: This displays custom text in a slim strip at the top
- **Mobile Information Bar**: This displays key contact information in a fat strip at the bottom, only on mobile devices

Unless you are a Squarespace superfan, it's unlikely that you'll want to use the Squarespace Badge—and even if you do, the configuration is self-explanatory. Therefore, we'll focus on the last two types of floating bars in this chapter. Each type of floating bar has its own configuration panel, accessed from the **Design** menu.

Using an Announcement Bar to highlight important information

If you are using Squarespace Commerce, you may recall we introduced the Announcement Bar as a method for highlighting discount codes back in *Chapter 7, Selling Online or Taking Donations with Squarespace Commerce*. However, you can also use an Announcement Bar for other types of information that you want to highlight, such as announcing a change of address, opening a new store, or winning an award.

If you are based in the EU, you may want to consider using an Announcement Bar for compliance with the EU Cookie Law (see `http://cookiepedia.co.uk/eu-cookie-law`), requiring all EU websites to notify users if their site uses cookies. Squarespace does use cookies, so you should definitely inform users of this in some way. The heavy-handed approach would be to use the custom code that Squarespace offers (see `http://help.squarespace.com/guides/eu-cookie-law-compliance`). This displays a rather unappealing alert box that gets in the way of usability, but may be the only solution that is fully compliant in some strict countries such as The Netherlands. The light-touch approach would be to simply include a link to a cookie/privacy page in your footer, but this may not comply with some countries' interpretation of the law. Using an Announcement Bar is a happy medium that uses the "implied consent" interpretation of the law applicable in many EU countries.

> Make sure to check the exact letter of the law in your country, but if you'd like to use an Announcement Bar, here is a good starting point for your wording:
>
> We use cookies to give you the best experience on our website. Read our **Cookie Policy** (link to your privacy/cookie page) to learn more.

To see an example and learn how to set up an Announcement Bar, refer to the *Using the Announcement Bar to highlight discount codes* section in *Chapter 7, Selling Online or Taking Donations with Squarespace Commerce*.

Making it easier for mobile site visitors to reach you

It's likely that many website visitors who access your site on their smartphone are looking for your address, contact details, or opening hours. It's a good idea to make this information easily accessible, especially because mobile browsers can be slow to load, or the person may be on the move. Enabling the **Mobile Information** bar can give mobile visitors quick access to directions, contact details, and your business hours. The black band at the bottom of the following screenshot is an example of a Mobile Information bar:

The Mobile Information bar uses information from **Settings | Business Information**, and displays it in a bar that runs across the bottom of the screen. The bar displays the following buttons and associated functions:

- **Email**: This opens the email application on the person's device, and prefills the **To:** field with your email address

- **Call**: This dials your phone number

- **Map**: This displays your physical location address and Google Map view in an overlay, with a link to open the Google Maps app for directions, as shown in the following screenshot:

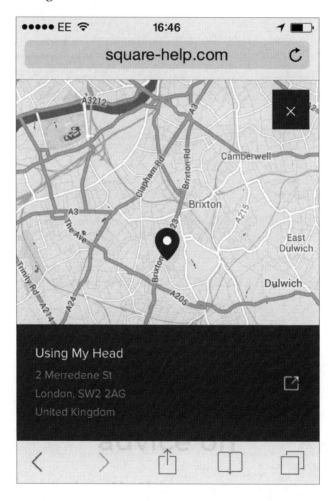

- **Hours**: This opens an overlay that shows your Business Hours, and a message at the top that indicates whether you are currently open or closed

As soon as the user scrolls down, the Mobile Information bar disappears, so it won't interfere with the use of your pages.

Enabling the Mobile Information bar is simply a matter of selecting whether you want a light or dark background, and checking the boxes next to the items you want to show.

Using Squarespace mobile apps

If you are one of the increasing number of people who rely on your smartphone or tablet for getting things done while on the move, you'll be pleased to know that Squarespace have a suite of iOS and Android apps that can allow you to monitor and manage your website (and more) using your handheld device.

There are currently four different apps, each designed for a different purpose, so you and your colleagues can use the app that suits your role on your Squarespace site, without having extra bits in the app that you may not need or want.

At the time of writing, only two of the four Squarespace apps are available for Android (Blog and Note). Check `http://squarespace.com/apps` for news about app developments.

Squarespace have provided helpful training videos and step-by-step instructions for each app, so we'll summarize the key points for each app here, and you can access the **Squarespace Help** link in each app summary for more information. There is also in-app support if you'd prefer to get started by installing and using them right away.

You can find the apps on the iTunes App Store by searching for `squarespace`, or you can find links to each app at `squarespace.com/apps`

You can manage multiple Squarespace sites through each app; you have the ability to easily switch between Squarespace sites in the app.

Let's go through each of the Squarespace apps now to learn what they do.

Blog

The **Blog** app allows you to control one or more blog pages on your Squarespace site, as follows:

- Write and save drafts, including adding images and video
- Edit, publish, or delete posts
- Manage comments: approve, delete, mark as spam, or reply
- Share (push) posts to your social media accounts

> Refer to the following guide for Blog app help: `http://help.squarespace.com/guides/the-blog-app`

Metrics

The **Metrics** app allows you to view and track statistics from Squarespace Metrics, and there are some nice details in the app that you don't get in the desktop Metrics panel. The following screenshot was taken from the Metrics app for iOS:

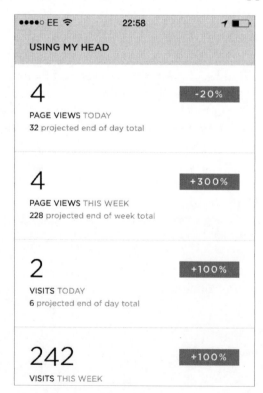

Some of these details are incredibly useful, bringing a much richer experience to the data than the plain vanilla reports you see in the desktop system. With the Metrics app, you can:

- View key figures such as page views and visits on a daily or weekly basis, with percentage increase/decrease compared to yesterday or last week shown in red or green, showing at a glance how well your site is performing

- See graphs and charts for your metrics, along with projections of future performance based on the current data

- Track the number of social followers for connected accounts such as Facebook and Twitter

Refer to the following guides for Metrics app help:
`http://help.squarespace.com/guides/the-metrics-app-for-the-iphone` and `http://help.squarespace.com/guides/the-metrics-app-for-the-ipad`

Portfolio

If you have a creative business and/or you have a rich set of images in Galleries on your website, the **Portfolio** app is a great way to showcase your work to clients and contacts in meetings. The app syncs with your Squarespace Galleries and can then display the images, even without a live Internet connection. The app gives the best experience with an iPad, but works on iPhone, too. The following screenshot shows the iOS Portfolio app with six Squarespace Galleries, showing the app settings menu along the bottom (you can swipe down to hide this menu for a minimal look):

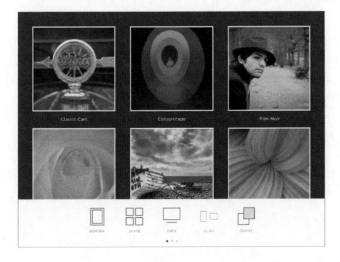

With the Portfolio app, you can:

- Always have the latest set of your images on you, wherever you are
- Display your Squarespace Gallery images and video in a minimalist viewer on a dark or light background, without the visual distractions you'd have on a web page
- Sync when you're on Wi-Fi, but still be able to show your images when offline (video is only available when online)
- Use simple tapping, swiping, and pinching to quickly move between or zoom in on images or galleries
- Customize the display to add/remove borders or titles, and adjust size, shape or alignment of images and thumbnails

[Refer to the following guide for Portfolio app help:
`http://help.squarespace.com/guides/`
`using-the-squarespace-portfolio-app.`]

Note

The **Note** app is a little different from the other apps, because it works not only with your Squarespace site, but also with your email, Twitter, Facebook, Dropbox, Google Drive, or Evernote accounts. Note is designed to be a simple, basic text tool that allows you to quickly jot down things that you want to remember, publish, or email to someone. With Note, you can:

- Use one single tool to publish a simple message through email, to your blog and/or social accounts, much more quickly than you could through a web interface or through multiple apps
- Type, and then swipe to send/publish, and you're done (yes, it's that simple)
- Work in a minimalist screen view to remove distractions
- Jot down all your ideas in one place, saving them as drafts until you're ready to publish later

[Refer to the following guide for Note app help: `http://help.`
`squarespace.com/guides/using-the-squarespace-note-app.`]

Summary

In this chapter, we've given you the skills you need to manage your website moving forward, and introduced some tools you can use to help do this while out and about. By now, you should hopefully be seeing activity on your website, through site visits, form submissions, purchases, and/or comments. Over the coming weeks, it's a good idea to keep an eye on your Squarespace Metrics and/or Google Analytics to look for any anomalies in the data, and to generally learn how your site is being used in the real world: this may not match your expectation or original plans. Analyze the data and think about whether you can improve your website's navigation, content, or functionality to make it even better than it is right now.

There are always ways to improve websites, and some of the techniques fall outside what you can do with the standard Squarespace tools. In the next chapter, we'll cover some of the more advanced techniques for enhancing your website, such as adding custom code or embedding external functionality. Don't worry if you're not a technical person: you'll also discover a range of resources that you can use to help achieve things you may not have dreamed possible, as well as learn where to ask for help if you get stuck.

11
Moving beyond Standard Squarespace Tools

Nearly everything we've covered so far has been achieved using the standard editing and configuration tools within Squarespace. These tools have been designed to enable non-designers/developers to create fairly sophisticated, professional websites without needing to use any code. However, when these tools don't suffice, it's possible to add or amend the Squarespace code to bend the templates or styles to fit your preferences. Alternately, if Squarespace doesn't include the functionality you need, you can also embed code from other places to complement the functions that come with Squarespace. If working with code seems outside your comfort zone, don't worry: there are plenty of resources that you can use as a guide. In this chapter, we'll introduce the different ways you can apply code adjustments and cover how and where you can get help—either from Squarespace directly, from the community of Squarespace users, or from an external professional designer/developer.

We will cover the following topics:

- Understanding advanced customization options
- What is and isn't covered by Squarespace support
- Where to find guides, code snippets, and advice
- Adding CSS, HTML, or JavaScript code to your website
- Finding a Squarespace designer or developer

Understanding advanced customization options

There are several different types of code you can use to change the appearance or functionality of your website and several different methods to add the code to Squarespace. These types of changes are called **advanced customizations**. Most changes can be carried out by simply copying and pasting the right code into the right place, so it's usually just a matter of knowing where to get the code and finding where to put it. While you don't have to be a coding expert to do this, you should ideally have a basic understanding of whatever **programming language** you are going to use (for example, **CSS**, **HTML**, or **JavaScript**), because Squarespace won't help you if you get stuck.

 Adding any type of code is considered an advanced customization, which is not covered by Squarespace support.

Although it's true that the Squarespace support teams won't help you with custom code through their chat or email support system, Squarespace does provide online step-by-step guides for some common code adjustments. Therefore, even if you are a total code newbie, you should still consider trying some of the less complex adjustments if you feel comfortable, especially if there is online guidance on how to do it. After all, you can simply delete the code if you can't get it to work properly.

Using the Squarespace Help Center for customization

The **Squarespace Help Center** (http://help.squarespace.com) is a great place to start if you're new to Squarespace customization. Here, you can find step-by-step guides, how-to videos, code snippets that you can copy and paste, and a space where you can ask questions to other Squarespace users. The Help Center is divided into three main areas that you can reach using the navigation at the top of every Help Center page:

- **Guides**: This includes step-by-step text and image guides covering nearly every aspect of using Squarespace, including common customizations.
- **Help Videos**: This includes training videos, covering key areas of getting started, and using Squarespace. Little (if any) customization is covered here.

- **Forum**: Although it can be accessed through the Help Center navigation, the Community Answers forum is actually located on a separate site: `http://answers.squarespace.com`. Community Answers is primarily a peer-to-peer support forum, with the occasional official Squarespace response. Many customizations can be found here.

 If you are based in New York, you can also sign up for 1:1 in-person workshops through the Squarespace Help Center.

You may be able to find the customization you need by simply searching within the Help Center or Community Answers forum. It's best if you know the type of customization to search for, and in some cases, you should include the name of your Squarespace template to get the best results.

Types of code customization

There are four types of code customization you can use on your Squarespace site.

 Many code customizations are not visible or behave differently when you are logged into your Squarespace site. If you apply any custom code and you can't see the effect (or it looks strange), try logging out of the editor to view it. Sometimes, code behaves differently because you are accessing the site via https:// when you are logged into the editor.

Code Block

You can use a **Code Block** to embed HTML, CSS, or JavaScript code into a part of a page. Code Blocks are the most common and best-supported type of customization in the Help Center. Some common uses for Code Blocks are:

- Pasting an HTML table into a page to display tabular data
- Embedding a third-party function, such as a Timely booking calendar, Hipmob chat, PayPal, or Google Translation button
- Displaying information in an iFrame, such as a Slideshare slideshow or Issuu PDF viewer
- Using JavaScript widgets, such as product reviews or ratings through RatingWidget

You can add Code Blocks in the same way as any block using the insert points that you see when editing pages, sidebars, or footers. When you add a Code Block, you will see the following screen:

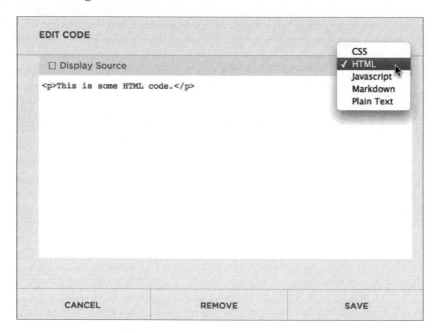

To add the code, simply paste or type into the code box, and select the correct programming language from the drop-down menu.

Code Blocks are the safest of all customizations for newbies, because you can usually find the code you need to copy and paste quite easily, and Code Blocks do not affect your entire site.

 Here are some Squarespace Guides for the most commonly used Code Blocks: `http://help.squarespace.com/guides/?cat egory=Third+Party+Integration`

CSS Editor

CSS is primarily used to control the aesthetics of your website. If you have been unable to achieve the look you'd like using the Style Editor, you can change the appearance of your website by overriding your template's CSS with your own. Although CSS can be used for a lot more, Squarespace only recommends that you use CSS to change fonts, colors, or backgrounds that are not controllable using your template's Style Editor Tools.

If you are confident using CSS, you could consider changing padding, margins, sizes, or positioning. However, be sure to check the effects on different screen sizes, and be aware that these kinds of CSS adjustments could be affected by future updates to your template or browsers.

You can use the **inspect element** function in Chrome, Firefox, or Safari browsers to see the CSS styles for any element on a Squarespace page. Search for inspect element CSS and the name of your browser on your favorite search engine for instructions and tips.

CSS adjustments are performed in the **Custom CSS** panel, which is accessible from the **Design** menu. Here is an example of the **Custom CSS** panel with some custom code applied:

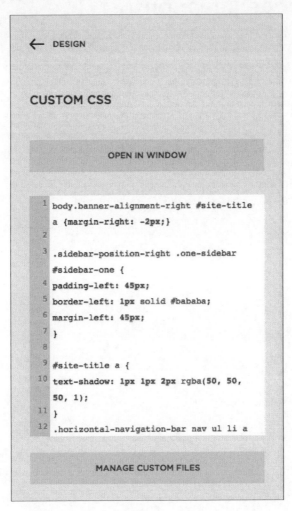

You can use the **Open in Window** button to open the code editor in a new, wider window to make it easier to see what you are doing. You can use the **Manage Custom Files** button if you need to upload files to the server (this is rarely used by beginners).

A Squarespace Guide for the CSS Editor is available at: `http://help.squarespace.com/guides/using-the-css-editor`

You can find some common CSS adjustments for your Squarespace template by searching `http://answers.squarespace.com` for your template's name and "CSS" or the item you want to adjust (such as the "heading" or "footer").

Sitewide code injection

If you need to apply HTML or JavaScript (such as jQuery or AJAX) to your entire website, you can do this using a **sitewide code injection**. You can insert code into the `<head>` tag or the footer area of every page. Using custom tracking scripts, icon fonts, animated sliders, or Facebook comments are just a few examples where a sitewide code injection may be useful. You can also use a sitewide code injection to add CSS by enclosing it in a `<style>` tag or by linking it to an external style sheet.

You should avoid using a sitewide code injection unless you are fairly confident with code, as mistakes can "break" your site.

You can apply a sitewide code injection by navigating to **Settings** | **Advanced** | **Code Injection**. Here's an example of the **Code Injection** panel with some custom code applied to the header:

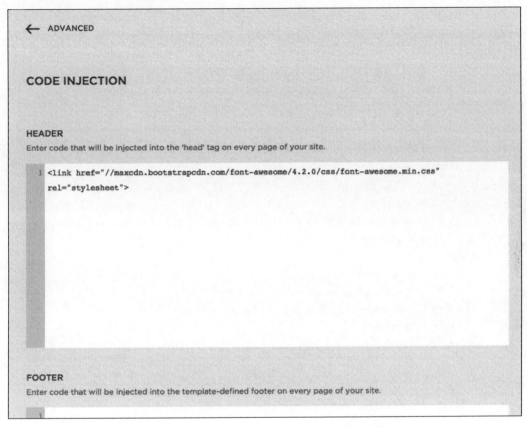

Sitewide code injection that links to an external style sheet

 The Squarespace Guide for Code Injection is available at http://help.squarespace.com/guides/using-code-injection

Per-page code injection

If you need to use code on just one or a few pages on your site, you may want to use a **per-page code injection** instead of a sitewide one. This will keep the rest of your pages lightweight and only increase the code load on those specific pages. You can add code to the `<head>` section of any page using the **Page Header Code Injection** box in the **Advanced** tab of any page's settings overlay, as shown here:

Per-page code injection with JavaScript applied

You can also add a **Post Blog Item Code Injection** to Blog pages. This will inject your HTML or script code directly after the end of each blog post. This is how you could add an *About the Author* box, for example. You'll see the **Post Blog Item Code Injection** box directly under the **Page Header Code Injection** box when you're in the **Advanced** area of Blog Settings. Here's an example of **Advanced** Blog Settings with code injections applied:

CONFIGURE BLOG   Basic   **Advanced**   Syndication

PAGE HEADER CODE INJECTION

Enter the code that will be injected onto the header for this page.

```
1  <style>
2  #aboutauthor {
3    background-color: #CCD3D9;
4    margin: 15px 0;
5    padding: 20px;
6    text-align: center;
7  }
8  </style>
```

POST BLOG ITEM CODE INJECTION

Enter the code that will be injected onto the page immediately after each blog content block (but before the blog post's footer block, if any). You can use the {permalink} variable to access the permalink and {title} variable to access the title for each item.

```
1  <div id="aboutauthor">
2  <h3>About the author</h3>
3  <p><strong>Miko Coffey</strong> is a web consultant with over
   17 years' experience helping people and businesses make the
   best of online communication tools, techniques and practices.
4  </p>
5  </div>
```

| CANCEL | DELETE | SAVE |

Blog code injections to style and insert an About the Author box

The Squarespace Answers post about adding an *About the Author* box is available at `http://answers.squarespace.com/questions/24911/post-blog-item-code-injection-aviator`.

There are also a couple of additional special code injection points for specific page types:

- **Lock Page**: This allows you to customize the text that appears on the Authentication page when you have set a sitewide or page-specific password

- **Order Confirmation Page**: This allows you to customize the message that appears when someone successfully orders a product

You can find these code injection points by navigating to **Settings** | **Advanced** | **Code Injection** below the sitewide **Header** and **Footer** boxes.

Finding Squarespace designers and developers

If you're scared by the idea of fiddling with code or you don't have the time or desire to do so, you can hire a professional to help you. You can also find someone to help you get your site set up, train you on how to manage your site, or help with any other aspect of your Squarespace website.

 As a very broad generalization, Squarespace **designers** tend to focus on the aesthetics and user experience of your website, whereas **developers** are best at helping with custom coding or building bespoke templates. Many people are skilled at both.

If you're an experienced frontend developer, you can sign up to the Squarespace Developer Platform and create your own bespoke Squarespace templates or modify existing Squarespace templates at the code level. We won't cover that in this book, but you can find out more at `http://developers.squarespace.com`.

Squarespace has its own directory of Squarespace Specialists: `http://specialists.squarespace.com`.

Each listing includes a couple of examples, a short summary, link, and guide prices, but the list is heavily weighted to big cities in the USA, and you can't filter the list by location. You can also find Squarespace professionals using Google or other search engines by typing your location and `Squarespace` plus the service you need (designer, developer, or training). If you don't live in a major US city, this may be an easier way to find someone local if you prefer to work face to face rather than remotely.

Summary

Using advanced customizations can give you nearly unlimited control over the appearance and functionality of your website by allowing you to introduce bespoke styles or third-party integrations. However, using custom code is not always easy for people who consider themselves "technically-challenged" or just plain busy. Although Squarespace provides a wide range of general guides and advice, one of the best places to find answers to specific problems is through the Community Answers forum, so don't be afraid to reach out if you get stuck. If you can't get the answers you need there, remember that most designers/developers who use Squarespace tend to have small businesses that offer reasonably priced services, so it may be worth investing in professional assistance to help bring your Squarespace website to its full potential.

A

Getting Help with Squarespace

There are a number of ways in which you can get help with your Squarespace website, all of which can be accessed through the Squarespace Help Center at http://help.squarespace.com/.

Knowledge Base

Search or browse topics to find how-to videos and step-by-step guides for the most common topics.

Community Answers

Search the peer-to-peer support forum or post your own question for the community to answer.

[Be sure to read the FAQ before posting your question at http://answers.squarespace.com/faq/]

Open a support ticket for 24/7 e-mail support

If you have already looked in the Knowledge Base and Community Answers but can't find the answer you need, you can open a ticket with Squarespace support using the button at the bottom of the Help Center homepage or by visiting `http://help.squarespace.com/open-a-ticket`.

 Make sure you provide specific details about your problem, including the page URL and/or the area of the system that is affected.

Live Chat

If you have a simple question or need instant answers, you can click on the **Open Live Chat** button at the bottom of the Help Center home page. Live Chat is available Monday to Friday between 3 AM and 8 PM Eastern Standard Time.

B
Squarespace Templates in a Nutshell

These charts compare the key features of all of the Squarespace templates:

Template	Adirondack	Adversary	Alex	Anya	Aubrey	Avenue	Aviator	Bedford	Boutique
Scale of control	L	M	M	XS	M	L	M	XS	M
Special Pages	Product	Index Scroll, Product	Index Scroll, Product	Index Scroll	Home	Index Grid	Home	Index Scroll	NO
Sidebar(s)	NO	NO	NO	Blog	NO	Blog	NO	Blog	NO
Header Images	YES +*	YES	YES	YES +*	YES BG	NO	YES BG	YES +*	NO
Main Nav	Horiz *	Horiz	Horiz	Horiz *	Horiz / Vert	Horiz	Horiz / Vert	Horiz *	Horiz
Fixed Navbar	YES +	YES +	YES +	NO	YES +	NO	YES +	NO	YES +
Other Nav	Folder, Footer	Footer	Footer	Folder, Footer	NONE	NONE	NONE	Folder, Footer	NONE
Social Icons	YES	NO	NO	NO	YES +	YES +	YES +	NO	YES +
Page Titles	YES *	YES +	YES +	YES +	NO	NO	NO	YES +	NO
Gallery	Grid + / Slide +	Grid + / Slide +	Grid + / Slide +	Grid + / Slide +	Grid +	Slide	Grid +	Grid + / Slide +	Grid + / Slide +
Blog Excerpt Images	NO	Wide Strip	Wide Strip	NO	NO	NO	NO	NO	NO
Promoted Blocks	NO	NO	NO	NO	YES *	YES	YES *	NO	YES *
Other Features	YES *+	YES *+	YES *+	YES *+	YES *+	NO	YES *+	YES *+	NO
Variant Of		Marquee	Marquee	Bedford	Aviator				

+ means the item is adjustable

* means the item has something special about it

Template	Bryant	Charlotte	Devlin	Dovetail	Encore	Five	Flatiron	Forte	Frontrow
Scale of control	XS	M	M	L	M	XL	M	XS	M
Special Pages	Index Scroll	Index Scroll	NO	NO	Home	NO	Index Grid	Index Slides	Gallery
Sidebar(s)	Blog	NO	Any page +	Blog	NO	Any page +*	NO	Blog	Blog
Header Images	YES +*	YES BG	YES +	NO	YES BG	YES +	NO	NO	NO
Main Nav	Horiz *	Horiz*	Horiz	Horiz	Horiz / Vert	Horiz / Vert	Horiz	Horiz *	Horiz *
Fixed Navbar	NO	YES +	NO	NO	YES +	NO	YES +	NO	NO
Other Nav	Folder, Footer	Footer	Folder	Folder, Footer	NONE	NONE	Index	NONE	NONE
Social Icons	NO	YES +	NO	YES +	YES +	YES +	YES +	YES +	YES +
Page Titles	YES +	YES	NO	YES +	NO	YES +	YES	NO	NO
Gallery	Grid + / Slide +	Grid + / Slide +	Grid + / Slide +	Grid + / Slide +	Grid +	Grid + / Slide +	Grid	Grid *	Slide +*
Blog Excerpt Images	NO	Lg Orig Aspect	NO	NO	NO	Square	NO	NO	NO
Promoted Blocks	NO	NO	NO	YES	YES *	NO	NO	NO	YES
Other Features	YES *+	YES+	NO	NO	YES *+	YES *+	YES *+	YES	NO
Variant Of	Bedford	Pacific			Aviator				

\+ means the item is adjustable

* means the item has something special about it

Template	Fulton	Galapagos	Hayden	Horizon	Ishimoto	Julia	Marquee	Momentum	Montauk
Scale of control	M	XS	M	M	M	M	M	S	M
Special Pages	Index Scroll	Product	Index Scroll	Index Scroll	Gallery	Index Grid	Index Scroll, Product	Index Slides, Gallery	Index Grid
Sidebar(s)	NO	Blog	NO	NO	Blog	Blog	NO	NO	Blog
Header Images	YES BG	NO	YES BG	YES BG	NO	YES +	YES	NO	YES +
Main Nav	Horiz*	Horiz *	Horiz*	Horiz*	Horiz	Horiz / Vert	Horiz	Horiz	Horiz / Vert
Fixed Navbar	YES +	NO	YES +	YES +	NO	NO	YES +	YES	NO
Other Nav	Footer	Footer	Footer	Footer	NONE	Index	Footer	NONE	Index
Social Icons	YES +	YES	YES +	YES +	YES +	YES +	NO	YES +	YES +
Page Titles	YES	NO	YES	YES	NO	YES +	YES +	YES +	YES +
Gallery	Grid + / Slide +	Grid + / Slide +	Grid + / Slide +	Grid + / Slide +	Grid *	Grid *	Grid + / Slide +	Slide & Grid *	Grid *
Blog Excerpt Images	Lg Orig Aspect	NO	Lg Orig Aspect	Lg Orig Aspect	Lg Orig Aspect	NO	Wide Strip	NO	NO
Promoted Blocks	NO	NO	NO	NO	YES	NO	NO	NO	NO
Other Features	YES+	YES	YES+	YES+	NO	NO	YES *+	YES *+	NO
Variant Of	Pacific		Pacific	Pacific		Montauk			

+ means the item is adjustable

* means the item has something special about it

Template	Naomi	Native	Om	Pacific	Peak	Shift	Supply	Wells	Wexley
Scale of control	M	S	M	M	L	M	XS	S	S
Special Pages	Index Scroll	NO	Index Grid	Index Scroll	NO	Index Scroll, Product	Index Grid, Product	NO	NO
Sidebar(s)	NO	NO	Blog	NO	NO	NO	NO	Blog	Blog
Header Images	YES BG	NO	YES +	YES BG	YES +	YES	YES BG	NO	NO
Main Nav	Horiz*	Horiz	Horiz / Vert	Horiz*	Horiz	Horiz	Vert	Vert	Horiz
Fixed Navbar	YES +	NO	NO	YES +	YES +	YES +	YES	YES +	NO
Other Nav	Footer	NONE	Index	Footer	NONE	NONE	2nd Vert	2nd Vert	NONE
Social Icons	YES +	YES +	YES +	YES +	YES +	NO	YES +	YES +	YES +
Page Titles	YES	NO	YES +	YES	YES +	YES +	NO	NO	NO
Gallery	Grid + / Slide +	Grid + / Slide +	Grid *	Grid + / Slide +	Grid + / Slide +	Grid + / Slide +	Grid *	Slide & Grid *	Slide & Grid *
Blog Excerpt Images	Lg Orig Aspect	Round	NO	Lg Orig Aspect	NO	Wide Strip	NO	Lg Orig Aspect	NO
Promoted Blocks	NO	YES *	NO	NO	YES	NO	NO	YES	YES
Other Features	YES+	NO	NO	YES+	YES *+	YES *+	NO	NO	NO
Variant Of	Pacific		Montauk			Marquee			

+ means the item is adjustable

* means the item has something special about it

These charts are correct at the time of printing. The available templates and their functions can change over time.

C

List of Online Resources Used in This Book

Chapter 1, Setting Up for Success – Your Website Toolkit

- Writing your slogan or strapline: http://thesaurus.com
- Creating idea boards:
    - http://pinterest.com
    - http://evernote.com
- Website inspiration: http://winners.webbyawards.com
- Creating wireframes:
    - https://moqups.com/
    - http://lumzy.com
- Finding a logo designer:
    - http://guru.com
    - http://freelancer.com
- Creating your own logo:
    - http://squarespace.com/logo
    - http://graphicsprings.com
- Stock photography and illustrations:
    - http://istockphoto.com
    - http://thinkstock.com
    - http://shutterstock.com
    - http://creativemarket.com

- Video hosting:
  - ○ http://YouTube.com
  - ○ http://Vimeo.com

- Streaming audio: http://Soundcloud.com

Chapter 2, Getting Started with Squarespace

- Signing up or logging into Squarespace: http://squarespace.com
- List of countries where Stripe is available: http://stripe.com/global
- Calculating the number of characters in a piece of text: http://charactercounttool.com
- Comparing Squarespace subscription plans: http://squarespace.com/pricing

Chapter 3, Working with Squarespace Templates

- Comparison chart of Squarespace templates and their features: http://square-help.com/templates
- Browsing Squarespace templates: http://squarespace.com/templates

Chapter 4, Creating Your Site Framework: Pages, Items, Collections, and Navigation

- Examples of creative ways to use different Squarespace page types: http://square-help.com/inspiration
- Guidance on importing a Squarespace 5, WordPress, Blogger, or Tumblr site into Squarespace 7: http://help.squarespace.com
- Finding out whether your chosen template displays Page Descriptions: http://square-help.com/templates
- Advice on using RSS on your Squarespace site: http://help.squarespace.com/guides/how-do-i-find-my-rss-feed-url
- Information about setting up your site for podcasting: http://help.squarespace.com/guides/podcasting-with-squarespace

Chapter 5, Adding, Editing, and Arranging Content in Your Web Pages

- Simulating different screen sizes and monitor resolutions: http://quirktools.com/screenfly
- Examples of different page layouts created with Squarespace's Blocks and LayoutEngine: http://square-help.com/inspiration

Chapter 6, Using Blocks to Add Functionality, Rich Media, and Special Features

- Email marketing tool that can integrate with Squarespace forms and Newsletter Blocks: `http://mailchimp.com`

- Cloud-based spreadsheet that can integrate with Squarespace forms and store all form data: `http://drive.google.com`

- Linking to a large, externally-hosted audio file: `http://help.squarespace.com/guides/using-the-audio-block`

- Step-by-step instructions for podcasting via your Squarespace blog: `http://help.squarespace.com/guides/podcasting-with-squarespace`

- More information about Content Blocks: `http://help.squarespace.com/guides`

- Service that allows restaurants to take reservations on Squarespace websites through an Opentable Block: `http://opentable.com`

- Service that allows you to display a feed of your latest location *check-ins*: `http://foursquare.com`

Chapter 7, Selling Online or Taking Donations with Squarespace Commerce

- Finding out about the Stripe payment gateway, and where it's available: `http://stripe.com/global`

- List of all country sales tax rates, in table format: `http://tradingeconomics.com/country-list/sales-tax-rate`

- Downloadable PDF with sales tax rates for all countries, including local taxes: `http://ey.com/GL/en/Services/Tax/Global-tax-guide-archive`

- Step-by-step instructions for importing products from Shopify: `http://help.squarespace.com/guides/importing-products-from-shopify`

- Step-by-step instructions for importing products from Etsy: `http://help.squarespace.com/guides/importing-products-from-etsy`

- Step-by-step instructions for importing products from BigCartel: `http://help.squarespace.com/guides/importing-products-from-big-cartel`

- Details of test credit card numbers you can use with Stripe: `http://stripe.com/docs/testing`

Chapter 8, Tailoring Your Site's Look and Feel

- Advice on choosing and combining fonts: `http://smashingmagazine.com/2010/11/04/best-practices-of-combining-typefaces`

- Using Typekit fonts that are not supplied through Squarespace: `http://help.squarespace.com/guides/using-typekit-with-squarespace`

- Browsing or downloading Google Fonts: `http://google.com/fonts`
- Browsing Adobe Typekit fonts: `http://typekit.com/fonts`
- Full list of the 60+ Typekit fonts including in Squarespace: `http://square-help.com/typekit-fonts-in-squarespace`
- Finding fonts that look similar to other fonts: `http://identifont.com`
- Finding similar fonts or general font inspiration: `http://typekit.com/lists`
- Free online image editing tool: `http://pixlr.com/editor`
- Designing your own free Squarespace logo: `http://squarespace.com/logo`
- Free color-picker plugin for Chrome or Firefox: `http://colorzilla.com`
- Add-ons for Firefox browser: `http://addons.mozilla.org`
- Extensions for Chrome browser: `http://chrome.google.com/webstore/category/extensions`
- Color schemes and color inspiration:
  - `http://colourlovers.com`
  - `http://colorschemer.com/schemes`
  - `http://kuler.adobe.com`
- Resources for textures and patterns:
  - `http://subtlepatterns.com`
  - `http://deviantart.com`
  - `http://colourlovers.com/seamless`
- Photography suitable for backgrounds or banners:
  - `http://unsplash.com/archive`
  - `http://creativemarket.com`
- Design inspiration: `http://square-help.com/inspiration`

Chapter 9, Going Live with Your Website and Driving Traffic to It

- Connecting to Dropbox to automatically publish Dropbox images to a Squarespace Gallery: `http://help.squarespace.com/guides/connecting-dropbox-with-squarespace`
- Converting an image to an icon: `http://converticon.com`
- Mapping an externally-purchased domain name to your Squarespace site: `http://help.squarespace.com/guides/mapping-a-domain-general-instructions`

- Submitting your website to the main search engines:
  - ○ `http://google.com/webmasters/tools/submit-url`
  - ○ `http://bing.com/toolbox/submit-site-url`
  - ○ `http://search.yahoo.com/info/submit.html`

- Setting up a Facebook page for your business: `http://facebook.com/about/pages`

Chapter 10, Managing Your Squarespace Website

- Google Analytics: `http://google.com/analytics`
- Advice on how to deal with *keyword not provided* data:
  - ○ `http://www.notprovidedcount.com/what-is-not-provided`
  - ○ `http://blog.kissmetrics.com/unlock-keyword-not-provided`

- News about search engine changes: `http://searchenginewatch.com`
- Creating a Google+ Profile: `http://plus.google.com`
- Information about Google Author Rank: `http://gplusgeek.com/authorship-authority-rank`
- Information about the EU Cookie Law: `http://cookiepedia.co.uk/eu-cookie-law`
- Using Squarespace's custom EU Cookie Law alert: `http://help.squarespace.com/guides/eu-cookie-law-compliance`
- App developments from Squarespace: `http://squarespace.com/apps`
- Help with the Squarespace Blog app: `http://help.squarespace.com/guides/the-blog-app`
- Help with the Squarespace Metrics app for iPhone and iPad:
  - ○ `http://help.squarespace.com/guides/the-metrics-app-for-the-iphone`
  - ○ `http://help.squarespace.com/guides/the-metrics-app-for-the-ipad`

- Help with the Squarespace Portfolio app: `http://help.squarespace.com/guides/using-the-squarespace-portfolio-app`
- Help with the Squarespace Notes app: `http://help.squarespace.com/guides/using-the-squarespace-note-app`

Chapter 11, Moving beyond Standard Squarespace Tools

- Squarespace Guides for the most commonly-used Code Blocks: `http://help.squarespace.com/guides/?category=Third+Party+Integration`
- Squarespace Guide for the CSS Editor: `http://help.squarespace.com/guides/using-the-css-editor`
- Squarespace Guide for Code Injection: `http://help.squarespace.com/guides/using-code-injection`
- Squarespace Answers post about adding an About the Author box: `http://answers.squarespace.com/questions/24911/post-blog-item-code-injection-aviator`
- Squarespace Developer Platform: `http://developers.squarespace.com`
- Directory of Squarespace Specialists: `http://specialists.squarespace.com`

Index

Symbol

500px
gallery, adding from 146, 147

A

add-ons
URL 249
Adobe's Lists page
URL 241
Adobe Typekit
about 240, 241
font-finders, using 238
fonts, URL 234
URL 240
advanced customizations 330
aesthetics, website 4
Album Pages
items, organizing 94, 95
settings 84
Album track properties 94
Amazon Blocks
using 169, 170
Annotations 25
Announcement Bar
used, for highlighting discount
    codes 218, 219
using, to highlight information 320
audience, website plan
customers 6
primary purpose 6
audio
adding, to website 173
Audio Block, using 173
settings, for podcasting 174

Soundcloud Block, using 174
streams, gathering for website 18
Twitter feed, adding 175
Aviary Image Editor
about 107
using 129, 130

B

background images
using 252-256
banner images
about **46**
adjusting 256
Basic Author
about 313
adding 318, 319
basic content
adding, to pages 113
images, adding with Image Blocks 115-117
text, adding with Text Blocks 113-115
text, formatting with Text Blocks 113-115
best template selection
brand, referring 57
content, referring 57
page structure, identifying 56
site's primary purpose, considering 56
special features, listing 56
Big Cartel
URL 203
billing information
setting up 40, 41
Bing
URL 287
Blog app 324
Blog Page Settings 83

constructing 2
content 4
contributor 311
contributor, permissions 311-313
custom domain, setting up 280
custom e-mail addresses, using custom
    domain 284
data, capturing 150, 151
domain, managing 285, 286
enquiries, handling 150, 151
existing domain name, using 282
existing website, moving from 283
final adjustments 274
fine-tuning 277
function 3
functions, testing 277
ideas, gathering 9
image-based logo, adding 244, 245
inspiration, gathering 9
making live 279
making visible, to Google 287
materials, gathering 9
media files 278
metrics reports 306
modifying 311
navigation, organizing 99
new domain, registering 281, 282
page elements, color controlling 251, 252

page elements, opacity controlling 251, 252
password protection, removing 280
POPULAR CONTENT report 305, 306
Search Queries report 303, 304
social blocks 278
social sharing, enabling 270-273
structure 3
tags, double-checking 278
testing, before launch 277
traffic 298-300
traffic, driving 286
visitors location, finding 301, 302
visitors, monitoring 298
working, at all sizes 277

website plan
audience 6
business 5
considerations 7
project 8
writing 4

Website Toolkit
raw materials, gathering 14

Y

Yahoo
URL 287

Thank you for buying
Building Business Websites with Squarespace 7

About Packt Publishing

Packt, pronounced 'packed', published its first book, *Mastering phpMyAdmin for Effective MySQL Management*, in April 2004, and subsequently continued to specialize in publishing highly focused books on specific technologies and solutions.

Our books and publications share the experiences of your fellow IT professionals in adapting and customizing today's systems, applications, and frameworks. Our solution-based books give you the knowledge and power to customize the software and technologies you're using to get the job done. Packt books are more specific and less general than the IT books you have seen in the past. Our unique business model allows us to bring you more focused information, giving you more of what you need to know, and less of what you don't.

Packt is a modern yet unique publishing company that focuses on producing quality, cutting-edge books for communities of developers, administrators, and newbies alike. For more information, please visit our website at www.packtpub.com.

Writing for Packt

We welcome all inquiries from people who are interested in authoring. Book proposals should be sent to author@packtpub.com. If your book idea is still at an early stage and you would like to discuss it first before writing a formal book proposal, then please contact us; one of our commissioning editors will get in touch with you.

We're not just looking for published authors; if you have strong technical skills but no writing experience, our experienced editors can help you develop a writing career, or simply get some additional reward for your expertise.

PUBLISHING

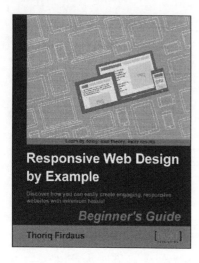

Responsive Web Design by Example Beginner's Guide

ISBN: 978-1-84969-542-8   Paperback: 338 pages

Discover how you can easily create engaging, responsive websites with minimum hassle!

1. Rapidly develop and prototype responsive websites by utilizing powerful open source frameworks.

2. Focus less on the theory and more on results, with clear step-by-step instructions, previews, and examples to help you along the way.

3. Learn how you can utilize three of the most powerful responsive frameworks available today: Bootstrap, Skeleton, and Zurb Foundation.

WordPress 3.7 Complete
Third Edition

ISBN: 978-1-78216-240-7   Paperback: 404 pages

Make your first end-to-end website from scratch with WordPress

1. Learn how to build a WordPress site quickly and effectively.

2. Find out how to create content that's optimized to be published on the Web.

3. Learn the basics of working with WordPress themes and playing with widgets.

Please check **www.PacktPub.com** for information on our titles

Joomla! 3 Beginner's Guide

ISBN: 978-1-78216-434-0   Paperback: 434 pages

A clear, hands-on guide to creating perfect content managed websites with the free Joomla! CMS

1.   Create a Joomla! website in an hour with the help of easy-to-follow steps and screenshots.

2.   Build and maintain your own website quickly, easily and efficiently, getting the most out of the latest release of the Joomla! content management system.

3.   Go beyond a typical Joomla! site to make a website meet your specific needs.

4.   Learn by doing: follow step-by-step instructions on how to design, secure, administrate, and fill your site with content.

Learning jQuery
Fourth Edition

ISBN: 978-1-78216-314-5   Paperback: 444 pages

Better interaction, design, and web development with simple JavaScript techniques

1.   An introduction to jQuery that requires minimal programming experience.

2.   Detailed solutions to specific client-side problems.

3.   Revised and updated version of this popular jQuery book.

Please check **www.PacktPub.com** for information on our titles

Printed in Great Britain
by Amazon.co.uk, Ltd.,
Marston Gate.